The
HIDDEN INNS
of
YORKSHIRE

including the
Yorkshire Dales and Moors

Edited by
Barbara Vesey

Published by:
Travel Publishing Ltd
7a Apollo House, Calleva Park
Aldermaston, Berks, RG7 8TN
ISBN 1-902-00763-8
© Travel Publishing Ltd

First Published:	*2001*

Regional Titles in the Hidden Inns Series:

Central & Southern Scotland	Southeast England
South of England	Wales
Welsh Borders	West Country
Yorkshire	

Regional Titles in the Hidden Places Series:

Cambridgeshire & Lincolnshire	Chilterns
Cornwall	Derbyshire
Devon	Dorset, Hants & Isle of Wight
East Anglia	Gloucestershire & Wiltshire
Heart of England	Hereford, Worcs & Shropshire
Highlands & Islands	Kent
Lake District & Cumbria	Lancashire and Cheshire
Lincolnshire	Northumberland & Durham
Somerset	Sussex
Thames Valley	Yorkshire

National Titles in the Hidden Places Series:

England	Ireland
Scotland	Wales

Printing by: Ashford Colour Press, Gosport
Maps by: © MAPS IN MINUTES ™ 2001 © Crown Copyright, Ordnance Survey 2001
Line Drawings: Sarah Bird
Editor: Barbara Vesey
Cover Design: Lines & Words, Aldermaston
Cover Photographs: Blacksmiths Arms, Lastingham; Buck Inn, Buckden;
White Lion, Kildwick

All information is included by the publishers in good faith and is believed to be correct at the time of going to press. No responsibility can be accepted for errors.

FOREWORD

The *Hidden Inns* series originates from the enthusiastic suggestions of readers of the popular *Hidden Places* guides. They want to be directed to traditional inns "off the beaten track" with atmosphere and character which are so much a part of our British heritage. But they also want information on the many places of interest and activities to be found in the vicinity of the inn.

The inns or pubs reviewed in the *Hidden Inns* may have been coaching inns but have invariably been a part of the history of the village or town in which they are located. All the inns included in this guide serve food and drink and many offer the visitor overnight accommodation. A full page is devoted to each inn which contains a line drawing of the inn, full name, address and telephone number, directions on how to get there, a full description of the inn and its facilities and a wide range of useful information such as opening hours, food served, accommodation provided, credit cards taken and details of entertainment. *Hidden Inns* guides however are not simply pub guides. They provide the reader with helpful information on the many places of interest to visit and activities to pursue in the area in which the inn is based. This ensures that your visit to the area will not only allow you to enjoy the atmosphere of the inn but also to take in the beautiful countryside which surrounds it.

The *Hidden Inns* guides have been expertly designed for ease of use. *The Hidden Inns of Yorkshire* is divided into 6 regionally based chapters, each of which is laid out in the same way. To identify your preferred geographical region refer to the contents page overleaf. To find a pub or inn simply use the index and locator map at the beginning of each chapter which refers you, via a page number reference, to a full page dedicated to the specific establishment. To find a place of interest again use the index and locator map found at the beginning of each chapter which will guide you to a descriptive summary of the area followed by details of each place of interest.

We do hope that you will get plenty of enjoyment from visiting the inns and places of interest contained in this guide. We are always interested in what our readers think of the inns or places covered (or not covered) in our guides so please do not hesitate to write to us. This is a vital way of helping us ensure that we maintain a high standard of entry and that we are providing the right sort of information for our readers. Finally if you are planning to visit any other corner of the British Isles we would like to refer you to the list of Hidden Inns and Hidden Places guides to be found at the rear of the book.

Travel Publishing

LOCATOR MAP

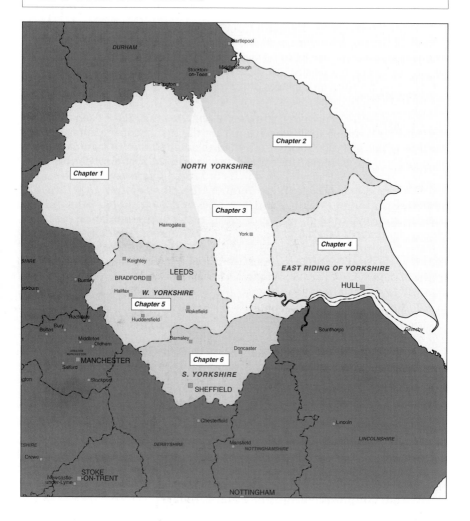

CONTENTS

1 The Yorkshire Dales

PLACES OF INTEREST:

PUBS AND INNS:

The Hidden Inns of Yorkshire

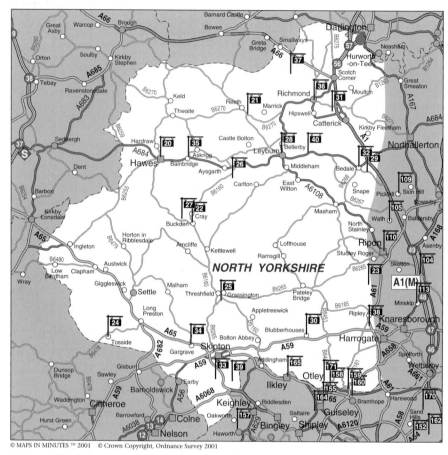

© MAPS IN MINUTES ™ 2001   © Crown Copyright, Ordnance Survey 2001

20	The Board Hotel, Hawes	**31**	King William IV, Brompton-on-Swale
21	The Bridge Inn, Grinton	**32**	The Kings Head, Bedale
22	The Buck Inn, Buckden	**33**	The New Inn, Cononley
23	Cross Keys Inn, Markington	**34**	The Old Swan Inn, Gargrave
24	The Dog & Partridge, Tosside	**35**	The Rose & Crown Hotel, Bainbridge
25	The Fountaine Inn, Linton-in-Craven	**36**	The Ship Inn, Richmond
26	The Fox & Hounds, West Burton	**37**	The Shoulder of Mutton, Kirby Hill
27	The George Inn, Hubberholme	**38**	The Three Horseshoes, Killinghall
28	The Golden Lion Hotel, Leyburn	**39**	The White Lion, Kildwick
29	The Green Dragon Country Inn, Exelby	**40**	Wyvill Arms, Constable Burton
30	Hopper Lane Hotel, Blubberhouses		

Please note all references refer to page numbers

The Yorkshire Dales

The Yorkshire Dales comprise Swaledale and Wensleydale in the north, and Nidderdale, Wharfedale, Airedale, Malhamdale and Ribblesdale to the south.   For many, Swaledale is the loveliest of the Yorkshire Dales. From historic Richmond town it runs westwards through countryside that ranges from the dramatic lower dale with its steep-sided wooded hills to austere upper reaches - a terrain where your nearest neighbour could be several miles away. Its rugged beauty makes quite a contrast to the pretty and busier Wensleydale just to the south.   Wensleydale perhaps above all the others is the one most people associate with the Yorkshire Dales. At some 40 miles long, it is certainly the longest dale, and it is also softer and greener than many of its neighbours. The pasture land, grazed by flocks of Wensleydale sheep, is broken only by the long lines of dry

Easby Abbey, nr Richmond

stone walls. This dale is, of course, famous for its cheese, whose fortunes have recently been given an additional boost by Wallace and Gromit, who have declared it to be their favourite! Wensleydale is also the only major dale not to be named after its river, the Ure, although until fairly recent years most locals still referred to the area as Yoredale, or Uredale. The dale's name comes from the once important town of Wensley, where the lucrative trade in cheese began in the 13th century.

Brimham Rocks

Of the southern dales, Niddledale is typically Yorkshire with its dry stone walls, green fields and pretty stone villages. It was christened Little Switzerland by the Victorians. Indeed, the upper reaches of the valley of the River Nidd are steep and wooded, with the river running through gorges, and with a covering of snow in winter it is easy to see the resemblance. It is this natural beauty that draws many people to the dale and there are also several remarkable features that are well worth exploring.   Wharfedale is one of the most spectacular and varied of the Yorkshire dales, and no one who sees the River Wharfe charging through the narrow gorge at The Strid, near Bolton Abbey, will deny that the power of the river is to be respected. There is much to see in Wharfedale and, in keeping with much of the Yorkshire Dales National Park, there is a variety of landscape to discover.   From the high moorland and fell to the deep, eroded limestone gorges the landscape varies almost, it seems, with every turn of the River Wharfe. This section of

4

Wharfedale has, over the years, inspired many of Britain's poets, writers, and painters. Both Coleridge and Wordsworth were taken with its beauty and, in the case of Wordsworth, with the local stories and legends. Ruskin enthused about its contrasts and Turner painted several scenes that also capture something of the dale's history and mystery. Airedale and its principal town, Skipton, have long been known as the *"Gateway to the Dales"*, a starting point for any tour of the Yorkshire Dales. The source of the River Aire lies in Malhamdale, just to the north of Malham, and it flows through both dales before finally joining the River Ouse. For some of its length, in Airedale, the river lies side-by-side with the Leeds and Liverpool Canal. Of the many and varied attractions in Airedale and the area sur-rounding Skipton, the most impressive feature is the beautiful limestone formations found to the north of Malham. The spectacular and enormous curved cliff of Malham Cove, cre-ated by glacial action during the last Ice Age, the limestone pavements above the cove, the deep gorge of **Gordale Scar**, and the remote natural lake, **Malham Tarn**, are all well worth a visit. This dramatic scenic area has been des-ignated a Site of Special Scientific Interest and, as well as the wonderful formations them-selves, the area supports a wide range of ani-mals, birds, and plant life. As there is a variety of terrain, from bleak, bracken strewn moor-land to coniferous plantations, there too is a wide variety of flora and fauna.

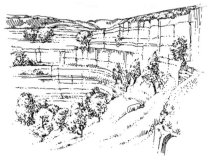

Malham Cove

The River Ribble, the source of which lies high up on bleak moorland to the northeast of Ingleton, flows through several ancient settlements before leaving the county of Yorkshire and flowing on into the mill town country of Lancashire. At the Aire Gap, and on opposite banks of the river, lie Settle and Giggleswick, which are overlooked by the towering white limestone cliffs of Castleberg Crag and Langcliffe Scar. Further north from these two market towns lies one of the most popular tourist centres in the Dales, Ingleton, and high above the village are the famous **Three Peaks** of Ingleborough, Pen-y-ghent and Whernside. The surrounding countryside is dominated by caves, potholes and waterfalls. It is ideal country for all those who enjoy the outdoors.

PLACES OF INTEREST

APPLETREEWICK

This peaceful village, which is known locally as Aptrick, lies between the banks of the River Wharfe and the bleak moorland, and is over-looked by the craggy expanse of **Simon's Seat**, one of Wharfedale's best loved hilltops. Dat-ing back to monastic times, lead has been mined on the surrounding moorland for many centu-ries and the northern slopes were the property of the monks of nearby Bolton Priory. The vil-lage was also the home of William Craven, a Lord Mayor of London who returned to spend much of his amassed wealth on improvements and additions to Appletreewick's fine old build-ings. The cottage where he was born was largely furnished by the similarly legendary Robert Thompson of Kilburn. Known as the Dick Whittington of the Dale, William Craven was born in 1548 and he moved to London when he became apprenticed to a mercer (a dealer in textiles and fine fabrics).

Just to the north of Appletreewick lie **Parcevall Hall Gardens**, a wonderful woodland garden which includes many varieties of unusual plants and shrubs. Though the 16 acre gardens are high above sea level (which provides the visitor with splendid views), many of the plants still flourish in these beautiful surroundings. The gardens, which are open between Easter and October, have a special quality of peace and tranquillity - appropriately enough, since the lovely old Hall is now a Bradford Diocesan Retreat and Conference Centre. The nearby gorge of **Trollers Gill** is said to be haunted by a fearsome ghost dog, with huge eyes and a shaggy coat, that drags a clanking chain. A little further down river is the stately ruin of **Barden Tower**, a former residence of Lord Henry Clifford, owner of Skipton Castle. It was built in the 15th century but allowed to fall into decay and, despite repair in 1657, it is once more a ruin. Nearby is the attractive **Barden Bridge**, a 17th century arch now designated as an ancient monument.

ASKRIGG

Once an important market town, Askrigg became better known to television viewers as Darrowby, a major location for the long-running series All Creatures Great and Small. The 18th century Kings Arms Hotel often featured as "The Drovers Arms", and Cringley House doubled as "Skeldale House", the fictional home of the TV vets. The village has been popular with tourists since the days of Turner and Wordsworth, when the chief attractions here were the two waterfalls at Whitfield and Mill Gill. Despite its olde worlde atmosphere, Askrigg was one of the first places in the dales to be supplied with electricity. That was in 1908, when the local miller harnessed the power of Mill Gill Beck.

Askrigg is bountifully supplied with footpaths radiating out to other villages, river crossings and farmsteads. One of the most scenic takes little more than an hour and takes in two impressive waterfalls, **Whitfield Gill Force** and **Mill Gill Force**. The route is waymarked from Mill Lane alongside the church.

AYSGARTH

This village is famous for the spectacular **Aysgarth Falls**, where the River Ure thunders through a rocky gorge and drops some 200 feet over three huge slabs of limestone which divide this wonderful natural feature into the Upper, Middle and Lower Falls. They provided a perfect location for the battle between Robin Hood and Little John in the film Robin Hood, Prince of Thieves.

Close to the falls stands the **Church of St Andrew**, home of the Jervaulx Treasures - a vicar's stall that is made from the beautifully carved bench ends salvaged from Jervaulx Abbey. During the Middle Ages, Aysgarth enjoyed the distinction of being the largest parish in England, though the parish has long been subdivided into more manageable areas.

Aysgarth Falls

The Dales National Park has a Visitor Information Centre here, with a spacious car park located close to the Church and Falls and also just a short walk from the **Yorkshire Carriage Museum** where a collection of nearly 60 Victorian coaches is housed in the 200-year-old mill which overlooks the Falls.

BAINBRIDGE

Back in the Middle Ages this area of Upper Wensleydale was a hunting forest, known as the Forest and Manor of Bainbridge. The village itself was established around the 12th century as a home for the foresters. One of their duties was to show travellers the way through the for-

6

est. Should anyone still be out by nightfall, a horn was blown to guide them home. The custom is still continued between the Feast of Holy Rood (September 27th) and Shrove Tuesday. The horn is blown every evening at 9 p.m.

Just to the east of Bainbridge is **Brough Hill** (private), where the Romans built a succession of forts known collectively as *Virosidum*. First excavated in the late 1920s, they now appear as overgrown grassy hummocks. Much easier to see is the Roman road that strikes south-westwards from Bainbridge, part of their trans-Pennine route to Lancaster. It passes close to the isolated lake of **Semer Water**, one of Yorkshire's only two natural lakes. (The other is Lake Gormire, near Thirsk.) Semer Water stretches for half a mile in length and teems with wild fowl. To the north the lake is drained by the River Bain which, at little more than 2 miles long, is the shortest named river in England.

BOLTON ABBEY

The village is actually a collection of small hamlets which have all been part of the estate of the Dukes of Devonshire since 1748. Bolton Abbey itself lies on the banks of the River Wharfe, while the hamlets of Storiths, Hazelwood, Deerstones and Halton East lie higher up.

The main attraction in the village is the substantial ruin of **Bolton Priory**, an Augustinian house that was founded in 1155 by monks from Embsay. In an idyllic situation on the banks of the River Wharfe, the ruins are well preserved, while the nave of the priory church, first built in 1220, is now incorporated into the parish church.

After the Dissolution of the Monasteries the priory was sold to the 2nd Earl of Cumberland,

Bolton Abbey

Henry Clifford, and it has since passed into the hands of the Dukes of Devonshire, the Cavendish family. The 14th century priory gatehouse, Bolton Hall, is the present duke's shooting lodge. Visitors walking to the priory ruins from the village pass through a hole in the wall which frames one of the most splendid views of the romantic ruins.

In and around this beautiful village there are some 75 miles of footpaths and nature trails, skirting the riverbanks and climbing up onto the high moorland. Upstream from the Priory, however, lies one of the most visited natural features in Wharfedale, a point where the wide river suddenly narrows into a confined channel of black rock through which the water thunders. This spectacular gorge is known as **The Strid** because, over the centuries, many heroic (or foolhardy) types have attempted to "stride" (leap) across it as a test of bravery.

The Strid

CASTLE BOLTON

Bolton Castle has dominated mid-Wensleydale for more than six centuries and is one of the major tourist attractions of the area. In 1379 the lord of the manor, Richard le Scrope, Lord Chancellor of England to Richard II, was granted permission to fortify his manor house and, using stone from a nearby quarry and oak beams from the Lake District, the building was completed some 18 years later. Today, this luxu-

Bolton Castle

One member of the family, Reginald Farrer, was an internationally renowned botanist and he was responsible for introducing many new plant species into the country. Many examples of his finds still exist in the older gardens of the village and in the hall's grounds. There is a particularly pleasant walk, the **Reginald Farrer Nature Trail**, which leads from Clapham to nearby Ingleborough Cave.

7

rious fortified manor house is still occupied by a direct descendant of the 1st Lord Scrope, and it remains an impressive sight with its four-square towers acting as a local landmark. The halls and galleries are remarkably well-preserved, as are some of the private apartments once used by Mary, Queen of Scots when she was a reluctant visitor here between 1568-69. Indeed, modern day visitors can take tea in the grand room where she spent many melancholy days. If you climb to the battlements you will be rewarded with some breathtaking views along the dale.

CATTERICK VILLAGE

Ever since the time of the Romans, when the settlement was known as Cataractonium, Catterick has been associated with the armed forces. Located on the Roman highway between London and Hadrian's Wall, the garrison was also close to the place where Paulinus, Bishop of York, baptised 10,000 Christians in the River Swale. Today the large army camp is some way from the village, but there are many reminders of its military connections. The connections with Nelson are not immediately obvious, but it was Alexander Scott, vicar of Catterick in 1816, who was at Nelson's side when he died at Trafalgar. Also, the Admiral's sister-in-law, Lady Tyrconnel, lived at nearby 6, a beautiful Jacobean country home famed for its wonderful interior plasterwork and medieval fishponds. The hall also contains many mementoes of Nelson and Lady Hamilton. On display in the Blue Room is a folding library chair from the Admiral's cabin on *HMS Victory*.

CLAPHAM

By far the largest building in Clapham is **Ingleborough Hall**, once the home of the Farrer family and now a centre for outdoor education.

Though the whereabouts of **Ingleborough Cave** were known for centuries, it was not until the 19th century that its exploration was begun. One of the explorers, geologist Adam Sedgwick, is quoted as saying *"we were forced to use our abdominal muscles as sledges and our mouths as candlesticks"*, which gives an excellent indication of the conditions the early potholers had to endure. However, their work proved very much worth while and the system is extremely extensive. Those visiting the caves today see only a small part of the 5 miles of caverns and tunnels - though, fortunately, this easily accessible portion is spectacular. As well as exotic cave formations and illuminated pools there is **Eldon Hall Cavern**, home to a vast mushroom bed! This is an area that has a great abundance of natural waterfalls, but the waterfall seen near the village church is one of the very few which owes its existence to man. In the 1830s the Farrer family created a large lake, covering some 7 acres of land, and the waterfall is the lake's overflow. As well as providing water for the village, a turbine was placed at the bottom of the waterfall and, with the help of the electrical power, Clapham was one of the first villages in the country to have street lighting. This is perhaps not as surprising as it might seem, as Michael Faraday, the distinguished 19th century scientist, was the son of the village blacksmith.

Overlooked by Ingleborough, close to the village, is the giant pothole known as **Gaping Gill**. Some 340 feet deep, the hole is part of the same underground limestone cave system as Ingleborough Cave, and the main chamber is similar in size to York Minster. Twice a year, the public can gain access via a bosun's chair on a winch operated by local caving clubs.

EAST WITTON

An attractive village set beside the confluence of the rivers Cover and Ure, East Witton was

8

almost entirely rebuilt after a great fire in 1796. The new buildings included the well-proportioned Church of St John although the old churchyard with its many interesting gravestones remains. Some two decades after that conflagration, the village was struck by another calamity. In 1820, 20 miners perished in a coal mine accident at Witton Fell. They were all buried together in one grave in the new churchyard.

Just to the west of the village is **Jervaulx Abbey**, one of the great Cistercian sister houses to Fountains Abbey. The name Jervaulx is a French derivation of Yore (or Ure) and Vale, just as Rievaulx is of Rye Vale. Before the Dissolution, the monks of Jervaulx Abbey owned huge tracts

Jervaulx Abbey, nr East Witton

of Wensleydale, and this now-solitary spot was once a busy trading and administrative centre. Despite its ruination, Jervaulx is among the most evocative of Yorkshire's many fine abbeys. The grounds have been transformed into beautiful gardens, with the crumbling walls providing interesting backdrops for the sculptured trees and colourful plants and shrubs.

GIGGLESWICK

This ancient village, which lies below the limestone scar that is part of the Craven fault, is home to several interesting places including the 15th century **Church of St Alkelda** and the well-known **Giggleswick School**. Alkelda is thought to have been a Saxon saint who was strangled for her faith, while the school, founded by James Carr, was granted a Royal Charter in 1553 by Edward VI. The school's fame stems from its observatory, which was used by the Astronomer Royal in 1927 to observe an eclipse of the sun. The school's chapel, the copper dome of which is a well-known local land-

mark, was built to commemorate the Diamond Jubilee of Queen Victoria by Walter Morrison, a school governor who lived at Malham Tarn House. Just to the north of Giggleswick can be found the famous **Ebbing and Flowing Well**, one of many in the area which owe their unusual name to the porous nature of the limestone of the area which causes there sometimes to be water here and sometimes not.

GRASSINGTON

One of the best loved villages within the Yorkshire Dales National Park, Grassington in many ways typifies the Dales' settlement with its characteristic market square. Known as the capital of Upper Wharfedale, the historically important valley roads meet here, and the ancient monastic route from Malham to Fountains Abbey passes through the village.

Grassington's origins are rooted in ancient history. There was certainly a Bronze Age settlement here, the remains of an Iron Age village have been found, a Celtic field system lies on nearby **Lea Green**, and the village was mentioned in the Domesday Book. However, the settlement seen today, having passed through various families, is now part of the estate of the Dukes of Devonshire. With its narrow streets lined with attractive Georgian buildings, Grassington is a delightful place to wander around.

Housed in two 18th century lead miners' cottages in Grassington Square, is the **Upper Wharfedale Folk Museum**. Containing many exhibits and displays relating to the lives of those who have lived in the dale, the museum is open (afternoons only) at weekends during the winter and daily throughout the summer. Throughout the year there are many festivals and holidays observed by the dales peoplep; one, the **Feast Sports**, still takes place here on a Saturday in October. Among the many traditional events which are carried out there is the tea cake eating race, where children have to eat a tea cake and race to the other end of the field. The winner is the first child to whistle a tune.

Some 3 miles northwest of Grassington, The striking outline of **Kilnsey Crag** is unmistakable as one side of this limestone hill was gouged out by a passing glacier during the Ice Age. One of the most spectacular natural features in the dales, the crag has a huge "lip" or overhang which presents an irresistible challenge to adventurous climbers.

Kilnsey Crag

street names relating to ancient trades: Dyer's Garth, Hatter's Yard and Printer's Square. Now the commercial and market centre of the upper dale, Hawes offers a good range of shopping, accommodation and visitor attractions.

Housed in the former railway station, the **Dales Countryside Museum** tells the story of how man's activities have helped to shape the Dales' landscape. Providing fascinating historical details on domestic life, the lead mining industry, hand-knitting and other trades, as well as archaeological material, the museum covers many aspects of Dales' life from as far back as 10,000BC.

One of those local industries was rope-making, and at **The Hawes Ropeworkers**, adjacent to the museum, visitors can still see it in operation, with experienced ropers twisting cotton and man-made fibres to make halters, hawsers, picture cords, dog leads, clothes lines and other 'ropy' items. The gift shop here stocks a comprehensive range of rope-related items along with an extensive choice of other souvenirs of the dale. Wensleydale's most famous product, (after its sheep), is its soft, mild cheese, and at the **Wensleydale Cheese Experience** not only can you sample this delicacy but also learn about its history through a series of interesting displays. With a museum, viewing gallery of the production area, cheese shop, gift shop and licensed restaurant, there's plenty here for the cheese lover to enjoy.

HARDRAW

Located in a natural amphitheatre of limestone crags, **Hardraw Force** is the highest unbroken waterfall in England above ground, a breathtaking cascade 98 feet high. Due to an undercut in the cliff, walkers can view the water from behind, as both Turner and Wordsworth famously did. It shows at its best after heavy rain as, generally, the quantity of water tumbling over the rocks is not great. On two separate occasions, in 1739 and 1881, the falls froze solid into a 100 foot icicle.

The amphitheatre here provides superb acoustics, a feature which has been put to great effect in the annual brass band competitions which began here in 1885 and have recently been resumed. Access to Hardraw Force is through the Green Dragon pub, where a small fee is payable. The inn itself is pretty venerable, with records of a hostelry on this site since at least the mid-13th century. At that time the land here was a grange belonging to the monks of Fountains Abbey, who grazed their sheep nearby.

HAWES

The present town expanded greatly in the 1870s after the arrival of the railways, but there's still plenty of evidence of the earlier settlement in

HORTON IN RIBBLESDALE

First mentioned in the Domesday Book, this village, whose name means literally "the settlement on the muddy land or marsh", was probably in existence long before the 11th century. The oldest building here is the 12th century **St Oswald's Church**, which still shows signs of its Norman origins in the chevron designs over the south door. Inside, peculiarly, all the pillars lean to the south and, in the west window, there is an ancient piece of stained glass showing Thomas à Becket wearing his bishop's mitre.

This village is the ideal place from which to explore the limestone landscapes and green hills of Upper Ribblesdale. To the east lies **Pen-y-ghent** (2273 feet high), one of the famous **Three Peaks**. For particularly energetic visitors to Horton there is the demanding Three Peaks

10 Challenge which is organised by the Pen-y-ghent Café. The 24 mile hike takes in not only Pen-y-ghent but the other two peaks, Ingleborough and Whernside, and those completing the trek within 12 hours qualify for membership of the Three Peaks of Yorkshire Club. Less energetic walkers will be glad to hear that the café not only supplies well earned refreshments but also has a host of local information and runs a highly efficient safety service.

The whole of this area has been designated as being of Special Scientific Interest, mainly due to the need to conserve the swiftly eroding hillsides and paths. This is an ancient landscape, well worth the efforts to preserve its relic ash woodlands, primitive earthworks and rare birdlife such as peregrine falcon, ring ouzel and golden plover. There are also a great many caves in the area, which add to the sense of romance and adventure one feels in this place. There are several listed buildings in the area, including Lodge Hall, which was formerly known as Ingman Lodge. Before the 20th century a judge would travel around the countryside on horseback stopping to try cases rather than villagers commuting to major towns for their trials. Here, if anyone was found guilty, they were brought to Ingman Lodge to be hanged.

Ingleton

INGLETON

Mentioned in the Domesday Book, the name means "Beacon Town", and Ingleton is certainly one of the most visited villages in the Dales. As a gateway to the Three Peaks, it is also popular with walkers. From as long ago as the late 18th century, Ingleton has been famous for the numerous caves and other splendid scenery that lie within a short distance, though some are harder to find and even harder to reach. The coming of the railway, which gave those working in the towns easy and cheap access to countryside, greatly increased the numbers of visitors looking for clean, country air. Though Ingleton is no longer served by trains, the village is still dominated by the railway viaduct that spans the River Greta. The river, which is formed here by the meeting of the Rivers Twiss and Doe, is famous for its salmon leaps.

Discovered in 1865 by Joseph Carr, the **Ingleton Waterfalls**, which were not immediately made accessible to the public, have been delighting visitors since 1885. Along the 4 miles of scenic walks, the stretch of waterfalls includes those with such interesting names as Pecca Twin Falls, Holly Bush Spout, Thornton Force, and Baxengill Gorge. The second principal network of caves in the area which are open to the public are **White Scar Caves**. Discovered in 1923, this cave network has been under exploration ever since and today the main features include two waterfalls, beautiful stalactites, and the longest show cave in Britain.

Finally, there is **Ingleborough** which, at 2375 feet, is the middle summit of the **Three Peaks**. For over 2,000 years the peak has been used as a beacon and a fortress. A distinctive feature of the horizon for miles around, as it is made of several layers of rock of differing hardnesses, there are several paths to the summit, most of which begin their journey in Ingleton. As well as the fine views, on a clear day there are also several interesting features on top of the peak. The most recent of these are the remains of a tower that was built by a local mill owner, Mr Hornby Roughsedge. Though the intended use of the building is not known, its short history is well documented. A grand opening was arranged on the summit and the celebrations, probably helped by a supply of ale, got a little out of hand when a group of men began tearing down the structure! At the highest point is a triangulation point while, close by, a cross-shaped shelter has been built which offers protection from the elements whatever their direction. The shelter acts as a reminder that the weather can change quickly in this area - a walk to the summit, however nice the day is at lower levels, should not be undertaken without careful thought as to suitable clothing. To the east, on the edge of the summit plateau, are the remains of several ancient hut circles and, beyond, the remains of a wall. The Romans are known to have used Ingleborough as a signal station, but the wall may have been built by the Brigantes, whose settlement on the mountain was called *Rigodunum*.

To the south of Keighley runs the line of the **Keighley and Worth Valley Railway** to Haworth. This restored steam railway line passes through some attractive small villages and some notable stations. Keighley Station itself is Victorian, and the 5 miles of railway that runs to Oxenhope is run by volunteers.

KELD

The little cluster of stone buildings that make up this village stand beside the early stages of the River Swale. The place is alive with the sound of rushing water, and it comes as no surprise that the word *keld* is Nordic for "spring". For lovers of green woodlands and breathtaking waterfalls, this village is definitely well worth a visit, and it has also managed to retain an impression of being untouched by modern life.

Wain Wath Force, with rugged Cotterby Scar providing a fine backdrop, can be found alongside the Birkdale road. **Catrake Force**, with its stepped formation, can be reached from the cottages on the left at the bottom of the street in the village. Though on private land, the falls and, beside them, the entrance to an old lead mine can still be seen. For less adventurous pedestrians, **Kisdon Force**, the most impressive waterfall in Swaledale, can be reached by a gentle stroll of less than a mile from the village along a well-trodden path. For really serious walkers, Keld is the most important crossroads in northern England. Here the south-to-north **Pennine Way** and the east-to-west **Coast to Coast** long distance walks intersect.

LEYBURN

The main market town and trading centre of mid-Wensleydale, Leyburn is an attractive town with a broad market place lined by handsome late-Georgian and Victorian stone buildings. Friday is market day, and the little town is even busier than usual. There's an interesting mix of traditional family-run shops and surprisingly large supermarkets behind deceptively small frontages.

The town has several interesting connections with famous people. Lord Nelson's surgeon, Peter Goldsmith, once lived in the Secret Garden House on Grove Square (and is buried in Wensley church, just a mile up the road). Flight Lieutenant Alan Broadley DSO, DFC, DFM, the 'F for Freddie' of Dam Busters fame, is named on the War Memorial in the main square, and just a few yards away is the birthplace of the *Sweet Lass of Richmond Hill*. Many believe that the popular song refers to Richmond Hill in Surrey rather than Richmond, North Yorkshire. Not so. Frances I'Anson was born in her grandfather's house on Leyburn High Street and his initials, WIA, can still be seen above the door of what is now an interior decorator's shop. It was her husband-to-be, Leonard McNally, who composed the immortal song.

The Shawl, to the west of the town, is a mile-long limestone scarp along which runs a footpath offering lovely panoramic views of the dale. A popular legend suggests that it gained its unusual name when Mary, Queen of Scots dropped her shawl here during her unsuccessful attempt to escape from Bolton Castle. However, a more likely explanation is that Shawl is a corruption of the name given to the ancient settlement here.

Spring is a good time to visit, since that is when both the Swaledale and Wensleydale festivals take place, as well as the prestigious Dales Music Festival. Continuing the musical theme, Leyburn is also home to **The Violin Making Workshop** where visitors have the rare opportunity of watching this ancient and fascinating craft. Little has changed in the art of violin making over the centuries, and the traditional tools and methods used by such master craftsmen as Stradivari are still employed today. The workshop is open every day during the high season, and every day except Saturday between Easter and the end of September.

Close by, at **The Teapottery**, you can see other craftspeople at work - in this case creating a whole range of witty and unusual teapots - anything from a grand piano to a bathtub complete with yellow duck. The finished pots can be purchased in the showroom where there's also a tea room with your tea served, naturally, in one of the astonishing teapots produced here.

About 2 miles west of Leyburn, off the A684, the **Sheepshop** at Cross Lanes Farm in Garriston is a treat for anyone who appreciates good knitwear which can be specially knitted to the cus-

12

tomer's requirements. You can see the raw material grazing in the surrounding fields - rare Wensleydale longwool sheep. The Sheepshop also stocks an extensive range of hand knitting yarns and patterns for the enthusiast.

LOFTHOUSE

This is a small dales' village lying in the upper valley of the River Nidd and, unlike neighbouring Wharfedale, the stone walls and rocky outcrops are of millstone grit though the valley bottom consists of limestone. As a result, only in excessive weather is there water under the bridge here as, in normal conditions, the river drops down two sumps: Manchester Hole and Goydon Pot. The monks of Fountains Abbey certainly had a grange here, but it is also probable that the village was first settled by Norsemen.

Nearby **How Stean Gorge**, in the heart of Nidderdale, is often called Yorkshire's Little Switzerland, and for good reason. This spectacular limestone gorge, which is up to 80 feet deep in places, through which the Stean Beck flows, is a popular tourist attraction though little known outside the area. A narrow path with footbridges guide the visitor along the gorge where the waters rush over the large boulders below. However, there are also many sheltered areas of calm water where fish hide under the rocks. As well as taking a stroll up this fascinating path, visitors can also step inside Tom Taylor's Cave and, along the walk, marvel at the wide variety of plant life that grows in this steep ravine.

MALHAM

Malham village was originally two settlements, Malham East and Malham West, which were separated by the beck. Each came under the influence of a different religious house: Bolton Priory and Fountains Abbey respectively. United after the Dissolution of the Monasteries, the focal point of Malham became the village green, where the annual sheep fairs were held. This pretty village of farms and cottages is one of the most visited places in the Yorkshire Dales, though it is not the charming stone built dwellings which visitors come to admire but the spectacular limestone scenery which lies just to the north. However, the two ancient stone bridges in the village centre are also worth

a second glance. The New Bridge, which is also known as the Monks' Bridge, was built in the 17th century, while the Wash-Dub Bridge dates from the 16th century and is of a clapper design (limestone slabs placed on stone supports).

The way to the ancient glacial grandeur of **Malham Cove** is from the Langcliffe road beyond the last buildings of the village, down a path alongside the beck that leads through a scattering of trees. The 300 foot limestone amphitheatre is the most spectacular section of the mid-Craven fault and, as recently as the 1700s, a massive waterfall that was higher than Niagara Falls cascaded over its edge! These days the water disappears through potholes at the top, called water-sinks, and reappears through the cavern mouth at Aire Head near the village. A steep path leads to the limestone pavement at the top, with its characteristic clints and grykes, where water has carved a distinctive natural sculpture through the weaknesses in the limestone.

From here it is not too far to reach the equally inspiring **Gordale Scar**, a huge gorge carved by glacial melt water with an impressive waterfall leaping, in two stages, from a fissure in its face. Further on still is another waterfall known as Janet's Foss. Beside the waterfall is a cave which Janet, a friendly fairy, is reputed to inhabit. Three miles north of the scar is **Malham Tarn**, a glacial lake which by way of an underground stream is the source of the River Aire, and Malham Tarn House, where such famous names as Ruskin, Darwin and Charles Kingsley (author of *The Water Babies*) received inspiration.

MIDDLEHAM

Middleham is an enchanting little town which, despite having a population of fewer than 800, boasts its own Mayor, Corporation and quaint Town Hall. It also is the site of one of Yorkshire's most historic castles, 12 of England's most successful racing stables, and not just one, but two, Market Places. It is almost totally unspoilt, with a wealth of handsome Georgian houses and hostelries huddled together in perfect architectural harmony.

Rising high above the town are the magnificent ruins of **Middleham Castle** (English Heritage), a once-mighty fortress whose most glorious days came in the 15th century when most of northern England was ruled from here by the Neville family. The castle's most famous resident was Richard III, who was sent here as a lad of 13 to be trained in the *"arts of nobilitie"*. Whatever crimes he may or may not have committed later down in London, Richard was popular locally, ensuring the town's prosperity by granting it a fair and a twice-yearly market. The people of Middleham had good reason to mourn his death at the Battle of Bosworth in 1485.

Middleham is often referred to as the "Newmarket of the North", a term you'll understand when you see the strings of thoroughbred racehorses clip-clopping through the town on their way to training runs on Low Moor. It was the monks of Jervaulx Abbey who founded this key industry. By the late 18th century races were being run across the moorland and the first stables established. Since then, they have produced a succession of classic race winners with one local trainer, Neville Crump, having three Grand National winners to his credit within the space of 12 years.

MOULTON

This small village is home to two fine 17th century manor houses that were built by members of the Smithson family. The Manor House, in the village centre, was originally built in the late 16th century and was improved greatly in the mid 17th century. Just to the south lies **Moulton Hall**, built by George Smithson following his marriage to Eleanor Fairfax in 1654. Similar in size to the original Smithson family home and somewhat resembling it, Moulton Hall is now in the hands of the National Trust.

PATELEY BRIDGE

Considered one of the prettiest towns in the Dales, Pateley Bridge is perfectly situated as a base from which to explore Upper Nidderdale. Considering its compact size, the town is remarkably well connected by roads which have been here since the monastic orders established trade routes through the town for transporting their goods. A street market, whose charter was granted in the 14th century, has however been abandoned for some time, although sheep fairs and agricultural shows still take place here.

Pateley Bridge is more than just a market centre - the nearby lead mines and spinning and hand-loom weaving also provided employment for the local community. The construction of the turnpike road to Ripon in 1751, followed by the opening of a road to Knaresborough in 1756, gave the town a further economic boost.

In the early 19th century, the brothers George and John Metcalfe moved their flax spinning business to nearby Glasshouses and they expanded rapidly. The lead mines too were expanding, due to the introduction of new machinery, and the town saw a real boom. The arrival of the railway in 1862 maintained this flourishing economy, making the transportation of heavy goods cheaper and the carriage of perishable foods quicker.

13

Much of the Pateley Bridge seen today was built in those prosperous years. A town of quaint and pretty buildings, the oldest is **St Mary's Church**, a lovely ruin dating from 1320 from which there are some fine panoramic views. Another excellent vista can be viewed from the aptly named **Panorama Walk**, part of the main medieval route from Ripon to Skipton.

The **Nidderdale Museum**, a winner of the National Heritage Museum of the Year, is housed in one of the town's original Victorian workhouses and presents a fascinating record of local folk history. The exhibits include a complete cobbler's shop, general store, Victorian parlour, kitchen and schoolroom, chemist's, haberdasher's, joiner's shop, solicitor's office as well as an agricultural, transport and industrial display.

The bridge at Pateley is a long established crossing which was used by the monks of Fountains Abbey. The original ford was replaced by a wooden bridge in the 16th century and the present stone structure dates from the 18th century.

Pateley Bridge

14

About 3 miles east of Pately Bridge are **Brimham Rocks** (National Trust), an extraordinary natural sculpture park. Formed into fantastic shapes by years of erosion, these great millstone grit boulders lie atop a steep hill amidst some 400 acres of heathland. Some of the shapes really do resemble their names - the "Dancing Bear" in particular, but perhaps the most awe-inspiring is "Idol Rock", a huge boulder weighing several tons which rests on a base just a foot in diameter. The National Trust has provided large scale maps showing suggested itineraries and the positions and names of the major formations.

REETH

Considered the capital of Upper Swaledale, this small town is poised at the junction of the River Swale and its main tributary, Arkle Beck. The local lead mining industry, which was begun by the Romans, served the town well for many years, until competition from abroad gradually caused its decline and Reeth became chiefly an agricultural centre. Noted in the Domesday Book, while everything else in the area was written off as untaxable wasteland, Reeth prospered and it is still today a much visited place.

Until the end of the 19th century a total of four fairs were held here annually, as well as a weekly market. Today, the annual agricultural show in September, held on the sprawling village green, is still a magnet for farmers from the entire length of the dale and beyond. Along the top of the green is **High Row**, with its inns and shops and outstanding Georgian architecture, reflecting the affluence of the town in the 17th century when the trade in wool and lead was booming.

The **Swaledale Folk Museum**, housed in what was once the old Methodist Sunday School, is the home for exhibits of local farming methods, crafts, and mining skills, as well as displays on local pastimes, the impact of Wesleyan Methodism, and the exodus of the population to the industrial areas of the south Pennines when the lead mines closed.

This little town is noted for its variety of craft shops. There's a cluster of them at the **Reeth Craft Workshops** near the green. Here you'll find a cabinet maker, a guitar maker, a pottery shop, a clock maker and restorer, "Shades of Heather" which has everything for rag rug making and "Stefs Models" where visitors can see

the production of beautifully crafted animal models.

Just to the south of Reeth lies the quiet village of **Grinton** whose parish **Church of St Andrew** served the whole of the dale for centuries. The building dates back to the 13th and 15th centuries, though there are still some Norman remains as well as a Leper's Squint (a small hole through which those afflicted by the disease could follow the service within). For those people living in the upper reaches of Swaledale who died, there was a long journey down the track to Grinton which became known as the **Corpse Way**.

Running northwestwards from Reeth, **Arkengarth-dale** is a small and remote valley. It was first settled by Norsemen and their presence is still reflected in the dale's place names - Booze, Eskeleth, and Wham. Overlooked completely during the Domesday survey, when it was considered of no value, lead mining brought about a period of prosperity in the 18th and 19th centuries.

RICHMOND

The former county of Richmondshire (which still survives as a parliamentary constituency), once occupied a third of the North Riding of Yorkshire. Alan Rufus, the 1st Earl of Richmond, built the original **Richmond Castle** in 1071 and the site, 100 feet up on a rocky promontory with the River Swale passing below, is imposing and well chosen. The keep rises to 109 feet with walls 11 foot thick, while the other side is afforded an impregnable defence by means of the cliff and the river. Richmond Castle was the first Norman castle in the country to be built, right from the foundations, in stone. Additions were made over subsequent years, but it reached its final form in the 14th century. Since then it has fallen into ruin, though a considerable amount of the original Norman stonework remains intact. With such an inspiring setting, it is hardly surprising that there is a legend suggesting that King Arthur himself is buried here, reputedly in a cave beneath the castle. The story goes that a simple potter called Thompson stumbled across an underground passage which led to a chamber where he discovered the king and his knights lying in an enchanted sleep, surrounded by priceless treasures. A voice warned him not to disturb the sleepers and he fled, predictably, then was unable to locate the passage again. Another legend associated with

Richmond Castle

the castle tells how a drummer boy was sent down the passageway. Beating his drum as he walked, the boy's progress was followed by the soldiers on the surface until, suddenly, the drumming stopped. Though the passageway was searched the boy was never seen again but, it is said, his drumming can still be heard.

In 1315, Edward II granted Richmond the right to protect the town by a stone wall after Scottish raiders had caused considerable damage in the surrounding area. By the 16th century, the walls were in a state of disrepair and little survives today. Two road bridges cross the River Swale in the town. The elder of the two, Green Bridge, was erected in 1789 to the designs of John Carr after the existing bridge had been swept away by flood water. Its picturesque setting is enhanced by the massive cliff crowned by Richmond Castle that towers above it.

During the Middle Ages, the markets of Richmond gave the town much of its prosperity, and its influence spread across Yorkshire to Lancashire. Also, like many North Yorkshire towns and villages, the textile industry played an important role in the continuation of the town's wealth and, for some time, Richmond became famous for its knitted stockings.

The **Green Howards Museum**, the regimental museum of the North Riding's infantry, is

based in the old Trinity Church in the centre of the cobbled market square. The regiment dates back to 1688, when it was founded, and the displays and collections illustrate its history with war relics, weapons, uniforms, medals, and regimental silver. Also housed in the museum is the town's silver. The church itself was founded in 1135 and, though it has been altered and rebuilt on more than one occasion, the original Norman tower and some other masonry has survived.

One of the grandest buildings in the town is the **Culloden Tower**, just off the town green. It was erected in 1747 by the Yorke family, one of whose members had fought at the Battle of Culloden the previous year. Unlike most follies, the interior of the 3-storey tower is elaborately decorated in the rococo style, and since it is now in the care of the Landmark Trust it is possible to stay there. It is not surprising that a town steeped in history should have several museums; the **Richmondshire Museum** traces the history of this old place and its county. There is also a reconstruction of James Herriot's veterinary surgery taken from the popular television series, as well as other period costumes and displays.

Richmond is also home to England's oldest theatre, the **Georgian Theatre Royal**, which originally formed part of a circuit that included Northallerton, Ripon and Harrogate. Built in 1788 by the actor and manager Samuel Butler, it had at that time an audience capacity of 400. The connection with the theatrical Butler family ended in 1830, and from then until 1848 it was used, infrequently, by travelling companies. After the mid 19th century right up until the 1960s, the theatre saw a variety of uses, as a wine cellar and a corn chandler's among others, and it did not re-open as a theatre until 1963, and only then after much restoration work had been carried out. The **Georgian Theatre Royal Museum** was also opened and it contains a unique collection of original playbills as well as the oldest and largest complete set of painted scenery in Britain.

Just outside the town lies **Easby Abbey**, a delightful monastic ruin which looks down to the River Swale. Founded in 1155 by Roald, Constable of Richmond Castle, its order of monks were of more modest leanings than the Cistercians, and the building certainly possesses none of the grandiose lines of Rievaulx and

16

Fountains, although the riverside setting is a common feature. The abbey's most notable feature is its replica of the Easby Cross, an Anglo-Saxon cross dating from the 9th century and the extensive ruins can be reached by a pleasant riverside walk that is well sign-posted.

RIPLEY

In the outer walls of the parish church at Ripley, built around 1400, are holes said to have been caused by musket balls from Cromwell's firing squad, who executed Royalist prisoners here after the battle of Marston Moor. Inside there is a fine Rood Screen dating from the reign of King Stephen and a mid-14th century tomb chest; the stone base of an old weeping cross (where one was expected to kneel in the stone grooves and weep for penance) survives in the churchyard.

Ripley, still very much an estate village, is a quiet and pretty place, with cobbled streets, a castle, a wonderful hotel, and an interesting history. The title was granted to Thomas Ingilby in the 1300s for killing a wild boar in Knaresborough Forest that was charging at King Edward III. Visitors strolling around Ripley cannot fail to notice the Hotel de Ville - the Town Hall. Sir William Amcotts Ingilby was responsible for this when, in 1827, he began to remodel the entire village on one which he had seen in Alsace Lorraine. The original thatched cottages were replaced with those seen today, and now Ripley is a conservation area with every pre-1980 dwelling being a Grade II listed building.

Magnificent **Ripley Castle** has been home to the Ingilby family for over 600 years. The castle is open to the public and is set in an outstanding "Capability" Brown landscape, with lakes, a deer park, and an avenue of tall beeches over which the attractive towers only just seem to peek. Its tranquillity belies the events that took place here after the battle at Marston Moor, when Cromwell, exhausted after his day's slaughter, camped his Roundheads here and chose to rest in the castle.

The Ingilbys, however, were Royalists and his intrusion was met with as much ill-will as possible; they offered neither food nor a bed. Jane Ingilby, aptly named "Trooper Jane" due to her fighting skills, was the house's occupant and, having forced the self-styled Lord Protector of England to sleep on a sofa with two pistols pointing at his head, declared the next morning, *"It was well that he behaved in so peaceable a manner; had it been otherwise, he would not have left the house alive."* Cromwell, his pride severely damaged by a woman ordered the immediate execution of his Royalist prisoners and left Trooper Jane regretting staying her hand during the previous night.

SETTLE

This small market town, which received its charter in 1249, still retains its thriving weekly market on Tuesdays. A busy stopping place in the days of the stagecoach, when travellers journeying between York and Lancaster and Kendal called here, Settle is now a popular place for visitors, walkers, and cyclists who stop in the town to take full advantage of the wide range of inns and hotels.

However, for most, Settle is the home of the famous **Settle-Carlisle Railway**, a proudly preserved memento of the glorious age of steam and the line is still flanked by charming little signal boxes and stations that are a real tourist magnet. This attractive railway was built in the midst of great controversy and even greater cost, in both money and lives, earning it the dubious title of *"the line that should never have been built"* . There is a churchyard at St Leonard's in Chapel-le-Dale, where over 100 of the workers and miners, who laboured under the most adverse conditions, lie buried. Today, the trains still thunder over the 21 viaducts, through the 14 tunnels, and over the numerous bridges for which they gave their lives.

Settle town itself is dominated by one of these huge viaducts as well as the towering limestone cliffs of **Castleberg Crag**, and it is worth spending some time here. Settle's architecture is very

Ribblehead Viaduct

distinctive, in the main being Victorian sandstone buildings that all look as if they are born of the railway culture. Buildings of note include the arcaded Shambles, originally butcher's slaughter houses, the French-style Town Hall, the Victorian Music Hall, and the oldest building, Preston's Folly, described as an extravaganza of mullioned windows and Tudor masonry, and so called because the man who created this anomalous fancy impoverished himself in the process! The composer, Edward Elgar, was a frequent visitor to the town; while here he stayed at the house of his friend, Dr Buck.

Apart from the grander structures on the main streets, there are charming little side streets lined with Georgian and Jacobean cottages and criss-crossed with quirky little alleyways and ginnels, with hidden courtyards and workshops of a time gone by. In Chapel Street is the **Museum of North Craven Life**, which gives a historical, topographical and geological background to the area. The imaginative displays tell the story of the local farming traditions and also the history of the building of the Settle-Carlisle Railway.

Just outside the town, housed in a refurbished 19th century cotton mill, is the **Watershead Mill Visitor Centre**. This charming place, on the banks of the River Ribble, offers a unique shopping experience, with the Dalesmade Centre offering a collection of 35 crafts all made in the region and much more besides.

The features of the surrounding countryside are equally interesting and, in particular, there is the fascinating Victorian Cave. Discovered in 1838 by Michael Horner, the cave has yielded finds of Roman relics, Stone Age artefacts, and even 120,000 year old mammoth bones. Unfortunately, the instability of the rock in the area has caused the cave and the surrounding land to be closed to the public.

Skipton

Often called the "Gateway to the Dales", Skipton's origins can be traced to the 7th century when farmers christened it Sheeptown. Featuring in the Domesday Book, the Normans decided to build a castle here to guard the entrance to Airedale, and Skipton became a garrison town. **Skipton Castle**, home of the Cliffords, was begun in 1090; the powerful stone structure seen today was devised in 1310 by Robert de Clifford, the 1st Earl of Skipton. The Cliffords were a fighting breed and, through-

out the Middle Ages, wherever there was trouble a member of the family was sure to be found. The 8th Lord Clifford, Thomas, and his son John were both killed while fighting for the House of Lancaster during the Wars of the Roses. Later, George Clifford, Champion to Queen Elizabeth I and a renowned sailor, fought against the Spanish Armada and, as well as participating in many voyages of his own, he also lent a ship to Sir Walter Ralegh.

One of the most complete and well preserved medieval castles in England, it is thanks to Lady Anne Clifford that visitors to Skipton can marvel at its buildings. Following the ravages of the Civil War, from which the castle did not escape, Lady Anne undertook a comprehensive restoration programme and, though little of the original Norman stonework remains, much of the work of the 1st Lord Clifford still stands.

As well as an enormous banqueting hall, a series of kitchens still remain with some of their original fittings, and a beautiful Tudor courtyard. There is also a rather unusually decorated room whose walls are lined with shells that were collected by George Clifford in the 19th century whilst he was travelling in the South Seas. However, the most striking feature of the castle is the impressive 14th century gateway, which is visible

Skipton Castle

18

from the High Street, and carries the Clifford family motto *Desormais*, meaning "Henceforth".

Adjacent to the castle, at the top of the High Street, lies the parish **Church of the Holy Trinity** which was originally built in the 12th century and replaced in the 1300s. There is a wealth of interest inside the building, which has been topped by a beautiful oak roof since the 15th century. It is possible to spend much time discovering the centuries of artefacts in the church; the various tombs and memorials are just as interesting and include the many tombs of the Clifford family. The church, too, suffered damage during the Civil War and, again, Lady Anne Clifford came to the rescue, restoring the interior and rebuilding the steeple in 1655. Inside the church, among the many tombstones is that of the Longfellow family, which included the uncle of the American poet, Henry Wadsworth Longfellow. As well as the fine castle and church, the Normans also established Skipton as a market town and it received its first charter in 1204. The market today is still thriving and is very much an important part of daily life in the area.

For many years Skipton remained a market town, then, with the development of the factory system in the 19th century, the nature of the town began to change. Textile mills were built and cottages and terraced houses were constructed for the influx of mill workers. However, not all were happy with the changes that the Industrial Revolution brought about and, in 1842, a group of men, women and children set out from the Pennine cotton towns and villages to protest at the mechanisation taking place. By the time the group had reached nearby Broughton, their number had grown to 3,000 and the Skipton magistrates urged them to turn back home. But the protesters continued, surging on Skipton, and the worried magistrates sent for military help. Moving from mill to mill, the mob stopped the looms. Special constables were quickly sworn in to help contain the situation, and the Riot Act was read from the town hall steps. Though the mob retreated to nearby Anne Hill, they refused to disperse and the soldiers were ordered to charge. During the ensuing violence, one soldier was killed and a magistrate blinded but the mob, bar six of the leaders who were arrested, fled as the first shots were fired.

The **Leeds and Liverpool Canal**, which flows through the town, provided a cheap form of transport as well as linking Skipton with the major industrial centres of Yorkshire and Lancashire. The first of three trans-Pennine routes, the 127 mile canal has 91 locks along the full length as well as two tunnels, one of which is over a mile long. Today the canal basin behind the town centre is busy with pleasure craft, and boat journeys can be taken along a section in the direction of Gargrave. The towpath was also restored at the same time as the canal, and there are a number of pleasant walks which include a stretch along the cul-de-sac Spring Branch beside the castle walls. Before the days of the canal, travelling by road, particularly in winter, was often a hazardous business. One local tale tells how, on Christmas Eve, during a bad snow storm, a young waggoner set out from the town for Blubberhouses. Though an innkeeper tried to dissuade him, the young man carried on into the night - thinking only of his betrothed, Ruth. He soon lost his way in a snow drift, and chilled by the fierce northerly winds, he fell to the ground in a comatosed sleep. Safe in her cottage, Ruth suddenly awoke and ran out of the house crying that her John was lost. Two men hurried after her and by the time they had caught up with Ruth she was digging out John with her bare hands. He was none the worse for his misadventure, and the couple married on New Year's Day.

A walk around the town is also worth while, and there are many interesting buildings to be found here. One, in particular, is the Town Hall which is now also the home of the **Craven Museum** (free). Dedicated to the surrounding area, there are many interesting displays relating to the geological and archaeological treasures that have been found locally, including a piece of Bronze Age cloth which is considered the oldest textile fragment in the country. Closer to the present day there are displays of furniture illustrating the fine craftsmanship that went into even the most mundane household item, and also farming exhibits which reflect the changing lives of many of the people who lived off the surrounding countryside.

Almost opposite the Town Hall, on the High Street, are the premises of the **Craven Herald**, a newspaper that was established in 1874, although the publication was produced for a short time in the 1850s. The building is fortunate in having retained its late Victorian shop front, as well as the passageway to one side, and it was first occupied by William Chippendale in the late 18th century. A trader in textiles, Chippendale made his money by buying then selling on the cloth woven by the farmers in their own homes. Close to the newspaper's offices is the **Public Library**, which opened in 1910 and was funded by Andrew Carnegie. A large, ornate building, it is in contrast to the town's older buildings and stands as a reminder of the change in character which Skipton underwent in the late 19th century. It seems fitting that, in a town which over many years has been dedicated to trade and commerce, Thomas Spencer, co-founder of Marks and Spencer, should have been born here in 1851. Skipton, too, was the home of Sir Winston Churchill's physician, Lord Moran, who grew up here as the son of the local doctor.

SNAPE

This quiet and unspoilt village, where the original timber-framed cottages stand side by side with their more modern neighbours, is still dominated by its castle as it has been for centuries. Reached via an avenue of lime trees, **Snape Castle** has a famous, if somewhat complicated, royal connection as it was the home of Lord Latimer of Snape (a member of the Neville family), the first husband of Catherine Parr, Henry VIII's last wife. The Nevilles owned the castle for over 700 years and its beautiful chapel, still used by the villagers, saw the marriages of many Latimers and Nevilles.

Set in over 1,000 acres of parkland, **Thorp Perrow Arboretum** is unique to Britain, if not Europe, in that it was the creation of one man, Col. Sir Leonard Ropner (1895-1977). Sir Leonard travelled all over the world collecting rare and unusual species for Thorp Perrow, and today the hundreds of trees he enthusiastically collected are in their prime. The arboretum was initially Sir Leonard's private hobby, but after his death his son, Sir John Ropner, decided to open the 85-acre garden to the public, and the arboretum is now one of the area's prime attractions. A treasure trove of specimen trees, woodland walks, nature trail, tree trails, a large lake, picnic area and children's play area, the Arboretum also embraces the **Milbank Pinetum**, planted by Lady Augusta Milbank in the mid-19th century, and the medieval Spring Wood dating back to the 16th century. Thorp

Perrow provides interest all year round, but perhaps the most popular time is the spring when you can witness one of the finest and most extensive plantings of daffodils in the north of England, among them some old and unusual varieties. In addition to the fascinating collection of trees, visitors will also find an information centre, a tea room and a plant sales area. An additional attraction at Thorp Perrow opened in the spring of 2000. The **Falcons of Thorp Perrow** is a brand new captive breeding, bird of prey and conservation centre which has been created within a large, formerly derelict walled garden.

THWAITE

Surrounded by dramatic countryside which includes Kisdon Hill, Great Shunnor, High Seat and Lovely Seat, this is a tiny village of ancient origins. Like so many places in the area the name comes from the Nordic language, in this case *thveit*, meaning a clearing in the wood. The woodlands which once provided shelter and fuel for the Viking settlers have long since gone.

To the southwest of the village lies *Buttertubs Pass*, one of the highest and most forbidding mountain passes in the country. The Buttertubs themselves are a curious natural feature of closely packed vertical stone stacks rising from some unseen, underground base to the level of the road. A local Victorian guide to the Buttertubs, perhaps aware that the view from above was not all that impressive, solemnly assured his client that "some of the Buttertubs had no bottom, and some were deeper than that". No one is quite sure where the Buttertubs name comes from. The most plausible explanation is that farmers used its deep-chilled shelves as a convenient refrigerator for the butter they couldn't sell immediately.

The narrow road from Thwaite across the Buttertubs Pass is not for the faint-hearted driver. Only a flimsy post and wire fence separates the road from a sheer drop of Alpine proportions. In any case, it's much more satisfying to cross the pass from the other direction, from Hawes: from the south as you crest the summit you will be rewarded with a stupendous view of Swaledale that stretches for miles.

19

20   The Board Hotel

Market Place,
Hawes,
North Yorkshire
DL8 3RD
Tel: 01969 667223
Fax: 01969 667970

Directions:

Hawes stands on the
A684 between Leyburn
and Sedbergh.

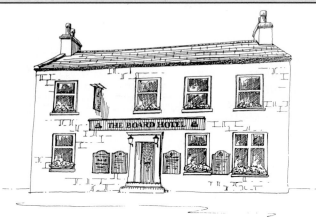

A warm Yorkshire welcome awaits visitors to the **Board Hotel**, an old coaching house constructed of sturdy stone in an excellent position in the heart of the market place. Popular with locals for its no-nonsense appeal and genuine hospitality, it also provides a good-value stopping place for visitors and tourists, whether for a drink, a meal or an overnight stay. Steve and Trudie, along with their very capable staff, take good care of their guests, and there's a comfortable, relaxed feel in the lovely light and airy bar-lounge and restaurant. Simple, unpretentious Yorkshire food ensures that no one leaves here hungry - and that can mean as many as 300 satisfied customers in a day. Home cooked pies and minted shoulder of lamb are among the specialities.

Overnight accommodation (Bed & Breakfast or Bed & Breakfast plus evening meal) comprises three rooms, two doubles and a twin, all with en suite facilities, tv and tea-making kit. AA 3 stars recommended. The Board has a little beer garden, and parking is available on the forecourt.

Hawes, a tiny place before the railway came in the 1870s, boasts several notable visitor attractions, including the Dales Countryside Museum (housed in the former railway station), its neighbour Hawes Ropemakers, and, most famously, the Wensleydale Creamery. Cheese was first made here, possibly by the monks of Jervaulx Abbey, some 700 years ago, and the first commercial cheese factory was opened at Gayle Beck, near Hawes, in 1897. Market day in Hawes is Tuesday. Hawes' neighbour Hardraw has the highest unbroken waterfall in England above ground (Turner and Wordsworth both walked behind it, and so can you) and further north, on the road to Thwaite, lies Butter Tubs Pass, one of the highest and most forbidding mountain passes in the country - not a route for the fainthearted!

Opening Hours: Mon-Sat, 11.00-23.00; Sun, 12.00-22.30
Food: Bar meals.
Credit Cards: All except Diners and Amex
Accommodation: 3 en suite rooms.

Local Places of Interest/Activities: Thwaite 10 miles, Hardraw, Askrigg 5 miles, Sedbergh 15 miles, Ribblehead Viaduct.

Internet/Website:
website: www.theboardhotel.co.uk
e-mail: theboardhotel1@netscapeonline.co.uk

The Bridge Inn 21

Grinton,
Nr. Richmond,
North Yorkshire
DL11 6HH
Tel: 01748 884224
Fax: 01748 884044

Directions:
1 mile south of Reeth
on the B6270

A fine old inn standing on a corner site next to the ancient packhorse bridge over the River Swale. The magnificent 12th century Church of St Andrew, known as the Cathedral of the Dale, stands opposite, completing a memorable backdrop. The ornate interior of the inn, which has changed little down the years, puts the emphasis on comfort, with open fires to take away a winter chill, and also makes the most of the location, with lovely views through the windows.

In the cosy public bars a selection of fine Jennings cask ales is waiting to be sampled, while in the bright, elegant restaurant (65 covers) diners are tempted with a wide-ranging menu dishes freshly prepared from prime ingredients and served in portions typical of Yorkshire hospitality. Wild boar and ale sausages - 'hog and hop' - were an intriguing item on a recent menu. The inn has a beer garden and ample parking space in a large private car park.

In a perfect position for exploring Swaledale and neighbouring Arkengarthdale, the **Bridge Inn**, which is run by Mark and Pauline Stephenson, provides a good night's rest in six well-appointed bedrooms - a single, four doubles and a family room - which all have bathrooms en suite, tv and hospitality tray. Central heating and double glazing ensure both warmth and peace. Prices are reasonable, and specials offers such as three nights for the price of two in winter show commendable enterprise. Friday night is quiz night. That superb church, which once served the whole of Swaledale, dates mainly from the 13th and 15th centuries, but also has some Norman traces and a 'leper's squint' - a small hole through which a leper could peep in at the service from outside. In nearby Reeth, local crafts and social history are the main topics in the Swaledale Folk Museum.

Opening Hours: Bar: Mon-Sat 11.00-23.00: Sun 11.00-22.30: Restaurant: 12.00-14.00, 18.30-21.00 daily

Food: A la carte.

Credit Cards: All except Diners

Accommodation: 6 en suite rooms.

Facilities: Car Park.

Entertainment: Quiz night Friday.

Local Places of Interest/Activities: Reeth 1 mile, Richmond 12 miles, Hudswell (King Arthur's Oven).

22   The Buck Inn

Buckden,
Upper Wharfedale,
North Yorkshire
BD23 5JA
Tel: 01756 760228
Fax: 01756 760227

Directions:

From Skipton (18 miles) take the B6265 then the B6160 through Thornfield and Kettlewell.

The Hayton family came to the **Buck Inn** over ten years ago, adding a friendly welcome and genuine hospitality to the abundant charm and character of their traditional Georgian coaching inn. The inn, an impressive sight with its long, creeper-covered stone frontage, faces southwest across the village green, and at the back the famous Buckden Pike rises dramatically to 2,300 feet. The Buck offers very high standards of comfort for guests staying overnight. The 14 beautifully furnished bedrooms, all en suite, with tv, telephone and tea-makers, comprise seven doubles, four twins, a single, a four-poster room and the splendid top-of-the-range Wharfedale Suite with a corner bath. Two of the rooms are on the ground floor.

The lounge bar, its open fire set in a massive stone surround, is a perfect place to relax - perhaps with a glass of Theakston's Best or one of the 35 malt whiskies in stock - and outstanding meals can be enjoyed in the atmospheric beamed restaurant built in the court-yard where wool auctions were once held. Local produce is very much to the fore through-out the tempting menus in the restaurant and in the bar, where lighter, informal meals are served. As well as offering everything that a guest could require, the Buck is open to non-residents for breakfast, morning coffee, bar lunches, afternoon teas and all meals. The kitchen is nothing if not versatile, with a team catering for all tastes: dishes on a recent menu - the choice changes constantly - included sea bass and roasted red pepper terrine, chargrilled lamb cutlets with a tomato and herb sauce, and confit duck leg on stir-fried noodles with an oriental-style sauce.

The little village of Buckden is at the heart of the wonderfully scenic Dales landscape with endless opportunities for exploring on foot or by car. Buckden was once the HQ of Norman officers hunting in the forest of Langstrothdale, and just south of the village can be seen an old stone cross that marked the forest boundary.

Opening Hours: Mon-Sat, 11.00-23.00; Sun, 11.00-22.30; Coffee available from 08.00 every day

Food: A la carte and bar meals.

Credit Cards: Access, Mastercard, Visa, JCB, Solo, Switch.

Accommodation: 14 en suite rooms.

Facilities: Off-road Parking.

Local Places of Interest/Activities: Artist shop across road with exhibitions, Kettlewell, Skipton (18 miles), Malham Cove, River Wharfe.

Internet/Website:
e-mail: thebuckinn@yorks.net
website: www.thebuckinn.yorks.net

Cross Keys Inn 23

High Street, Markington,
Nr. Harrogate,
North Yorkshire HG3 3NR
Tel: 01765 677555

Directions:

From Harrogate A61 north through Killinghall and Ripley. 5 miles after Ripley turn left on to minor road signposted Markington.

A well-established roadside hostelry in the middle of a pleasant village off the A61 between Harrogate and Ripon. The **Cross Keys** are emblazoned on the pub sign and also adorn the front of the tiny copper-topped bar in the beamed main room. Behind the pub is a beer garden

with a patio area, and there's plenty of off-road parking space. Tiggy and Frank arrived here as leaseholders two years ago, bringing with them plenty of experience in the licensed trade.

Tiggy does the cooking, and the fruits of her labour can be enjoyed in the little dining room or anywhere else in the pub. The menu and blackboard specials provide a good choice, but many of the regulars will tell you that Tiggy's steak pie is the best there is. Food is served Saturday lunchtime, all day Sunday, and Monday to Friday evenings. Two real ales (Tetley's and John Smith's), Webster's Green Label and a good selection of draught lagers take care of thirsts. Pool, darts and dominoes are all played with gusto, and Thursday night is quiz night. The bars are closed Monday to Friday lunchtimes except when it's a Bank Holiday. Three upstairs bedrooms with wash basins and shared bathroom facilities are available for Bed & Breakfast accommodation throughout the year.

The area round Markington is particularly well endowed with castles and grand ecclesiastical buildings: the magnificent Cathedral of St Peter and St Wilfrid at Ripon; the imposing ruins of Knaresborough Castle; Ripley Castle set in a lovely Capability Brown landscape; Robert Adam's Newby Hall at Skelton; and the evocative ruins of Fountains Abbey, the only World Heritage Site in Yorkshire.

Opening Hours: Mon-Fri, 17.00-23.00; Sat: 12.00-15.00, 17.00-23.00; Sun: 12.00-22.30

Food: Bar meals.

Credit Cards: None.

Accommodation: 3 rooms with shared facilities.

Facilities: Car Park.

Entertainment: Quiz night Thursdays

Local Places of Interest/Activities: Harrogate 8 miles, Ripon 6 miles, Fountains Abbey.

24   The Dog & Partridge

Tosside,
Nr. Skipton,
North Yorkshire
BD23 4SQ
Tel: 01729 840668

Directions:

On the B6478
between Long
Preston (A65) and
Slaidburn.

The Dog and Partridge is a 17th century hostelry in the quiet hamlet of Tosside, with fine views and easy access to Skipton, Settle, the Yorkshire Dales National Park and the Lakes. Betty Rigby, who owns the pub, is a superb cook, and along with her daughter Susan and some dedicated staff has really put the Dog & Partridge on the map. Starting life as an inn, it was later a gathering place where farmers came to pay their rent, then a temperance hotel owned by a local vicar, then the HQ of an animal sanctuary; it has now thankfully turned full circle, resuming its role as a hostelry and retaining all its erstwhile charm.

The bar has a quarry-tiled floor, the main lounge handsome old beams, the second lounge a feature fire, and old prints and memorabilia adorn the walls throughout. Betty's cooking is the undoubted main attraction, with lovely classic dishes like rabbit pie or steak & kidney pie among the highlights, or a really mouthwatering dish of Somerset pork with peaches. The day's roast is always in great demand, while for lighter or quicker meals there are plenty of snacks and sandwiches. The selection of real ales is particularly good, and Theakston's is the favourite local brew.

One of the eating areas is designated non-smoking, as are all the bedrooms. The four letting rooms, all on the first floor, are warm and cosy, not en suite but sharing good bathrooms. They are all equipped with tv and tea-making facilities. Gisburn Forest, which is part of the ancient Forest of Bowland, starts immediately behind the inn, offering superb scenery and miles of waymarked walking and cycling trails: a few hours gentle exercise here and you'll certainly be ready for one of Betty's pies!

Opening Hours: Tue-Sat 11.00-15.00, 19.00-23.00: Sun 12.00-15.00, 19.00-22.30 Closed Monday

Food: Homecooked bar meals

Credit Cards: None

Accommodation: 4 rooms with shared facilities

Facilities: Car Park

Entertainment: Pianist occasionally

Local Places of Interest/Activities: Gisburn Forest, close to Yorkshire Dales, walking, cycling

The Fountaine Inn   25

Linton-in-Craven,
Nr. Skipton,
North Yorkshire
BD23 5HJ
Tel: 01756 752210

Directions:

1 mile off B6265
Skipton-Grassington
road. Pass through
Cracoe towards
Grassington and
look for Linton signs
on the right.

Good food, good ale and a great atmosphere. That's the recipe for success at the **Fountaine Inn**, which enjoys a superb setting opposite the village green. Built as a row of three cottages in the 17th century, it has recently been refurbished throughout, and the interior is outstanding, with both decor and furnishings of a very high standard in the bar area, snug (with an open fire) and dining section. Food is served all day, from noon to 9pm, and at the weekend the 45 covers fill up quickly, so it's definitely best to book. The menus are splendidly varied, with something for everyone, and the portions are very generous. On the beer front, a minimum of six real ales are available, including brews from Black Sheep and Theakston's, and a further good range of draught bitter, lager, cider and stout.

Tenant Alan Betteridge, who took over here in June 2000, has ten years experience in the licensed trade and he has really put the Fountaine Inn back on the map. It's a very popular spot that attracts a loyal and ever-growing local trade, and the regular monthly themed food evenings have proved a notable success. Motorists can park their cars in the delightfully unspoilt village, which boasts a fine example of rural medieval architecture.

The Church of St Michael and All Angels lies a little way from the centre but its handsome bell-cote is an easy-to-spot landmark. Among the 14th century roof bosses can be seen the Green Man, an ancient fertility symbol that was widely adopted by the Christian church. Spanning Linton Beck is a graceful 14th century packhorse bridge that was repaired by Dame Elizabeth Redmayne in the late 17th century. During the work she had a narrow parapet added to prevent carts from crossing, because, it is said, the local farmers refused to chip in with the repair bill!

Opening Hours: Mon-Sat 11.00-23.00: Sun 12.00-22.30

Food: Bar meals.

Credit Cards: Access, Mastercard, Visa.

Accommodation : None.

Facilities: Outside Seating

Entertainment: Darts, Cards, Dominoes

Local Places of Interest/Activities:
Grassington 2 miles, Wharfedale, Embsay Moor, Embsay Railway.

26   The Fox & Hounds

West Burton,
Bishopdale,
North Yorkshire
DL8 4JY
Tel: 01969 663111
Fax: 01969 663544

Directions:

Off the B6160 7 miles west of Leyburn, 3 miles south of Aysgarth Falls (A164).

In the centre of an unspoilt, picturesque village, the **Fox & Hounds** is a traditional Wensleydale pub of immense charm. John Furniss and his family and staff provide a warm, friendly welcome in their newly refurbished pub, where low oak beams contribute to an old-world scene in the bar and dining room. Traditional Yorkshire fare, all prepared and cooked on the premises, is served in both areas - daily specials are in demand at lunchtime, and an à la carte menu is served from 6.30 to 9 in the evening, when the popularity of the place makes booking advisable. Hand-pulled Yorkshire ales quench thirsts and taste good, too. Picnic tables at the front of the pub overlook the pretty village green, and at the back is a private car park. Well-behaved dogs are allowed, but no children under the age of 14.

This is very much a place for lingering, and for visitors staying overnight there are seven comfortably appointed, centrally heated bedrooms, all en suite, with tvs and tea-making facilities. Guests are invited to join the locals in the fun of the quiz nights, music nights and karaoke sessions that are all held regularly.

The village of West Burton is one of the prettiest in all Wensleydale; it lies in a conservation area and is best known for its large and beautiful village green. Just to the east of the village a path leads across a small packhorse bridge to Mill Force, perhaps the most photogenic of the Wensleydale waterfalls. These are a major feature hereabouts, the most spectacular being Aysgarth Falls, where the River Ure thunders through a rocky gorge and tumbles 200 feet over limestone slabs.

Opening Hours: 11.00-23.00 high season; 11.00-15.00 & 18.00-23.00 low season.

Food: Bar meals and à la carte.12.00-14.00, 18.30-21.00

Credit Cards: Access, Mastercard, Visa, Delta, Switch.

Accommodation: 7 en suite rooms.

Facilities: Car Park.

Entertainment: Live music, karaoke and quiz nights.

Local Places of Interest/Activities: Leyburn 7 miles, Aysgarth 3 miles, Bolton Castle (a fortified manor house where Mary Queen of Scots was detained).

The George Inn

27

Kirk Hill,
Hubberholme,
Nr. Skipton,
North Yorkshire
BD23 5JE
Tel: 01756 760223
Fax: 01756 760808

Directions:

Just off the B6160
between Kettlewell
and Kidstones, 15
miles north of
Skipton.

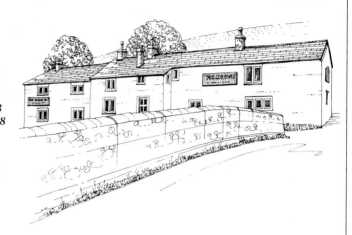

The George Inn is a traditional Dales inn, with flagstone floors, stone walls, mullion windows, old beams and open fires. The inn's location is one of its chief assets, with the glorious dales and fells all around and the River Wharfe running by - a tranquil and secluded setting, but by no means remote, as it's an easy drive to Hawes in one direction and Skipton in the other. Owners Jenny and Terry Browne, in the licensed trade for more than 20 years, are the most delightful hosts, and a warm welcome is guaranteed for all who drop in, whether locals with familiar faces or first-timers touring this wonderful part of the world.

Home-cooked meals based on local produce are served in the two cosy bars; hot and cold snacks provide light lunchtime sustenance, while for something more substantial the Yorkshire puddings with onion gravy and sausage or beef are always popular. Dishes such as sirloin steak or herby halibut steak are served lunchtime and evening, and the full dinner menu expands the choice with the likes of Dales lamb chops or lamb casserole made with Black Sheep ale from Masham brewery.

For guests staying overnight the George has seven letting bedrooms, four en suite and three with shared facilities. All the rooms have tv and tea-making kit.

The tiny hamlet of Hubberholme has a 13th century church with a rood loft (the crucifix was installed in 1558). The pews are the work of the renowned Robert 'Mouseman' Thompson of Kilburn - look for his signature carved mice. On the first day of the year the Hubberholme Parliament meets at the inn to perform the ancient tradition of land-leasing.

Opening Hours: Closed 2 weeks early January. Normal hours 11.00-15.00 and 18.00-23.00 but phone for details

Food: Bar meals and à la carte.

Credit Cards: Access, Mastercard, Visa.

Accommodation: 7 bedrooms, 4 en suite.

Facilities: Car Park.

Local Places of Interest/Activities: Aysgarth Falls 10 miles, Hawes 10 miles, Skipton 15 miles, Yorkshire Dales National Park.

Internet/Website:
e-mail: thegeorgeinn@virgin.net

28 The Golden Lion Hotel

Market Place,
Leyburn,
North Yorkshire
DL8 5AS
Tel: 01969 622161
Fax: 01969 623836

Directions:

Leyburn lies at the
junction of the A684
(Northallerton-
Hawes) and the
A6108 (Ripon-
Richmond).

A traditional family hotel, **The Golden Lion** lies on the broad market place of mid-Wensleydale's main market town and trading centre. Dating from 1765, Anne Wood's fine little hotel offers facilities usually associated with much larger establishments. The 15 tastefully furnished bedrooms, all en suite, have tv, telephone, radio and tea-making kit, and a lift to the first and second floors eases access for disabled guests, for whose needs many of the rooms have been adapted.

In the 70-cover restaurant, murals of Dales scenes by local artist Lynn Foster provide a pleasant backdrop to good wholesome Yorkshire fare freshly prepared from local ingredients - the roast beef is famous throughout the Dales! Diners can choose between à la carte and fixed-price menus, or go for something lighter from the informal snack menu served in the bar areas. The oak-panelled bars are at their busiest on market day, which has been a Friday ever since Charles ll granted the town its market charter in 1686.

Leyburn rewards exploring on foot with its many handsome old buildings, shops and craft centres - the Teapottery (witty and unusual teapots) and the Violin Making Workshop are two of the most fascinating. The Shawl, to the west of town, is a mile-long escarpment that offers wonderful views east and west; it was here that Mary Queen of Scots is said to have been recaptured after escaping from nearby Bolton Castle. Middleham, just two miles away, has two claims to fame, as a major centre for the training of racehorses (the legendary Sam Hall was here for many years) and as the site of Middleham Castle, where Richard lll was sent as a lad for part of his education in the noble arts.

Opening Hours: 08.00-23.00.

Food: Bar meals and snacks. A la carte and table d'hote. 12.00-14.00, 18.30-21.00 (restaurant 19.00-21.00)

Credit Cards: Access, Mastercard, Visa, Delta.

Accommodation: 15 en suite rooms.

Facilities: Car Park, function room.

Local Places of Interest/Activities: Aysgarth Falls, Middleham Castle, Jervaulx Abbey.

Internet/Website:
 e-mail: annegoldenlion@aol.com

The Green Dragon Country Inn   29

Exelby,
Bedale,
North Yorkshire
DL8 2HA
Tel: 01677 422233

Directions:

Exelby is located on the B6285 between Bedale and Theakston, very close to the A1.

Built in the early 1800s and little changed in appearance down the years, the **Green Dragon** is all that's best in a country pub. Owner Irene Shields puts the comfort of her customers high on her list of priorities, and the main bar area is roomy and inviting, with log fires, leather sofas to sink into, lots of intimate little snugs and plenty of elbow room for downing a pint.

But the biggest attraction of this large pub in a small village is the food, and the reputation of the kitchen has spread to the far corners of the county and well beyond. Everything is prepared and cooked on the premises from the pick of the season's produce, and few would disagree with Irene's claim that the pies, made the proper way with shortcrust pastry, are unrivalled in the whole of Yorkshire. Food is served in the bars and the restaurant from 12 to 2 at lunchtime (till 3 in high season) and from 6 to 9 in the evening (till 10 in high season). There's a pleasant beer garden in which to enjoy a glass of hand-pulled ale in the sun. The car park is well able to cope with the number of hungry customers, and visitors in touring caravans can use the adjacent caravan park, which is owned by the pub. The pub also offers Bed & Breakfast accommodation in two double bedrooms with private showers. Tuesday night is quiz night at this really outstanding pub, which stands in a prime site in the village's main street.

Exelby is signposted from the A1, which is only two minutes' drive away. Places of interest in the locality include the agreeable little market town of Bedale and the castle and arboretum at Snape.

Opening Hours: 11.00-23.00 every day

Food: Bar meals and à la carte.

Credit Cards: All except Diners.

Accommodation: 2 double rooms, 1 singl room all with showers.

Facilities: Car Park.

Entertainment: Quiz night Tuesday.

Local Places of Interest/Activities: Bedale 3 miles, Catterick 10 miles, Richmond 12 miles, Ripon 12 miles.

30 Hopper Lane Hotel

Skipton Road,
Blubberhouses,
Nr. Otley,
West Yorkshire
LS21 2NZ
Tel/Fax:
01943 880246

Directions:

8 miles from
Harrogate, 10 miles
from Skipton on
the A59.

Simon and Catherine, both very experienced in the licensed trade, have held the lease at **Hopper Lane** since July 1999. The two linked buildings, a former ale house and farmhouse, date from the 16th century and enjoy a superb location in the picturesque Washburn Valley. The beautiful countryside of the Yorkshire Dales surrounds the village, but it's also an easy drive to Ilkley, Skipton, Harrogate and other historic towns. open fires warm the public areas, and in the cosy stone-walled dining room a floodlit well (covered of course!) is an interesting feature.

A minimum of four real ales is always available, and the pub enjoys a growing reputation for the excellence of its cooking. Bar meals, cream teas and restaurant meals are all produced with equal care and enthusiasm, and when the weather's fine a meal can be enjoyed in the pleasant surroundings of the beer garden. The specials board always makes mouthwatering reading, with dishes drawn from both local recipes and the world's cuisines. Representing the 'home' team could be Yorkshire puddings with onion gravy and home-made sausages with bubble and squeak, while the 'visitors' could include Scottish rope-grown mussels with garlic, herbs and cream, chicken espagnol, Bengali balti with three different meats and Peking duck served on a bed of rice or noodles with an apple, mango, ginger and orange sauce.

For guests staying overnight, year-round accommodation comprises five comfortable bedrooms, all with en suite facilities, tv and hairdryer, and all located on the ground floor.

Opening Hours: All day, every day

Food: Bar meals and à la carte.

Credit Cards: Access, Diners, Mastercard, Visa.

Accommodation: 5 en suite rooms.

Facilities: Off-road parking space, function room.

Entertainment: Varies - phone for details

Local Places of Interest/Activities: Harrogate 8 miles, Skipton 10 miles, Bolton Priory.

King William 1V

31

Brompton-on-Swale,
Nr. Richmond,
North Yorkshire
DL10 7HN
Tel: 01748 811416

Directions:
Brompton-on-Swale
is located on the
A6136 three miles
south of Richmond.

A typical rural pub in a little village three miles south of the historic town of Richmond. The two-tier lounge has a separate bar, and the main area is comfortably carpeted, with excellent seating and lots of intimate little corners. Run in fine style by Graham and DebbieVickers, the **King William IV** is a favourite meeting place for the locals, who come for the relaxed atmosphere that always prevails, for the good beer and for the freshly prepared home-cooked bar food that is served every lunchtime and every evening. Families are always made very welcome, and children can keep themselves amused in their own special play area. Thursday night is quiz night. Motorists touring with a caravan should note that there is a very large caravan park nearby.

It's an easy drive to the town of Richmond, where the places of interest on any tourist's itinerary should include the imposing castle, the Green Howards Museum and Culloden Tower, built in 1747 by the Yorke family, one of whose members had fought at the Battle of Culloden the year before. Just outside the town are the romantic ruins of Easby Abbey. A little way to the west, off the A6108, is the ancient village of Hudswell, where a walk down steps through woodland leads to King Arthur's Oven, a horizontal crack in the limestone that is said to have connections with Richmond Castle and the Arthurian legend. Even closer to the King William is Catterick Bridge, whose popular racecourse stage horseracing under both Flat and National Hunt rules.

Opening Hours: 12.00-23.00 (Wed: 17.00-23.00 only)

Food: Bar meals.

Credit Cards: None

Accommodation: None.

Facilities: Car Park, Beer garden

Entertainment: Darts, dominoes, bull ring, Sky TV, quiz nights every other Thursday

Local Places on Interest/Activities:
Richmond 3 miles, Catterick 2 miles, Constable Burton Hall & Gardens, Jervaulx Abbey.

32 The Kings Head

40 Market Place,
Bedale,
North Yorkshire
DL8 1EQ
Tel: 01677 422763
Fax: 01677 427700

Directions:

12 miles east of
Leyburn on the
A684.

This delightful old pub enjoys a prime main-street location in the centre of Bedale over-looking the wide market place. **The Kings Head** is one of many attractive Georgian buildings in this largely unspoilt little town, and the broad alley to one side, leading to a garden, reveals its origins as a coaching inn. Behind the imposing stonework the interior has changed little down the years, and comfort and hospitality have always been the watchword.

Hosts Steve Reed and Adam Lawrence have their fingers on the pulse of Bedale and have made their inn a popular meeting place for the young of the town as well as the older generation of regulars. Adam is the chef, offering a well-balanced menu of made-to-order dishes with the emphasis on variety. The Kings Head is also highly regarded for its selection of ales. Entertainment here takes the form of regular karaoke sessions and a disco on Friday and Saturday evenings.

Bedale is handily placed as a base for touring Wensleydale, and guests staying overnight at the inn have the use of two double rooms with en suite facilities, tvs and tea-makers - there are plans to add more rooms. There is plenty to see and do in and around Bedale itself, a pleasant market town developed from the point where the Saxon track from Ripon joined the route from Northallerton to Wensleydale. At Crakehall, two miles west, the mighty water mill and the Museum of Badges and Battledress are both well worth a visit, while attractions at Snape, two miles south of town, include a castle, an arboretum and pinetum, and a bird of prey centre.

Opening Hours: Mon-Sat 12.00-23.00; Sun 12.00-22.30

Food: Bar meals.

Credit Cards: None

Accommodation: 1 family, 1 twin and 5 singles all en suite.

Entertainment: Disco, karaoke.

Local Places of Interest/Activities: Leyburn 12 miles, Northallerton 10 miles, Richmond 10 miles, Catterick races.

The New Inn   33

Main Street,
Cononley,
Nr. Keighley,
North Yorkshire
BD20 8NR
Tel: 01535 636302

Directions:

From Skipton A6069,
then A629, turn
right on to minor
road signposted
Cononley.

The New Inn is a lovely old pub dating back some 400 years, on a corner site in a village just off the main road from Skipton to Keighley. Plants and hanging baskets produce a fine show of colour in season, and the interior is particularly homely and cosy, with an old stone fireplace and a collection of gleaming copper and brass ornaments. Tenants Andrew and Helen Garside, who moved here from another Yorkshire pub in 1999, welcome all ages in their delightful inn and beer-drinkers happy with a full range of draught ales, including Timothy Taylor's championship-winning Landlord and, in winter, the smashing Ram Tam.

Helen is a first-class cook, and in the bar or in the grand upstairs restaurant a good variety of dishes is served lunchtime and evening (except Saturday and Sunday evenings). A splendid and very reliable butcher supplies the main ingredients for many of the most popular dishes, among them steak sizzlers, mixed grills and really tasty meat & potato pies. At the back of the pub is a beer garden where children can play in safety. Tuesday is quiz night. Street parking.

Among the many delightful places to visit in the vicinity of Cononley are Kildwick, a picturesque little village on the north bank of the River Aire. The village church is unusually long - hence its local name of Lang Kirk o'Craven. The village of Lothersdale, a neighbour of Cononley, is on a dramatic stretch of the Pennine Way. Stonegappe, a residence on a hillside near its church, was the model for the house called Gateshead in Charlotte Brontë's *Jane Eyre.* Also within an easy drive is Keighley, a bustling textile and engineering town with many grand buildings from its Victorian heyday.

Opening Hours: 12.00-15.00, 18.00-23.00;
Sat & Sun 12.00-23.00

Food: Bar meals and à la carte.

Credit Cards: All the major cards except
Amex

Accommodation: None.

Facilities: Function room seating 40

Entertainment: Quiz night Tuesday.,
occassional "Blues Night"

Local Places of Interest/Activities: Skipton
5 miles, Keighley (Worth Valley Railway) 6
miles, Wharfedale, Embsay Steam Railway.

34   The Old Swan Inn

20 High Street,
Gargrave,
Nr. Skipton,
North Yorkshire
BD23 3RB
Tel: 01756 749232

Directions:

4 miles northwest of
Skipton on the A65
road to Kirkby
Lonsdale.

Locals, walkers, cyclists and motorists are all equally welcome at the **Old Swan Inn**, which stands on the A65 on the edge of the village of Gargrave. The old building was sensitively refurbished early in 2000 to provide four main public areas: a non-smoking lounge/dining room with seats for 40+; a cosy parlour complete with rocking chair; a flagstone snug with an open fire; and the convivial main bar. Since the refurbishment the inn has been run by Adrian and Veronica Shaw, whose first venture as leaseholders this is

They are maintaining and indeed enhancing the inn's reputation for providing hearty home-cooked food in a relaxed, informal setting. Ingredients are obtained fresh from local farmers and producers wherever possible, the basis of a broad range of traditional dishes and daily specials prepared by the kitchen team, with an experienced and talented chef. Food is served lunchtime and evening every session and all day in the summer. It's advisable to book for Sunday lunch. Timothy Taylor's Landlord is a favourite among the real ales, and there's also a good choice of bottled, keg and draught ales, as well as an extensive wine list including fruit wines.

The Old Swan has five letting bedrooms of different sizes, all with en suite facilities and with TV and drink making facilities. Tuesday night is quiz night (with prizes!) open to all-comers. The inn is situated just moments from the Pennine Way, the Leeds & Liverpool Canal and the River Aire, so it's a fine base for walking, cycling and even boating holidays, as well for those exploring the area by car. Local places of interest include the historic market town of Skipton, Malham Cove with its limestone causeway and the Embsay & Bolton Abbey steam railway.

Opening Hours: Mon-Sat, 11.00-23.00; Sun 12.00-22.30

Food: Bar meals and restaurant. Sunday lunchtime carvery - advisable to book.

Credit Cards: All the major cards.

Accommodation: 5 en suite rooms.

Facilities: Car Park to the right hand side, Beer garden. Private functions catered for.

Entertainment: Quiz night Tuesday, occasional music nights, 1st Thu of the month theme menu - international flavour.

Local Places of Interest/Activities: Skipton 4 miles, Malham, Pennine Way.

Internet/Website:
e-mail: adyshaw007@hotmail.com
www.yourlocal.co.uk/theswanatgargrave

The Rose & Crown Hotel | 35

Bainbridge,
North Yorkshire DL8 3EE
Tel: 01969 650225
Fax: 01969 650735

Directions:
Bainbridge is on the A684 between Hawes and Leyburn.

In business as a hostelry since 1445, the **Rose & Crown**, owned and run by David and Sue Collinson, lives up to its long-established reputation as the 'Pride of Wensleydale'. Overlooking the village green with its set of old stocks, it has an unrivalled tradition of hospitality, and its 12 prettily furnished bedrooms, all with private facilities, tv, radio, tea-making kit and hairdryers, provide an excellent night's sleep. Some of the rooms boast four-poster beds. A cosy residents' lounge is at the disposal of guests, and among the other day rooms are a lounge bar with an open log fire in winter, a snug and a bar known as the Dust & Diesel, ideal for meeting and mixing with the locals.

In the 100-cover Dales Room restaurant the emphasis is on traditional food, with the best of local produce freshly prepared in the hotel's kitchens. The mighty mixed grill is guaranteed to satisfy even the most ravenous diner! Lighter meals and snacks are served in the bars. Parking for 65 cars. Fishing can be arranged on the River Ure.

Bainbridge originally stood in the ancient Forest of Wensleydale, and the famous Bainbridge Horn was blown to guide travellers from the forest to the safety and shelter of the village. The Horn is no longer needed as the forest has disappeared, but it is still blown every evening from Holy Rood (September 27) to Shrovetide; it is kept in the hall of the hotel. Nearby attractions include the Wensleydale Creamery at Hawes, home of Wensleydale cheese; the falls at Aysgarth and Hardraw; and the tiny River Bain, said to be the shortest in England. This is the perfect hotel from which to go walking in the dales.

Opening Hours: Mon-Sat, 09.00-23.00; Sun, 11.00-22.30

Food: Bar meals and à la carte; Mon-Sat, 12.00-14.00; Sun 12.00-14.30

Credit Cards: All except Amex and Diners.

Accommodation: 12 en suite rooms.

Facilities: Function room, Car Park.

Entertainment: Just the hornblowing.

Local Places of Interest/Activities: Aysgarth, Hawes 5 miles, Bolton Castle.

Internet/Website:
www.theprideofwensleydale.co.uk
e-mail: stay@rose-and-crown.freeserve.co.uk

36   The Ship Inn

Frenchgate, Richmond,
North Yorkshire DL10 7AE
Tel: 01748 823182

Directions:
Richmond lies on the A6136, just off the A1 between Leeming and Scotch Corner.

Frenchgate is in one of the choicest parts of town, with streets of handsome old houses interspersed with a few hotels and restaurants - and this lovely little pub. **The Ship Inn** was first launched in 1750, and subsequent alterations and upgrading have in no way detracted from its charm.

Behind its modest street frontage the Ship is surprisingly large, extending back some 50 yards and featuring impressively thick walls and elaborately decorated doors and windows. The games room, where pool, darts and dominoes are the main activities, is also used as a venue for various meetings and small functions, and this very sociable pub also hosts weekly live music sessions (Friday) and quiz nights (Sunday). Out at the back is pleasant, secluded beer garden where children can have fun in their own play area, complete with a wooden play house. Real ales, including regularly changing guest brews, take care of grown-up thirsts.

Mark McCulloch, the landlord, will not be short of custom, either from the citizens of Richmond or from the thousands who visit this important North Yorkshire town each year. The best known of its many historic buildings are the imposing Norman castle on a rocky promontory above the River Swale, and the elaborate Culloden Tower, built in 1747 by the Yorke family to honour a relative who fought at the eponymous battle the year before. It is not surprising that a town so steeped in history should have several museums: among the most notable are the Richmond Museum of Local History and the Green Howards Museum in the old Trinity Church. Richmond is also home to England's oldest theatre, the Georgian Theatre Royal built in 1788 and lovingly preserved (and used).

Opening Hours: 12.00-15.00, 18.00-23.00; Fri, Sat & Sun 12.00-23.00
Food: Restaurant planned for the future
Credit Cards: None
Accommodation: None

Entertainment: Sunday Quiz nights, Fridays light music, darts, dominoes

Local Places of Interest/Activities: Historic Richmond, Catterick 5 miles, Hudswell (King Arthur's Oven) 3 miles.

The Shoulder of Mutton | 37

Kirby Hill,
Nr. Richmond,
North Yorkshire
DL11 7JH
Tel: 01748 822772

Directions:
Kirby Hill lies on a
minor road 4 miles
north of Richmond;
or look out for the
village on the A66
five miles north of
Scotch Corner.

In a tiny, picturesque village four miles north of Richmond, the **Shoulder of Mutton** enjoys magnificent views of Holmedale and beyond. Built as a row of cottages in 1780, but with a license from the beginning, it is a fine example of a traditional inn, with a healthy covering of creeper adorning the outside. Log fires burn in the bar, and the stone walls and original beams make an attractive backdrop to a meal in the dining room. Much of the wall space in all the public areas is taken up by pints, plates, brasses and other assorted ornaments. It is even reputed that Charles Dickens stayed here.

The Shoulder of Mutton, as befits its name, is very much food-driven, with both bar and restaurant menus available. The cooking is traditional English, and among the all-time favourites are a superb steak & kidney pie, rabbit pie and, naturally, shoulder of lamb. Sunday lunch is a real bargain, and the hearty, packed-with-flavour food is complemented by a range of cask and draught ales and well-chosen wines. In fine weather picnic benches are set out under sunshades in the front garden. Besides keeping the inner man happy, landlords John and Polly Bacon offer comfortable accommodation in five letting bedrooms, all with en suite facilities, tv and hospitality tray. Four of the rooms are doubles, the fifth a family room with bunk beds for the children.

The moorland that stretches to the west of the village, unbroken except for the occasional minor road, is wonderful walking country. A short drive in the other direction, across the A66, brings the traveller to East Layton, where a new attraction, Miniature World, is home to dozens of small tame animals, and Stanwick Camp, a series of 2,000-year-old banks and ditches that make an impressive sight. To the south is the historic town of Richmond, to the north, just over the border in County Durham, the equally interesting town of Barnard Castle.

Opening Hours: 12.00-23.00; off season 12.00-15.00 & 18.00-23.00.

Food: Bar meals and à la carte.

Credit Cards: All the major cards

Accommodation: 5 en suite rooms.

Facilities: Car Park.

Entertainment: Mondays Jam session - been going for 25 years; Fridays quiz night

Local Places of Interest/Activities: Richmond 4 miles, Barnard Castle.

Internet/Website:
e-mail: john@holmedale.com
website: holmdale.com

38 | The Three Horseshoes

Ripon Road,
Killinghall,
Nr. Harrogate,
North Yorkshire
HG3 2DH
Tel: 01423 506302

Directions:
Killinghall lies on
the A61 2 miles
north of Harrogate.

Darren Pike and his wife Louise have recently taken over **The Three Horseshoes**, which enjoys a lovely setting in a village a short drive north of Harrogate. They set about refurbishing the 1950s building from top to bottom, and its bright, eyecatching outward appearance is matched by an immaculate interior which has clearly benefited from a keen eye for detail and design. It's a really super spot to pause on a journey, at once civilised and lively, and the growing band of regulars give full marks to the ambience, the excellent cask ales and the traditional bar food. The menu is very well conceived and the dishes are always appetising and full of flavour; food is served lunchtime and evening Tuesday to Friday, and from noon to 7 o'clock on Saturday and Sunday - no food Monday. Wednesday night is quiz night, and there's live music most Saturdays. The pub has a garden and a car park.

The renowned spa town of Harrogate, only five minutes away by car, has a multitude of attractions for the visitor, including the Royal Pump Room Museum in a building beneath which the sulphur water still rises. Knaresborough, too, with its dominating ruined castle, is very close by, and even closer, off the main road that runs north to Ripon, is the majestic Ripley Castle. Home to the Ingleby family for over 600 years, the castle, which is open to the public, is set in a superb Capability Brown landscape with lakes, a deer park and an avenue of tall beech trees. Also of interest in Ripley is the parish church, built around 1400 and bearing the scars of the aftermath of the Battle of Marston Moor.

Opening Hours: 11.00-23.00.

Food: Bar meals.

Credit Cards: Access, Mastercard, Visa, Switch.

Accommodation: None.

Facilities: Car Park.

Entertainment: Quiz Wednesday

Local Places of Interest/Activities: Harrogate 3 miles, Knaresborough 4 miles, Ripley 2 miles.

The White Lion

39

Priest Bank,
Kildwick,
Nr. Skipton,
North Yorkshire
BD20 9BH
Tel: 01535
632265/636586

Directions:

Look for the
Kildwick sign off
the main Skipton-
Keighley road
(A629).

Likeable landlord Alistair Maclennan spent five years working in bars and restaurants all over the world and he celebrated the new millennium by settling in at the **White Lion**, an imposing pub opposite the church in a picturesque village on the north bank of the River Aire. Behind the handsome brick frontage the look is charmingly old-fashioned, with old beams, exposed stone, darkwood panelling and rustic furniture - all playing their part in the inviting, traditional picture. A dartboard and a tv screen are neighbours in the bar, where a minimum of three real ales are available.

In the restaurant, where horse brasses, pewter tankards and old prints adorn the walls, diners have a plentiful choice of dishes. The main menu is supplemented by weekly specials which probably owe something to the landlord's recent globetrotting: nachos grande, Thai green curry, mixed cheese ravioli, garlic mushroom and mascarpone lattice. Food is served from 12 till 2 and from 6 till 8.30 every day except Monday evening. At 9 o'clock sharp every Wednesday the weekly quiz gets under way, and once in a while there's a live folk music session - visitors are welcome to bring their own instruments and join in the fun. As we went to press the amenities of this fine old hostelry were about to be expanded with the coming on stream of three en suite double bedrooms for Bed & Breakfast accommodation.

The church opposite the pub is the Church of St Andrew, dating mainly from the 14th and 15th centuries and known for its unusually long choir (hence the local name Lang Kirk o'Craven). The village lies on the River Aire and also on the Leeds & Liverpool Canal, no longer used commercially but popular with pleasure craft.

Opening Hours: 12.00-15.00, 18.00-23.00; all day Fri, Sat & Sun.

Food: A la carte and specials menu daily

Credit Cards: Access, Diners, Mastercard, Visa.

Accommodation: 3 en suite bedrooms April 2001.

Facilities: Car Park,

Entertainment: Quiz night Wednesday.

Local Places of Interest/Activities: Keighley, Skipton, Ilkley.

40   Wyvill Arms

Constable Burton,
Wensleydale,
North Yorkshire
DL8 5LH
Tel: 01677 450581

Directions:

4 miles east of
Leyburn on the
A684.

Built in 1920, the **Wyvill Arms** occupies an elevated site with spectacular gardens and plenty of car parking space. Its dry-stone walls are covered in ivy, giving it a much older look than its 80 years. Inside, all is spick and span, with open log fires. well-spaced tables and lots of elbow room to enjoy a pint at the bar. This is very much a food-driven establishment and the owner Nigel Stevens is himself a chef. He sets great store by his menus, which always make excellent use of fresh ingredients - many of them local - in producing dishes to excite the palate as well as satisfy country appetites.

The Wyvill Arms is a good place to stay as well as to eat, and the three en suite bedrooms, all with tv and tea-making kit, offer very comfortable accommodation with the bonus of pleasant views. Well sited at the foot of Wensleydale on the main road (A164) to Bedale, the inn is an excellent base for touring this exceptionally beautiful part of the world. In the village itself, surrounded by walled and wooded parkland, Constable Burton Hall is famous for its gardens and in particular its spacious, romantic terraces; the gardens are open to the public from March to October. The market towns of Leyburn and Bedale have much to attract the visitor, and other places of interest in the vicinity include Jervaulx Abbey near East Witton, in ruins but still one of the most evocative of Yorkshire's many fine abbeys; and the extraordinary Marmion Tower, a Tudor gatehouse overlooking the River Ure at West Witton.

Opening Hours: 11.00-15.00,18.00-23.00.

Food: A la carte.

Credit Cards: Access, Mastercard, Visa, Switch, Delta.

Accommodation: 3 en suite rooms.

Facilities: Car Park.

Entertainment: Occasional quiz nights.

Local Places of Interest/Activities: Leyburn 4 miles, Catterick races (Flat & National Hunt), Richmond 10 miles, Jervaulx Abbey, Bedale 9 miles.

Internet/Website:
website: www.wyvillarms.com

2

North York Moors, Heritage Coast & the Vale of Pickering

PLACES OF INTEREST:

PUBS AND INNS:

The Hidden Inns of Yorkshire

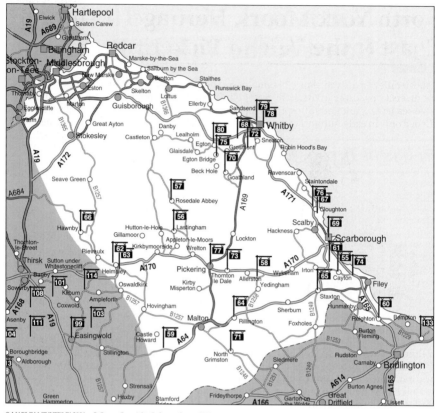

© MAPS IN MINUTES ™ 2001   © Crown Copyright, Ordnance Survey 2001

55	**Blacksmiths Arms**, Cayton		**68**	**The Huntsman**, Aislaby
56	**The Blacksmiths Arms**, Lastingham		**69**	**Ivanhoe Hotel**, Scarborough
57	**The Blacksmiths Country Inn**, Rosedale Abbey		**70**	**Mallyan Spout Hotel**, Goathland
58	**The Coachman Inn**, Snainton		**71**	**Middleton Arms**, North Grimston
59	**The Crown & Cushion**, Welburn		**72**	**Netherby House**, Sleights
60	**The Dotterel Inn**, Reighton		**73**	**The New Inn**, Thornton-le-Dale
61	**Eastfield Hotel**, Eastfield		**74**	**The Ox Inn**, Lebberston
62	**The Feathers**, Helmsley		**75**	**The Postgate**, Egton Bridge
63	**The Feversham Arms**, Helmsley		**76**	**The Red Lion**, Cloughton
64	**The Fleece Inn**, Rillington		**77**	**The Rose Inn**, Pickering
65	**The Hare & Hounds**, Staxton		**78**	**The Tap & Spile**, Whitby
66	**Hawnby Hotel**, Hawnby		**79**	**The Wheeldale Hotel**, Whitby
67	**Hayburn Wyke Inn**, Cloughton		**80**	**Ye Horseshoe Inn**, Egton Bridge

Please note all references refer to page numbers

North York Moors, Heritage Coast & the Vale of Pickering

Some 40 miles across and about 20 miles deep, the North York Moors encompass a remarkable diversity of scenery. There are great rolling swathes of moorland rising to 1,400 feet above sea level, stark and inhospitable in winter, still wild and romantic in summer, and softened only in early Autumn when they are mantled by a purple haze of flowering heather.

Gisborough Priory, Guisborough

Almost one fifth of the area is woodland, most of it managed by Forest Enterprise, which has established many picnic sites and forest drives. Settlements are few and far between: indeed, there may have been more people living here in the Bronze Age (1500-500 BC) than there are now, to judge by the more than 3,000 "howes", or burial mounds, that have been discovered. (The climate was much warmer and drier then.) Also scattered across these uplands is a remarkable collection of medieval stone crosses. There are more than 30 of them and one, the **Lilla Cross**, is reckoned to be the oldest Christian monument in northern England. It commemorates the warrior Lilla who in AD626 died protecting his King, Edwin, from an assassin's dagger. Most of them have names - such as Fat Betty which has a stumpy base surmounted by the top of a wheelhead cross. Perhaps the finest of these monuments is **Ralph Cross**, high on Westerdale Moor. It stands nine feet tall at almost precisely the geographical centre of the moors and has been adopted by the North York Moors National Park as its emblem.

Wild as they look, the moors are actually cultivated land, or perhaps managed by fire is the better term. Each year, gamekeepers burn off patches of the old heather in carefully limited areas called "swiddens" or "swizzens". The new growth that soon appears is a crucial resource for the red grouse, which live only in heather moorland, eat little else but heather and find these young green shoots particularly appetising. The older heather that remains provides the birds with protective cover during their nesting season.

Just as the Yorkshire Dales have large areas of moorland, so the North York Moors have many dales - Eskdale, Ryedale, Farndale, more than a hundred of them in all. They cut deep into the great upland tracts and are as picturesque, soft and pastoral as anywhere in Yorkshire. To the west lies the mighty bulk of the Cleveland Hills; to the east the rugged cliffs of the Heritage Coast. This is marvellously unspoilt countryside, a happy state of affairs that has come about as a result of the Moors being designated a National Park in 1952, a status which severely restricts any development that would

Ryedale Folk Museum, Hutton-le-Hole

44

adversely affect either its natural or man-made beauty. Between Saltburn and Filey lies some of the most striking coastal scenery in the country. Along this stretch of the Heritage Coast you'll find the highest cliffs in the country, a shoreline fretted with rocky coves, golden with miles of sandy beaches, a scattering of picture postcard fishing villages, and, at its heart, the historic port of Whitby dramatically set around the mouth of the River Esk. This glorious seaboard was designated as a Heritage Coast in 1979 in recognition of its beauty and its long history.

Not all that long ago, the Vale of Pickering was the Lake of Pickering, an immense stretch of water far larger than any English lake today, about 32 miles long and four to eight miles wide. As the Ice Age retreated, the waters gradually drained away leaving a low-lying plain of good arable soil based on Kimmeridge clay. Much of it remained marshy, however, and at Star Carr, near Seamer, archaeologists have uncovered a late Stone Age lake community, dating back some 7,500 years, where the houses were built on stilts above the water. It is only in comparatively recent times that the Vale has been properly drained, which explains why most of the towns and villages lie around its edge in a rough kind of horseshoe formation.

PLACES OF INTEREST

BECK HOLE

When the North Yorkshire Moors Railway was constructed in the 1830s (designed by no less an engineer than George Stephenson himself), the trains were made up of stage coaches placed on top of simple bogies and pulled by horses. At the pretty little hamlet of Beck Hole, however, there was a 1 in 15 incline up to Goathland so the carriages had to be hauled by a complicated system of ropes and water-filled tanks. (Charles Dickens was an early passenger on this route, and wrote a hair-raising description of his journey.) The precipitous incline caused many accidents so, in 1865, a "Deviation Line" was blasted through solid rock. The gradient is still one of the steepest in the country at 1 in 49, but it opened up this route to steam trains. The original 1 in 15 incline is now a footpath, so modern walkers will understand the effort needed to get themselves to the summit, let alone a fully laden carriage.

Every year, this little village plays host to the **World Quoits Championship**. The game, which appears to have originated in Eskdale, involves throwing a small iron hoop over an iron pin set about 25 feet away. Appropriately enough, one of the houses on the green has a quoit serving as a door knocker. On the hillside a mile or so to the west of Beck Hole is the curiously-named **Randy Mere**, the last place in

England where leeches were gathered commercially. An elderly resident of Goathland in 1945 recalled how as a young man he had waded into the lake and emerged in minutes with the slug-like creatures firmly attached to his skin. For those interested, the leeches are still there.

CASTLE HOWARD

Lying in the folds of the Howardian Hills about 5 miles southwest of Malton stands one of the most glorious stately homes in Britain, **Castle Howard**. Well known to television viewers as the Brideshead of *Brideshead Revisited*, Castle Howard has astonished visitors ever since it was completed in the early 1700s. Even that world-weary 18th-century socialite Horace Walpole was stirred to enthusiasm: *"Nobody had informed me"* he wrote *"that at one view I should see a palace, a town, a fortified city, temples on high places ... the noblest lawn in the world fenced by half the horizon and a mausoleum that would tempt one to be buried alive: in short, I have seen gigantic places before, but never a sublime one."* Perhaps the most astonishing fact of all concerns the architect of Castle Howard, Sir John Vanbrugh. Vanbrugh had been a soldier and a playwright, but until he began this sublime building had never overseen the placing of one block of masonry on another.

Yet another attraction at Castle Howard is **Jorvik Glass**, housed in the handsome 18th

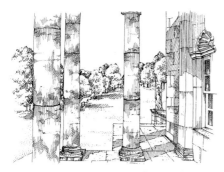

Castle Howard

York Moors National Park. The Centre is housed in a former shooting lodge and set in 13 acres of riverside, meadow, woodland, formal gardens and picnic areas. Visitors can either wander on their own along the waymarked woodland walks and nature trails or join one of the frequent guided walks. Inside the Lodge various exhibits interpret the natural and local history of the moors, there's a bookshop stocked with a wide range of books, maps and guides, and a tea room serving refreshments.

45

Downstream from The Moors Centre is a narrow medieval packhorse bridge, one of three to be found in Eskdale. This one is known as **Duck Bridge**, but the name has nothing to do with aquatic birds. It was originally called Castle Bridge, but re-named after an 18th-century benefactor, George Duck, a wealthy mason who paid for the bridge to be repaired. To the south of Duck Bridge are the remains of **Danby Castle**, now a private farmhouse and not open to the public. Built in the 14th century, and originally much larger, it was once the home of Catherine Parr, the sixth wife of Henry VIII. In Elizabethan times the justices met here - the Danby Court Leet and Baron, which administers the common land and rights of way over the 11,000 acres of the Danby Estate, still meets here every year in the throne room. One of the court's responsibilities is issuing licences for the gathering of sphagnum moss, a material once used for stuffing mattresses but now more commonly required for flower arranging.

century stable yard, featuring a beautifully crafted range of functional and decorative glassware, all of it manufactured on the premises.

Three miles south of Castle Howard, in a lovely, peaceful setting beside the River Derwent, stand the remains of **Kirkham Priory**. According to legend the priory was founded in 1125 by Walter l'Espec after his only son was thrown from his horse and killed at this very spot. (A few years later, Walter was to found another great abbey at Rievaulx.) Visitors to Kirkham pass through a noble, exquisitely decorated gatehouse - but one of the most memorable sights at the Priory, perhaps because it is so unexpected, is the sumptuous lavatorium in the ruined cloister. Here the monks washed their hands at two bays with lavishly moulded arches supported by slender pillars, each bay adorned with tracery.

CASTLETON

Spread across the hillside above the River Esk, Castleton is a charming village which at one time was the largest settlement in Eskdale. It still has a weekly market and a station on the scenic **Esk Valley Railway** that runs between Whitby and Middlesbrough. Its amber-coloured **Church of St Michael and St George** was built in memory of the men who fell in the First World War; inside there is some fine work by Robert Thompson, the famous "Mouseman of Kilburn". The benches, organ screen and panelling at each side of the altar all bear his distinctive ``signature'' of a crouching mouse.

DANBY

A visit to **The Moors Centre** at Danby Lodge provides an excellent introduction to the North

EGTON BRIDGE

This little village tucked around a bend in the River Esk plays host each year to the famous **Gooseberry Show**. Established in 1800, the show is held on the first Tuesday in August. It attracts entrants from all over the world who bring prize specimens in an attempt to beat the current record of 2.18oz. for a single berry. The village is dominated by the massive **Church of St Hedda**, built in 1866. It has a dazzling roof painted blue with gold stars, and the altar incorporates some distinguished Belgian terracotta work. Appropriately, St Hedda's is a Roman Catholic church, since it was at Egton Bridge that the martyr Nicholas Postgate was born in 1596. He was ordained as a priest in France but returned to the moors to minister to those still loyal to the outlawed Catholic faith.

46

He travelled disguised as a jobbing gardener and eluded capture for many years but was finally betrayed for a reward of £20. He was 81 years old when he was hung, drawn and quartered at York. A sad story to be associated with such a delightful village.

FILEY

With its six-mile crescent of safe, sandy beach, Filey was one of the first Yorkshire resorts to benefit from the early 19th-century craze for sea bathing. Filey's popularity continued throughout Victorian times, but the little town always prided itself on being rather more select than its brasher neighbour just up the coast, Scarborough. Inevitably modern times have

Filey Bay

brought the usual scattering of amusement arcades, fast food outlets and, from 1939 to 1983, a Butlin's Holiday Camp capable of accommodating 10,000 visitors. But Filey has suffered less than most seaside towns, and with its many public parks and gardens still retains a winning, rather genteel atmosphere.

Until the Local Government reforms of 1974, the boundary between the East and North Ridings cut right through Filey. The town lay in the East Riding, the parish church and graveyard in the North. This curious arrangement gave rise to some typically pawky Yorkshire humour. If, as a resident of Filey town, you admitted that you were feeling poorly, the response might well be *"Aye, then tha'll straightly be off t'North Riding"* - in other words, the graveyard. Just to the north of the town, the rocky promontory known as **Filey Brigg** strikes out into the sea, a massive mile-long breakwater protecting the town from the worst of the North Sea's winter storms. From the Brigg there are grand views southwards along the six-mile-long bay to the cliffs that rise up to Flamborough Head and Scarborough Castle. Despite the fact that

there is no harbour at Filey, it was once quite a busy fishing port and one can still occasionally see a few *cobles* - direct descendants of the Viking longships that arrived here more than a millennium ago - beached on the slipways. Filey's parish church, the oldest parts of which date back to the 12th century, is appropriately dedicated to St Oswald, patron saint of fishermen, and the Fishermen's Window here commemorates men from the town who died at sea. At the **Filey Folk Museum**, housed in a lovely old building dating back to 1696, you can explore the town's long history, while the **Edwardian Festival**, held every June, re-creates the pleasures of an earlier, more innocent age.

GILLAMOOR

This pleasant little village is well worth a visit to see its very rare and very elegant four-faced sundial erected in 1800 and to enjoy the famous **Surprise View**. This is a ravishing panoramic vista of Farndale with the River Dove flowing through the valley far below and white dusty roads climbing the hillside to the heather-covered moors beyond.

Also of interest is the village church, which was once the church at Bransdale, about six miles away. In the late 1700s Bransdale Church was in good repair but little used; Gillamoor's was dilapidated but the villagers wanted a place of worship. This was achieved by appointing a single stonemason, James Smith, to remove Bransdale church stone by stone and re-erect it at Gillamoor.

GLAISDALE

Glaisdale is a picturesque village set at the foot of a narrow dale beside the River Esk, with

Beggar's Bridge, Glaisdale

Arncliffe Woods a short walk away. The ancient stone bridge here was built around 1620 by Thomas Ferris, Mayor of Hull. As an impoverished young man he had lived in Glaisdale and fell in love with Agnes Richardson, the squire's daughter. To see Agnes, he had to wade or swim across the river. He swore that if he prospered in life he would build a bridge here. Fortunately, he joined a ship which sailed against the Spanish Armada and captured a galleon laden with gold. Tom returned to Glaisdale a rich man, married Agnes and later honoured his promise by building what has always been called the **Beggar's Bridge**.

GOATHLAND

Goathland today is perhaps best known as "Aidensfield" - the main location for the television series *Heartbeat*. This attractive village 500 feet up on the moors, where old stone houses are scattered randomly around spacious sheep-groomed greens, was popular long before television. Earlier visitors mostly came in order to see **Mallyan Spout**, a 70 foot high waterfall locked into a crescent of rocks and trees. They were also interested in Goathland's rugged church, and the odd memorial in its graveyard to William Jefferson and his wife. The couple died in 1923 within a few days of each other, at the ages of 80 and 79, and chose to have their final resting place marked by an enormous anchor.

Goathland Station, Goathland

47

In the award-winning **Goathland Exhibition Centre** you'll find a full explanation of the curious tradition of the **Plough Stots Service** performed at Goathland every January. It's an ancient ritual for greeting the new year which originated with the Norsemen who settled here more than a thousand years ago. "Stots" is the Scandinavian word for the bullocks which would drag a plough through the village, followed by dancers brandishing 30-inch swords. This pagan rite is still faithfully observed, but with the difference that nowadays Goathland's young men have replaced the "stots" in the plough harness. The Exhibition Centre can also provide you with information about the many walks in the area, and guide you to one of the oldest thoroughfares in the country, **Wade's Way**. If you believe the legend, it was built by a giant of that name, but it is actually a remarkably well-preserved stretch of Roman road.

HELMSLEY

One of North Yorkshire's most popular and attractive towns, Helmsley lies on the banks of the River Rye at the edge of the North York Moors National Park. The spacious market square is typical of the area, but the Gothic memorial to the 2nd Earl of Feversham that stands there is not. This astonishingly ornate construction was designed by Sir Giles Gilbert Scott and looks like a smaller version of his famous memorial to Sir Walter Scott in Edinburgh.

The Earls of Feversham lived at **Duncombe Park**, whose extensive grounds sweep up to within a few yards of the Market Place. Most of the original mansion, designed by Vanbrugh, was gutted by a disastrous fire in 1879; only the north wing remained habitable, and that in its turn was ruined by a second fire in 1895. The Fevershams lavished a fortune on rebuilding the grand old house, largely to the original design, but the financial burden eventually forced them to lease the house and grounds as a preparatory school for girls. Happily, the Fevershams were able to return to their ancestral home in 1985 and the beautifully restored house and lovely grounds are now open to the public.

Before they were ennobled, the Fevershams' family name was Duncombe; it was Sir Thomas Duncombe, a wealthy London goldsmith,

48

who established the family seat here when he bought **Helmsley Castle** (English Heritage) and its estate in 1687. Founded in the early 1100s, seriously knocked about during the Civil War, the castle was in a dilapidated state but its previous owner,

Helmsley Castle

the Duke of Buckingham, had continued to live there in some squalor and discomfort. Sir Thomas quickly decided to build a more suitable residence nearby, abandoning the ruins to lovers of the romantic and picturesque.

Just to the west of Helmsley rise the indescribably beautiful remains of **Rievaulx Abbey** (English Heritage), standing among wooded hills beside the River Rye - *"the most beautiful monastic site in Europe"*. JMW Turner was enchanted by this idyllic landscape; Dorothy Wordsworth, *"spellbound"*. Founded in 1131, it was the first Cistercian abbey in Yorkshire and, with some 700 people - monks, lay brothers, servants - eventually living within its walls, became one of the largest. Like Kirkham Abbey a few years earlier, Rievaulx was endowed by Walter l'Espec, Lord of Helmsley, still mourning the loss of his only son in a riding accident. The Abbey was soon a major landowner in the county, earning a healthy income from farming - at one time owning more than 14,000 sheep. The Abbey also had its own fishery at Teesmouth, and iron-ore mines at Bilsdale and near Wakefield.

Looking down on the extensive remains of the Abbey is **Rievaulx Terrace** (National Trust), a breathtaking example of landscape gardening completed in 1758. The cunningly contrived avenues draw your eyes to incomparable views of the Abbey itself, to vistas along the Rye Valley and to the rolling contours of the hills beyond. At each end of the terrace is a classical temple, one of which is elaborately furnished and decorated as a dining room.

Rievaulx Abbey

LEALHOLM

The houses in the attractive village of Lealholm houses cluster around a 250 year old bridge over the Esk. A short walk leads to some picturesque stepping stones across the river. A much-travelled foreign journalist remarked, "Elsewhere, you have to go in search of beautiful views; here, they come and offer themselves to be looked at." On one of the stone houses, now a tea room and restaurant, a carved inscription reads "Loyal Order of Ancient Shepherds" together with the date 1873 in Roman numerals. The Loyal Order ran their lodge on the lines of a men-only London club, but their annual procession through the village and the subsequent festivities were one of the highlights of the autumn. In recent years, Lealholm has become very popular with naturalists, who come to study the wealth of trees, ferns, flowers and rare plants in the deep, dramatic ravine known as **Crunkley Gill**. Sadly, the ravine is privately owned and not open to the public.

MALTON

Malton has been the historic centre of Ryedale ever since the Romans came. They built a large fort and called it "Derventio" after the river Derwent beside which it stands. For many years, archaeologists were puzzled by the large scale of the fort, a mystery solved in 1970 when a building dedication was uncovered which revealed that the fort housed a cavalry regiment, the Ala Picentiana - the extra space was needed to accommodate their horses. Many relics from the site, showing the sophisticated lifestyles of the Roman centurions and civilians, can be seen in the **Malton Museum**, along with items from the Iron Age settlement that preceded the Roman garrison.

The River Derwent was vitally important to Malton. The river rises in the moors near Scarborough, then runs inland through the Vale of Pickering, bringing an essential element for what was once a major industry in Malton - brewing. In the 19th century there were nine breweries here; now only the Malton Brewery Company survives. It operates in a converted stable block behind Suddabys Crown Hotel in Wheelgate and welcomes visitors, but telephone them first on 01653 697580.

Old Malton is located just to the north of the **Roman Fort**, an interesting and historic area on the edge of open countryside. Nearby villages such as Settrington and their secluded country lanes are home to many famous racehorse stables: if you are up and about early enough you will see the horses out on their daily exercises. In the centre of Old Malton stands a beautiful fragment of **St Mary's Priory**, incorporating a particularly fine Norman doorway. The Priory was built around 1155 by the only monastic order in Christendom to have originated entirely in England - the Gilbertines. The order was founded in 1148 by a Lincolnshire parish priest, St Gilbert of Sempringham. Parts of the parish church are quite as old as the Priory, but one of its most interesting features is relatively modern, the work of the "Mouseman of Kilburn", Robert Thompson. A gifted woodcarver and furniture maker, Thompson ``signed'' all his pieces with a discreetly placed carving of a mouse. There's one on the stout oak door of the church and, inside, the stalls are carved elaborately with all manner of wondrous beasts and historical and mythical scenes.

A mile or so north of Old Malton is **Eden Camp**, a theme museum dedicated to re-creating the dramatic experiences of ordinary people living through the Second World War. This unique museum is housed in the huts of a genuine prisoner of war camp, built in 1942. Sound, lighting effects, smells, even smoke generators are deployed to make you feel that you are actually there, taking part. Visitors can find out what it was like to live through an air raid, to

be a prisoner of war, or a sailor in a U-boat under attack. Among the many other exhibits are displays on

Fashion in the 1940s, Children at War, and even one on Rationing. In 1941, one discovers, the cheese ration was down to 1oz (28 grams) a week! Right next door to Eden Camp is **Eden Farm Insight**, a working farm with a fascinating collection of old farm machinery and implements (including a very old horse wheel), lots of animals, a blacksmith's and a wheelwright's shop, as well as a choice of farm walks, all clearly signposted and with useful information boards. The Farm also offers a café, gift shop and a picnic and play area.

PICKERING

This busy little town developed around the important crossroads where the Malton-to-Whitby and the Thirsk-to-Scarborough roads intersect. It's the largest of the four market towns in Ryedale and possibly the oldest, claiming to date from 270 BC when (so it's said) it was founded by a King of the Brigantes called Peredurus. William the Conqueror's attempts to dominate the area are recalled by Pickering's ruined castle, and the many inns and posting houses reflect the town's prosperity during the stage coach era. Lying at the heart of the fertile Vale of Pickering, the town's reputation was originally based on its famous pigs and horses. Vast quantities of pork were transported across the moors to Whitby, salted and used as shipboard rations. The famous Cleveland Bay horses, with their jet-black manes and tails, were extensively bred in the area. (In Eskdale, a little further north, they still are.) These sweet-natured, sturdy and tireless animals have always been in great demand. During the 19th century, their equable temperament made them ideal for pulling Hansom cabs and street-cars, and nowadays they are often seen in more dignified events such as State Processions.

The parish church of **St Peter and St Paul** is well worth visiting for its remarkable 15th-century murals. During the glum days of Puritanism, these lively paintings were denounced as idolatrous and plastered over. They stayed forgotten for some 200 years, but were rediscovered when the church was being restored in 1851. Unfortunately, the vicar at that time shared the Puritans' sentiments and, despite opposition from his parishioners and even from

50

his bishop, had them smothered again under whitewash. A more liberal successor to the Vicar had the murals restored once again in 1878, and they now give one a vivid idea of how cheerful, colourful and entertaining many English churches were before the vandalism of the Puritan years. These superb paintings, sharp, vigorous and well-observed, happily embrace scenes from the Bible, old legends and actual history: a real insight into the medieval mind that had no difficulty in accepting both the story of St George slaying the dragon and the martyrdom of St Thomas à Becket as equally real, and inspiring, events.

Also not to be missed in Pickering is the **Beck Isle Museum**, housed in a gracious Regency mansion. Its 27 display areas are crammed with a *"magnificent assortment of items curious, mysterious, marvellous and commonplace from the last 200 years"*. There are intriguing re-creations of typical Victorian domestic rooms, shops, workshops and even a pub. The comprehensive collection of photographs by Sydney Smith presents a remarkable picture of the Ryedale area as it was more than half a century ago. The exhibition is made even more interesting by its acquisition of the very cameras and other photographic equipment used by Sydney Smith.

If you catch a whiff of sulphurous smoke, then you must be close to the station. Pickering is the southern terminus of the **North York Moors Railway**, and here you can board a steam-drawn train for an 18-mile journey along one of the oldest and most dramatically scenic railways in the country. And at the **Pickering Trout Lake** you can hire a rod and tackle and attempt to beat the record for the largest fish caught here - it currently stands at a mighty 25lb 4oz (11.45 kg).

ROBIN HOOD'S BAY

Artists never tire of painting this "Clovelly of the North", a picturesque huddle of red-roofed houses clinging to the steep face of the cliff. Bay Town, as locals call the village, was a thriving fishing port throughout the 18th and 19th centuries. By 1920, however, there were only two fishing families left in the Bay, mainly because the harbour was so dilapidated, and the industry died out. Today, small boats are once again harvesting the prolific crab grounds that lie along this stretch of the coast.

Robin Hood's Bay

Because of the natural isolation of the bay, smuggling was quite as important as fishing to the local economy. The houses and inns in the Bay were said to have connecting cellars and cupboards, and it was claimed that "a bale of silk could pass from the bottom of the village to the top without seeing daylight." These were the days, too, when press gangs from the Royal Navy were active in the area, since recruits with a knowledge of the sea were highly prized. Apparently, these mariners were also highly prized by the local women: they smartly despatched the press gangs by means of pans and rolling pins.

Shipwrecks in the Bay were frequent, with many a mighty vessel tossed onto its reefs by North Sea storms. On one memorable occasion in the winter of 1881, a large brig called the *Visitor* was driven onto the rocks. The seas were too rough for the lifeboat at Whitby to be launched there, so it was dragged eight miles through the snow and let down the cliffside by ropes. Six men were rescued. The same wild seas threatened the village itself, every storm eroding a little more of the chalk cliff to which it clings. Fortunately, Robin Hood's Bay is now protected by a sturdy sea wall.

The most extraordinary building in Robin Hood's Bay is undoubtedly **Fyling Hall Pigsty**. It was built in the 1880s by Squire Barry of Fyling Hall in the classical style, although the pillars supporting the portico are of wood rather than marble. Here the Squire's two favourite pigs could enjoy plenty of space and a superb view over the Bay. The building is now managed by the Landmark Trust, who rent it out to holidaymakers.

RUNSWICK BAY

Runswick Bay is a picturesque fishing village with attractive cottages clinging to the steep sides of the cliff. This perilous position proved disastrous in 1682 when the cliff face collapsed and the whole of Runswick, with the exception of a single cottage, tumbled into the sea. A disaster fund was set up and a new village established.

At Runswick, as in most of Yorkshire's remote communities, superstition was once widespread. Even at the beginning of the 20th century, many still believed in witches and almost everyone would avert their gaze or cross the road to avoid someone afflicted with the "Evil Eye". The Revd Cooper, Vicar of Filey, visited the village at the turn of the century and came across a "perfectly horrible superstition". Apparently, it was considered unlucky to save a drowning man. The Vicar was told of "men nearly dragged ashore, and then, by the advice of the elders, abandoned to their fate lest ill-fortune should result from saving them".

SALTBURN-BY-THE-SEA

The charming seaside resort of Saltburn lies at the northern end of the Heritage Coast. It was custom-built in Victorian times and designed for affluent middle-class visitors - so much so that in the early years excursion trains were barred from calling there. Created in the 1860s

Inclined Tramway, Saltburn

by the Quaker entrepreneur Henry Pease, Saltburn is set on a cliff high above a long sandy beach. To transport

visitors from the elegant little town to the promenade and pier below, an ingenious water-balanced **Tramway** was constructed. It is still in use, the oldest such tramway to have survived in Britain. Saltburn's Victorian heritage is celebrated in mid-August each year with a full programme of events, many of them with the participants clad in appropriate costume. It seems appropriate, too, that such an olde-worlde town should be well-known for its many shops selling antiques and collectables.

Saltburn's genteel image in Victorian times was a far cry from its notoriety in the late 18th century when it was one of the northeast's busiest centres for smuggling. The "King of the Smugglers", John Andrew, had his base here; during a long and profitable career he was never apprehended. His story, and that of his partners in villainy, is colourfully recalled at **The Saltburn Smugglers Heritage Centre** near the Ship Inn, of which Andrew was once landlord. From the sea front, a miniature railway will take you to the splendid **Italian Gardens** - another Victorian contribution to the town. Here you can take tea on the lawn and explore the **Woodlands Centre** set between the formal pleasure gardens and the wild natural woodlands beyond.

SCARBOROUGH

With its two splendid bays and dramatic cliff-top castle, Scarborough was targeted by the early railway tycoons as the natural candidate for Yorkshire's first seaside resort. The railway arrived in 1846, followed by the construction of luxury hotels, elegant promenades and spacious gardens, all of which confirmed the town's claim to the title *"Queen of Watering Places"*. The *"quality"* - people like the eccentric Earls of Londesborough - established palatial summer residences here, and an excellent train service brought countless thousands of 'excursionists' from the industrial cities of the West Riding.

Even before the advent of the railway, Scarborough had been well-known to a select few. They travelled to what was then a remote little town to sample the spring water discovered by Mrs Tomyzin Farrer in 1626 and popularised in a book published by a certain Dr Wittie who named the site "Scarborough Spaw".

52

Anne Brontë came here in the hope that the spa town's invigorating air would improve her health, a hope that was not fulfilled. She died at the age of 29, and her grave lies in St Mary's churchyard at the foot of the castle. **Scarborough Castle** itself can be precisely dated to the decade between 1158 and 1168; surviving records show that construction costs totalled £650. The castle was built on the site of a Roman fort and signal station, and its gaunt remains stand high on Castle Rock Headland, dominating the two sweeping bays. The spectacular ruins often provide a splendid backdrop for staged battles commemorating the invasions of the Danes, Saxons and the later incursions of Napoleon's troops. The surrounding cliffs are also well worth exploring - just follow the final part of the famous Cleveland Way.

If you happen to be visiting the resort on Shrove Tuesday, be prepared for the unusual sight of respectable citizens exercising their ancient right to skip along the highways. This unexpected traffic hazard is now mostly confined to the area around Foreshore Road. Another tradition maintained by local people around this time is the sounding of the Pancake Bell, a custom started by the wives of the town to alert their menfolk in the fields and in the harbour that they were about to begin cooking the pancakes.

As befits such a long-established resort, Scarborough offers a vast variety of entertainment. If you tire of the two sandy beaches, there's **Peasholm Park** to explore, with its glorious gardens and regular events, among them the unique sea battle in miniature on the lake. Or you could seek out the intellectual attractions of the **Rotunda Museum** on Vernon Road, *"the finest Georgian museum in Britain"*, which includes among its exhibits a genuine ducking stool for ``witches''; the art collections at the **Scarborough Art Gallery**; or the futuristic world of holograms at **Corrigans Arcade** on Foreshore Road. **The Stephen Joseph Theatre in the Round** is well-known for staging the premiere performances of comedies written by its resident director, the prolific playwright Alan Ayckbourn. And at Scalby Mills, on the northern edge of the town, **Sea-Life** offers the chance of close encounters with a huge variety of marine creatures from shrimps to sharks, octopi to eels.

Also worth visiting is the **Wood End Museum of Natural History** on The Crescent, once the home of the eccentric Sitwell family. There are permanent displays of their books and photographs, as well as changing exhibitions of local wildlife. The double-storeyed conservatory and the aquarium here are particularly interesting.

STAITHES

Visitors to this much-photographed fishing port leave their cars at the park in the modern village at the top of the cliff and then walk down the steep road to the old wharf. Take care - one of these narrow, stepped alleys is called **Slippery Hill**, for reasons that can become painfully clear. The old stone chapels and rather austere houses testify to the days when Staithes was a stronghold of Methodism.

The little port is proud of its associations with Captain James Cook. He came here, not as a famous mariner, but as a 17-year-old assistant in Mr William Sanderson's haberdashery shop. James didn't stay long, leaving in 1746 to begin his naval apprenticeship in Whitby with Thomas Scottowe, a friend of Sanderson.

Staithes is still a working port, with one of the few fleets in England still catching crabs and lobsters. Moored in the harbour and along the river are the fishermen's distinctive boats. Known as cobles, they have an ancestry that goes back to Viking times. Nearby is a small sandy beach, popular with families (and artists), and a rocky shoreline extending north and south pitted with thousands of rock pools hiding starfish and anemones. The rocks here are also rich in fossils and you may even find ingots of "fools gold" - actually iron pyrites and virtually worthless. A little further up the coast

Staithes Harbour

North York Moors, Heritage Coast & the Vale of Pickering

rises Boulby cliff, at 666 feet the highest point on the east coast of England.

WHITBY

Whitby is one of North Yorkshire's most historic and attractive towns. Whitby is famed as one of the earliest and most important centres of Christianity in England; as Captain James Cook's home port, and as the place where, according to Bram Stoker's famous novel, Count Dracula in the form of a wolf loped ashore from a crewless ship that had drifted into the harbour. The classic 1931 film version of the story, starring Bela Lugosi, was filmed in the original locations at Whitby, and there were several reports of holidaymakers being startled by coming across "the Count", cloaked and fanged, as he rested between takes.

High on the cliff that towers above the old town stand the imposing and romantic ruins of **Whitby Abbey**. In AD664, many of the most eminent prelates of the Christian Church were summoned here to attend the Synod of Whitby. They were charged with settling once and for

Whitby Abbey

all a festering dispute that had riven Christendom for generations: the precise date on which Easter should be celebrated. The complicated formula they devised to solve this problem is still in use today.

A short walk from the Abbey is **St Mary's Church**, a unique building "not unlike a house outside and very much like a ship inside". Indeed, the fascinating interior with its clutter of box-pews, iron pillars and long galleries was reputedly fashioned by Whitby seamen during the course of the 18th century. The three-decker pulpit is from the same period; the huge ear trumpets for a rector's deaf wife were put in place about fifty years later. St Mary's stands

atop the cliff: the old town clusters around the harbour mouth far below. Linking them are the famous 199

steps that wind up the hillside: many a churchgoer or visitor has been grateful for the frequent seats thoughtfully provided along the way.

The old port of Whitby developed on the slim shelf of land that runs along the east bank of the River Esk, an intricate muddle of narrow, cobbled streets and shoulder-width alleys. Grape Lane is typical, a cramped little street where ancient houses lean wearily against each other. Young James Cook lived here during his apprenticeship: the handsome house in Grape Lane where he lodged is now the **Captain Cook Memorial Museum**.

By the early 19th century, old Whitby was full to bursting and a new town began to burgeon on the west bank of the River Esk. The new Whitby, or "West Cliff", was carefully planned with the nascent industry of tourism in mind. There was a quayside walk or "promenade", a bandstand, luxury hotels, and a Royal Crescent of upmarket dwellings reminiscent of Buxton or Cheltenham but with the added advantage of enjoying a sea air universally acknowledged as "invariably beneficial to the health of the most injured constitution".

Captain Cook's Endeavour

The Hidden Inns of Yorkshire

54

In a dominating position on West Cliff, a bronze statue of Captain Cook gazes out over the harbour he knew so well and nearby the huge jawbone of a whale, raised as an arch, recalls those other great Whitby seafarers, the whalers. Between 1753 and 1833, Whitby was the capital of the whaling industry, bringing home 2761 whales in 80 years. Much of that success was due to the skills of the great whaling captains William Scoresby and his son, also named William. The elder William was celebrated for his great daring and navigational skills, as well as for the invention of the crow's nest, or masthead lookout. His son was driven by a restless, enquiring mind and occupied himself with various experiments during the long days at sea in the icy Arctic waters. He is most noted for his discoveries of the forms of snow crystals and the invention of the "Greenland" magnet which made ships' compasses more reliable. The whaling industry is now, thankfully, long dead, but fortunately the fishing industry is not, as many of Whitby's restaurants bear witness, being famous for their seafood menus.

One of Whitby's unique attractions is **The Sutcliffe Gallery** in Flowergate. The Gallery celebrates the great photographer Frank Meadow Sutcliffe who was born in Whitby in 1853. His studies of local people, places and events powerfully evoke the Whitby of late-Victorian and Edwardian times in photographs that are both beautifully composed and technically immaculate. Few visitors to the Gallery can resist the temptation to purchase at least one of the nostalgic prints on sale.

Another popular souvenir of the town is jet stone, a lustrous black stone which enjoyed an enormous vogue in Victorian times. After the death of Prince Albert, jewellery in jet was the only ornament the Queen would allow herself to wear. The Court and the middle classes naturally followed her example, and for several decades Whitby prospered greatly from the trade in jet. By 1914, workable deposits of the stone were virtually exhausted and a new generation shunned its gloomy association with death. Recent years have seen a revival of interest in the glossy stone, and several shops have extensive displays of jet ornaments and jewellery.

Blacksmiths Arms | 55

Cayton,
Nr. Scarborough,
North Yorkshire
YO11 3RP
Tel: 01723 582272

Directions:

A64 from
Scarborough to
Eastfield, turn left at
roundabout on to
B1261 fro 1 mile.

There's no shortage of good pubs in this part of the worlds, so it is well worth noting that the **Blacksmiths Arms** is the preferred choice of many of the locals - and they should know! An imposing late-19th century building on the corner of the main road through the village (B1261) and Church Lane, it has a bright, cheerful look that is even more bright and cheerful since a recent repaint.

The promise of the outside is more than fulfilled within, where the roomy lounge, public bar and restaurant have atmosphere in abundance. There's a separate games room where pool is played, and throughout the pub a detailed history of its past is displayed on the walls. Friday and Saturday nights bring in the crowds for, respectively, quiz night and karaoke night. The pub has a large car park and a beer garden with a children's play area. The new tenant is Diane Durrant, who has ambitious plans for the pub.

Cayton is one of only 31 'Thankful Villages' in England. They were so named after the First World War because all their men returned safely from service. Cayton had all the more reason to be thankful, since 43 of its men returned, more than any other 'Thankful Village'. Visitors to Cayton should not leave without looking in at the Stained Glass Centre, where the showroom is an Aladdin's Cave of lampshades, mirrors and assorted gifts; an exhibition in the studio charts the history of stained glass. Minor roads lead up from the village to the A165 and the coast at lovely Cayton Bay.

Opening Hours: 12.00-23.00

Food: A la carte, bar snacks

Credit Cards: Access, Mastercard, Visa, Switch.

Accommodation: None

Facilities: Pool room

Entertainment: Friday- karaoke, Saturday- live entertainment, Sunday- quiz

Local Places of Interest/Activities: Scarborough 3 miles, Filey 6 miles, Ayton Castle.

56   The Blacksmiths Arms

Lastingham,
North Yorkshire
YO62 6TL
Tel/Fax: 01751
417247

Directions:

Lastingham is situated on a minor road north of the A170 between Pickering and Helmsley.

Opposite a very famous church in a tiny conservation village, the **Blacksmiths Arms** has a history dating back to 1673. Behind a sturdy stone frontage shaded by tall trees on either side of the road, the pub has a simple, homely look and a traditional appeal that brings visitors back time and time again. But there is much more to Craig Miller's pub than old-fashioned charm. In a 32-cover restaurant separate from the bar. Yorkshire and British dishes are freshly prepared using local ingredients as far as possible. Seafood gets a look in too. People flock from miles around when the word gets out that cod is on the menu!

There's a lot to explore in this lovely part of Yorkshire, and the Blacksmiths Arms is an ideal base for trips. Overnight accommodation comprises three double bedrooms, all recently refurbished, with en suite facilities, tv, tea/coffee-makers and great views. In summer, the beer garden is a pleasant spot for relaxing with a drink. The pub is always a convivial place, and never more so than on the regular theme evenings - Burns Night being one of many causes for celebration.

Lastingham is best known for its 11th century Church of St Mary, the sole surviving part of a priory founded in the 7th century. The site draws upwards of 30,000 visitors every year, and those in the know make sure that their visit also includes the Blacksmiths Arms. It's an easy drive to the delightful town of Pickering, where the car can be swapped for a ride on the steam-hauled North Yorkshire Moors Railway.

Opening Hours: 12.00-15.00 and 19.00-23.00

Food: A la carte.

Credit Cards: Mastercard, Visa, Amex

Accommodation: 3 en suite rooms.

Facilities: Beer garden, terrace

Entertainment: Themed food events.

Local Places of Interest/Activities: Pickering 8 miles, Hutton-le-Hole (Ryedale Folk Museum), Helmsley 8 miles

The Blacksmiths Country Inn   57

Hartoft End,
Rosedale Abbey,
Pickering,
North Yorkshire YO18 8EN
Tel: 01751 417331
Fax: 01751 417167

Directions:
From Pickering take the A170 towards Kirkbymoorside; half a mile past Aislaby turn right at Wrelton, sign for Cropton, Hartoft, Rosedale Abbey. 2.5 miles past Cropton down a dip, up a slope.

Built round a farmhouse with origins in the 16th century, **the Blacksmiths** is a hotel of immense charm, run with warm friendliness by resident owners Paul and Jennifer Cusworth. Its first advantage is the setting, high on a ridge overlooking moorland and forest at the heart of the North Yorkshire Moors National Park. Behind the handsome facade - the stones of the original farmhouse came from the ruins of Rosedale Abbey - the past and the present combine happily and seamlessly, and the recent extension (the Millennium Wing) demonstrates the care and attention to detail that are evident throughout this outstanding hotel for discerning guests.

The Blacksmiths has 18 bedrooms, each one furnished and equipped to the highest standards, and all with full en suite facilities. Fourteen standard rooms, six with balconies, are situated on the first floor, while on the ground floor are four superb superior rooms with French doors opening on to stunning views of Cropton Forest. All the rooms are non-smoking. There is ample parking space (the car park has the look of a high-class car showroom!) and pets are welcome by arrangement. Hospitality is the keyword, and guests will find instant relaxation in the warm, inviting bars and lounges. In the Stable Restaurant an à la carte menu features the best of traditional Yorkshire and modern European cuisine, and more informal bar meals are available lunchtime and evening. All in all, the Blacksmiths Country Inn is a perfect base for exploring the scenic delights and historical sights of a glorious part of the country.

Opening Hours: Bar:12.00-15.00, 18.00-midnight: Restaurant: 12.00-14.00, 18.00-21.00

Food: A la carte and bar meals.

Credit Cards: All except Diners & Amex

Accommodation: 18 en suite rooms.

Facilities: Car Park.

Local Places of Interest/Activities: Pickering 7 miles, Cropton Brewery Visitor Centre, Goathland (Mallyan Spout waterfall).

Internet/Website:
e-mail: blacksmiths.rosedale@virgin.net
website: blacksmithsinn-rosedale.co.uk

58   The Coachman Inn

Pickering Road West,
Snainton,
Nr. Scarborough,
North Yorkshire YO13 9PL
Tel: 01723 859231/859984

Directions:

From Pickering take the A170 to Snainton and turn on to the B1258. The inn is on the edge of the village just off the B1258.

New owners Graham and Judith Senior are carrying on the tradition of 230 years at their handsome Grade ll listed coaching inn with a large garden and spacious car park. The look and style are very much that of a country house, but the warmth and hospitality are on a much more intimate level. Laid back and informal, the Coachman has a huge open fire warming the bar.

The owners take great pride in the food they serve, taking every care to find the best local sources and trying to provide something for everyone (no food Monday). Complementing the food is a fine selection of wines and real ales. Eight recently refurbished en suite bedrooms with tv and tea/coffee-makers promise quiet, comfortable accommodation for the night, while a well-maintained caravan site alongside the inn caters for visitors in touring caravans. Quiet and well screened by trees, the site is equipped with electrical hook-up points, showers and WC.

Two redwood trees and two weeping ash make an impressive approach to the inn, which stands just off the B1258 on the edge of the village. The A170, seconds along the road, offers ready access west to Scarborough and east to Pickering, with several attractive villages en route - none more so than Thornton-le-Dale, one of the prettiest villages in the whole country and a regular star on chocolate boxes and biscuit tins and in jigsaw puzzles. A great stretch of forest lies to the north. On the very edge of the forest, beyond the village of Ebberston, stands Ebberston Hall, built in the 18th century for an MP for Scarborough and a contender for the title of smallest stately home in England.

Opening Hours: 19.00-23.00 daily, 12.00-14.00 Sundays; (Also 12.00-15.00 daily in summer)

Food: A la carte.

Credit Cards: None

Accommodation: 5 en suite rooms.

Facilities: Car Park.

Local Places of Interest/Activities: Pickering 11 miles, Scarborough 11 miles, Thornton-le-Dale, Ebberston.

The Crown & Cushion   **59**

Welburn,
North Yorkshire
YO60 7DZ
Tel/Fax:
  01653 618304

Directions:

5 miles southwest
of Malton off the
A64. Welburn lies
near the southern
end of the
approach to
Castle Howard.

On the main street of a village by the approach to Castle Howard, the **Crown & Cushion** is a charming old inn which has always borne its rather unusual name. The interior is decorated and furnished in a style entirely appropriate to its 18th century origins, and the ambience is just right for enjoying a glass or two of the excellent cask ales on offer. In addition to the public bar there's a lovely little lounge and a comfortable, spacious restaurant. The husband-and-wife team of John and Maggie Tate-Smith set themselves very high standards, and the kitchen produces home cooking at its best that brings regular visitors from all over Yorkshire. The menu, which is available v Tuesday to Sunday lunchtimes and evenings, provides plenty of variety, with dishes inspired by the cuisines of the world. The pub is a warm and cosy refuge in the winter, while in the summer the action shifts to the lovely beer garden, which is a winner of Pubmaster in Bloom competitions.

The great attraction in the locality is of course Castle Howard, one of the most glorious stately homes in Britain, set in 1,000 acres of parkland with sweeping lawns, lakes and fountains. The house itself, which is full of family treasures, was, almost unbelievably, the first work of the architect Sir John Vanbrugh. Two miles south of Welburn, in a lovely peaceful setting beside the River Derwent, stand the remains of Kirkham Priory, founded in 1125 by Walter l'Espec, who later also founded the wonderful Rievaulx Abbey. The first delight for visitors to Kirkham is the exquisitely decorated gatehouse but the most memorable sight, and one that is completely unexpected by first-time visitors, is the sumptuous *lavatorium*, where monks washed their hands at two bays with lavishly moulded arches supported by slender pillars.

Opening Hours: 11.30-14.30 (except Mondays) and 17.30-23.00. Open all day Saturday and Sunday

Food: A la carte.

Credit Cards: Access, Mastercard, Visa.

Accommodation: None.

Facilities: Car Park.

Entertainment: Occasional quiz nights.

Local Places of Interest/Activities: Castle Howard 3 miles, York 15 miles, Kirkham Priory 2 miles.

60   The Dotterel Inn

Reighton,
Nr. Filey,
North Yorkshire
YO14 9IU
Tel: 01723 890300

Directions:

6 miles south of Filey, 6 miles north of Bridlington on the A165.

The Dotterel is a sizeable roadside inn with a modern appearance but traditional standards of hospitality. Recently refurbished inside and out, it has a really welcoming atmosphere and plenty of room in the bars, where a good selection of real ales is on tap. It's an excellent place to come with an appetite, as the à la carte menu proposes a wide choice and brilliant value for money. The chef is rightly proud of the variety he offers on the menu, which is always supplemented by several dishes of the day. Friday night is karaoke night and there's live music on Saturday.

Reighton is a quick and easy drive from Filey and Bridlington, which both have all the amenities expected from their status as seaside resorts. A vast stretch of sandy beach runs south from above Filey right down to Reighton. Flamborough Head provides some of the most spectacular views on the east coast, and at Bempton, on the road to Flamborough, Bempton Cliffs, 400 feet high, mark the northernmost tip of the great belt of chalk that runs diagonally across England from the Isle of Wight to Flamborough Head. The Cliffs are now an RSPB bird sanctuary, a refuge during the April to August breeding season for upwards of 200,00 seabirds. To get right into the seaside mood a trip to Carnaby, four miles from Bridlington on the A166, is in order. Here, John Bull - World of Rock tells of the delights and the techniques of producing sticks of rock; visitors can try their hand at making their own personalised stick. John Dinan is the manager of the Dotterel, which is in the same ownership as the Blacksmiths Arms at nearby Cayton.

Opening Hours: 12.00-23.00.

Food: A la carte.

Credit Cards: Access, Mastercard, Visa, Switch.

Accommodation: B&B 3 doubles, 2 singles

Facilities: Car Park.

Entertainment: Karaoke Friday, live music Saturday.

Local Places of Interest/Activities: Filey 6 miles, Bridlington 6 miles, Flamborough 6 miles, Carnaby 10 miles.

Eastfield Hotel 61

Manham Hill,
Eastfield,
Nr. Scarborough,
North Yorkshire
YO11 3LA
Tel: 01723 583437

Directions:

3 miles south of
Scarborough near
the junction of the
A64 and B1261.

Good food at sensible prices is one of the chief assets of **Eastfield Hotel**, a very substantial structure in red brick. With the appearance more of a church or a court than a pub, it was clearly designed to play host to very large numbers. Behind the imposing facade there is a great deal of space; the place is kept in excellent order and the restaurant has very recently been refurbished. Owner Heather Williams sees that the place has almost unlimited potential and is very hopeful that the crowds will soon return to enjoy the full range of options the pub has to offer - these include regular quiz nights and live music sessions.

The North Sea coast is a short drive away (nearest point Osgodby) and the resorts of Scarborough and Whitby are also near. Scarborough has been one of the east coast's most popular resorts ever since the railway arrived as long ago as 1846. This event was followed by the construction of grand hotels, elegant promenades and spacious gardens. But even before the advent of the railway the spring water discovered in 1626 had been attracting a select few to what was then a remote little town. Among the visitors who came looking for a cure for various ills was Anne Brontë - alas the springs could not help her and she died there at the age of 29. Her grave is in St Mary's churchyard at the foot of the castle. From the coast at Filey, on a rocky promontory known as Filey Brigg, there are grand views north to Scarborough Castle and south to Flamborough Head. Inland, near East Ayton, Forge Valley is one of the loveliest if Yorkshire's many beauty spots, its hills clothed in over-arching trees to create superb woodland walks. Even closer to the hotel are the ruins of Ayton Castle, built around 1400 as a defence against marauding Scots.

Opening Hours: 12.00-23.00 every day

Food: Bar Meals with all the trimmings

Credit Cards: Most with cash back

Accommodation: None

Facilities: Childerns play area, beer garden, function room

Entertainment: Quiz nights and live music nights.

Local Places of Interest/Activities:
Scarborough 3 miles, Osgodby 2 miles, Ayton Castle, Forge Valley.

62   The Feathers

Market Place,
Helmsley,
North Yorkshire
YO62 5BH
Tel: 01439 770275
Fax: 01439 771101

Directions:

Helmsley is situated
on the A170 20 miles
north of York.

Standing on the broad market place of what was originally a Saxon village, **the Feathers** was built as a merchant's house that in its day commanded the highest rent in town. Later it became two cottages and now, united once again, it is a hotel offering a winning combination of old-world charm and up-to-date comfort, seasoned with a generous dash of true Yorkshire hospitality. After nearly 40 years - from 1958 - in the ownership of the Feather family (hence the name), it is now owned by Studford Inns, a local company which also has the Feversham Arms in Helmsley.

The Feathers has 14 letting bedrooms, four twins and ten doubles, all with en suite facilities, tv and tea/coffee-making kit. One of the rooms is a family suite and three rooms have the luxury of four-poster beds. Fresh fruit and bottled water are among the thoughtful touches that await visitors in their rooms. In the Feversham and Pickwick bars a full menu is available lunchtime and evening, seven days a week; breakfast is served from 8 to 10.30 to residents and non-residents, morning coffee through till noon and afternoon tea in the summer. The whole of the ground floor of the Feathers is accessible to guests in wheelchairs, including male and female toilets (but not the bedrooms, which are located on the first and second floors).

The Ryedale Room, with seats for up to 100, is the hotel's function room and can also be equipped for meetings. Regular entertainment includes quiz nights, live music and karaoke. There's ample car parking space behind the hotel. Helmsley is a historic village with many interesting buildings, and there are several more historic houses and other attractions within an easy drive.

Opening Hours: 11.00-23.00.

Food: A la carte.

Credit Cards: All except Diners or Amex

Accommodation: 14 en suite rooms.

Facilities: Function room, Car Park.

Entertainment: Live music, karaoke, quiz nights.

Local Places of Interest/Activities:
Duncombe Park, Castle Howard, Beningborough Hall (NT), York 20 miles, Hutton-le-Hole (Ryedale Folk Museum), Rievaulx Abbey & Terrace.

Internet/Website:
e-mail: feathershotel@aol.com

The Feversham Arms | 63

High Street,
Helmsley,
North Yorkshire
YO62 5AG
Tel: 01439 770766
Fax: 01439 770346

Directions:

Helmsley is situated
on the A170 20 miles
north of York.

The Feversham Arms has long been a favourite Yorkshire retreat, and since a major refurbishment its appeal is even stronger. Owners Studford Inns have totally transformed the place, upgrading what was already a fine hotel into one of real quality. Occupying a corner site at the top of the town, the inn was built in 1855 using the finest stone, and its handsome facade is more than matched by a stunningly updated interior where modern design is combined with tastefully lavish decor and furnishings.

The 17 bedrooms, including five top-of-the-range suites, are appointed to the highest standards, offering one of the very finest bases for touring this lovely part of the world. The new dining room provides the best in local and international cuisine, while the Brasserie at the Fev, in a magnificent new building, serves superb informal meals, with food styles ranging from Escoffier to Jamie Oliver, accompanied by beers and wines from around the world. One of the most impressive new amenities on site is the Feversham Health & Fitness Club, a state-of-the-art fitness suite with an outdoor swimming pool and a tennis court. The Club is open for residents and for private membership.

The Feversham Arms is a sister establishment to the Feathers in the market place here at Helmsley. Feversham is the name of a leading local family, and the centrepiece in the broad market square is a memorial to the 2nd Baron Feversham, whose home was at Duncombe Park just outside town. The memorial bears more than a passing resemblance to London's Albert Memorial, both being the work of the distinguished architect Sir George Gilbert Scott.

Opening Hours: 11.00-23.00.

Food: Brasserie & Fine Dining menus.

Credit Cards: All except Diners

Accommodation: 17 en suite rooms.

Facilities: Health & Fitness Club, Meeting rooms, Car Park.

Local Places of Interest/Activities:
Duncombe Park, Castle Howard, Beningborough Hall (NT), York 20 miles, Hutton-le-Hole (Ryedale Folk Museum), Rievaulx Abbey & Terrace.

Internet/Website:
e-mail:fevershamarms@hotmail.com

64   The Fleece Inn

Westgate,
Rillington,
North Yorkshire
YO17 8LN
Tel: 01944 758464
Fax: 01944 758097

Directions:

5 miles east of
Malton/Norton on
the A64 Scarborough
road.

Built in the 19th century and sympathetically upgraded down the years, **the Fleece Inn** presents a smart face to motorists on the main Scarborough road (A64). Inside, there's plenty of space, and the carpeted main bar lounge is bright and modern, very warm and welcoming, and very well furnished.

The adjoining rooms house the restaurant, the Rillington Grill, which is also kept in apple-pie order. This is where local diners head to relax in comfort and enjoy top-quality meat, poultry and fish, simply and unpretentiously prepared and served in generous portions. Food is available from noon onwards all day, every day. Families are made very welcome by partners Bob Dunford and Jennie, Lynn and Trevor Hodgson, who organise a very popular live music session every Saturday night, as well as the occasional theme night. Their pub has a beer garden and plenty of off-road parking spaces. It's a short drive along the A64 to Malton, which has been the historic centre of Ryedale since Roman times.

Malton was the site of one of the largest of all the Roman garrisons, and many relics from the excavations carried out at the site can be seen in Malton Museum. Just north of Malton is another fascinating insight into history, but this time more recent: Eden Camp is a theme museum that recreates the lives of ordinary people during World War ll.

Opening Hours: Summer; 11.30-23.00 every day: Winter; 12.00-23.00 every day

Food: A la carte.

Credit Cards: All the major cards except Amex

Accommodation: None

Facilities: Car Park for 40 cars at side.

Entertainment: Live music Saturday.

Local Places of Interest/Activities: Malton 5 miles, Norton 5 miles, Scarborough 20 miles, Wharram Percy (deserted village), Flamingo Land Zoo at Kirby Misperton.

Internet/Website:
e-mail: jen@the fleece.fsnet.co.uk

The Hare & Hounds 65

Main Road,
Staxton,
Nr. Scarborough,
North Yorkshire
YO12 4TA
Tel: 01944 710243

Directions:

From Scarborough take the A64 to Staxton 6 miles. From Filey A1039 6 miles.

Sue and John Anderson arrived at this unpretentious little pub in the middle of 2000 and are already making their mark. Built in 1773 as a coaching inn, **the Hare & Hounds** is easy to find on the main road (A64) that runs from Scarborough to York, sidestepping Malton en route. Behind the substantial cream-painted facade the interior is cosy and relaxing, a very pleasant spot for enjoying a quiet drink with friends. It is also warmly recommended for its food, a range of home-cooked dishes that offer plenty of variety and outstanding value for money (no food Monday night). Open fires warm both lounges, and if the sun shines the beer garden is a very agreeable place to be. Beer is also important here with a new guest beer every week.

Entertainment includes the occasional live music night and charity theme nights. The village of Staxton lies at the junction of the A64 and A1039, making access easy to the bright lights of Scarborough to the north, the safe, sandy beaches of Filey Bay to the east, and the town of Malton to the west.

Running south from the village, the B1249 crosses the Wolds on its way to Driffield, a busy little town at the heart of an important corn-growing area. A cattle market is held every Thursday, and the annual agricultural show has been going strong since 1854. There are many pretty little villages hereabouts, and one, on a minor road off the Filey road, is Hunmanby, larger than most and with an information centre for its many visitors. A curiosity here is the ancient village lock-up, with two cells and tiny windows. This is excellent walking country, and the Wolds Way passes a short distance south of Staxton.

Opening Hours: Mon-Fri, 12.00-16.00, 19.00-23.00; Sat -Sun, 12.00-23.00

Food; Bar meals.

Credit Cards: None.

Accommodation: None.

Facilities: Car Park.

Entertainment: Occasional live music and charity nights

Local Places of Interest/Activities: Wolds Way, Scarborough 6 miles, Filey 6 miles.

66 Hawnby Hotel

Hilltop, Hawnby,
Nr. Helmsley,
North Yorkshire
YO62 5QS
Tel: 01439 798202
Fax: 01439 798344

Directions:

From Helmsley take the B1257; after 6 miles turn left on a minor road to Hawnby.

David Young, a Canadian who married a local nurse, runs a most appealing little hotel in a peaceful, out-of-the-way rural setting. Built of local stone in the early 19th century, it makes a delightful base for lovers of the great outdoors: ramblers and hikers will find many miles of waymarked paths and trails, while more strenuous exercise is provided by the gradients of the Hambleton Hills. But without even stirring from the hotel guests can enjoy the stunning views, and from the bay window in the splendid dining room they can drink in the views while enjoying a superb meal.

The menus here would do justice to many a top restaurant, and the results on the plate do not disappoint. There really is something for everyone on a list that visits all parts of the globe for its inspiration, and the regular themed dinner nights are always popular occasions. The hotel has a pleasant beer garden - with more of those great views, of course and each of the rooms is decorated to a very high standard in Laura Ashley co-ordinated themes. All rooms have TV, tea and coffee making facilities, ironing boards, telephones and alarm clocks.

As well as the natural glories of the countryside - Arden Great Moor, Helmsley Moor, the Rye and Seph rivers - the major attraction hereabouts, and one that brings visitors in their thousands is the wonderful Rievaulx Abbey, which stands, a hauntingly beautiful ruin, among the wooded hills beside the River Rye. Looking down on the Abbey is the National Trust's Rievaulx Terrace, a stunning example of landscape gardening that was completed in 1758. Just beyond Rievaulx is the agreeable little town of Helmsley, famous for its castle, the Gothic market square memorial by Sir Giles Gilbert Scott and the grand house and gardens at Duncombe Park.

Opening Hours: 11.00-23.00; limited hours off season.

Food: A la carte menu.

Credit Cards: All the major cards.

Accommodation: 6 en suite rooms.

Facilities: Restaurant, beer garden with panoramic views over Ryedale.

Local Places of Interest/Activities: Helmsley 8 miles, Rievaulx Abbey, Cleveland Way, York, Scarborough,Castle Howard, Duncombe Park.

Internet/Website:
website: www.hawnbyhotel.co.uk

Hayburn Wyke Inn 67

Newlands Road,
Cloughton,
Nr. Scarborough,
North Yorkshire
YO13 0AU
Tel: 01723 870202
Fax: 01723 871474

Directions:

From Scarborough
A171 four miles
north to Cloughton.

A half-mile winding lane leads from the main road to **Hayburn Wyke Inn**, a distinctive stone building fronted by a red-tiled veranda, neat rows of picnic tables on a hardstanding and a supply of large toys to keep young visitors happy. At the side is a garden with trim lawns. The present owner, Sharon Simpson, who runs the place with her family, is a vivacious lady with a welcome for all-comers. The interior of the hotel is bright and spacious, with huge open fires in the bar and lounge to keep out the North Sea chill.

Visitors can quench their thirsts with Real Ales and the usual range of drinks and deal with outdoor appetites with generous helpings of delicious home- made, traditional food from a list that is supplemented by daily specials. Being close to the sea, this is a good base for a healthy holiday, and overnight accommodation is provided in three en suite bedrooms equipped with tea & coffee making facilities, tv, radio-alarm and hairdryer. Sharon has plans to bring more bedrooms on stream.

Cloughton, and in particular Cloughton Wyke, hit the national headlines in 1932 when a huge whale beached itself. Press photographers and postcard publishers rushed to the scene and paid the smallest local children they could find to pose by the giant creature. The fun lasted only until the six-ton monster began to rot, and the problem then was not how to exploit it but how to get rid of it. The air has been pure ever since, with the breezes bringing either the tang of ozone or the scent of heather from the moors. It's an easy drive to Scarborough and Whitby, while inland the scenic delights of moors and dales and forest beckon. One of the most picturesque local places is Forge Valley, south of Hackness, a steep wooded ravine with splendid walks along a two-mile stretch of the River Derwent (the name refers to ancient iron workings which totally disappeared long ago).

Opening Hours: 11.00-15.00 and 19.00-23.00 Mon-Fri; All day Sat and Sun

Food: Bar meals.

Credit Cards: Access, Mastercard, Visa.

Accommodation: 3 en suite rooms.

Facilities: Car Park.

Entertainment: Live music occasionally

Local Places of Interest/Activities: Scarborough 4 miles, Whitby 10 miles, Hackness (Forge Valley).

68   The Huntsman

22 Main Road,
Aislaby,
Nr. Whitby,
North Yorkshire
YO21 1SW
Tel/Fax:
 01947 810637

Directions:

A171 1 mile out of
Whitby, turn left on
to minor road
signposted Aislaby.

A neat, well-kept little pub that started life as a coaching inn 180 years ago. It stands on the edge of the Moors above the valley of the River Esk, but is only a couple of miles from Whitby and the sea, thus offering easy access to all the varied delights that this lovely part of the world has to offer.

The congenial owner, Gary Moutrey, puts a great emphasis on food, and folk in the know travel for miles to tuck into plates of cod and haddock fresh from the boats at Whitby. Quality is also to the fore in the meat dishes, for which the main ingredients are supplied by a first-class local butcher. Chargrilled steaks are a speciality of the house. The pub's convenient best-of-both-worlds location naturally attracts overnight guests, for whom two en suite bedrooms - a double and a family room with TV and tea/coffee making facilities - provide warm, comfortable accommodation. The locals play darts here with an enthusiasm unmatched in the area, and the regulars don their thinking caps every other Tuesday for the popular quiz nights.

Moorland and riverside walks are great for building up a thirst while drinking in the local scenery, and motorists do not have to travel far to reach some of the other attractions. These include Grosmont, where the car can be temporarily swapped for the delights of a ride behind a steam engine on the gloriously scenic North Yorkshire Moors Railway; Glaisdale, a picturesque village with a historic stone bridge; Goathland - known as Aidensfield in the tv series *Heartbeat*; and the Moors Visitor Centre at Danby.

Opening Hours: 12.00-15,00; 19.00-23.00
Food: Bar meals.
Credit Cards: Access, Mastercard, Visa.
Accommodation: 1 double and 1 family en suite
Facilities: Car Park, Front Terrace

Entertainment: Quiz night every second Tuesday.
Local Places of Interest/Activities: Whitby 2 miles, Grosmont 5 miles, Danby 9 miles.

Ivanhoe Hotel 69

Burniston Road,
Scarborough,
North Yorkshire
YO12 6QX
Tel: 01723 366063
* or 01723 355447*
Fax: 01723 353621

Directions:

A64 from Malton,
A170 from Pickering,
A165 from Hull,
A171 from Whitby;
on the north side of
town.

A family-oriented pub/hotel on the north side of Scarborough, overlooking the sea, the castle and the golf course. It's the perfect choice for a seaside holiday, offering comfortable accommodation and good food at very competitive prices. The 12 well-appointed modern bedrooms are all en suite, with tv, radio-alarms and hairdryers; they range from a single to a family room for two adults and two children. The three cheerful bars offer lots of space for socialising, along with pool and other traditional pub games, and an extensive lunch and dinner menu is served in the lounge, conservatory and snug, or out in the garden when the sun shines.

On Thursday afternoon pensioners get special deal. Access for wheelchairs is provided from the rear entrance, and there's a toilet with facilities for disabled visitors on the ground floor. When some pubs call themselves child-friendly they might mean a see-saw in the garden, but when Les and Lynne Price's hotel calls itself child-friendly it really means it. The chief centre of attraction for youngsters is a double-decker bus parked permanently in the garden, with a slide, soft playing areas and videos. Children can amuse themselves for hours in the bus while parents relax inside the hotel; like most buses this one is also available for private hire - in this case for children's parties! Also in the garden are a play cottage and an aviary. The Ivanhoe hotel was winner of 'Family Pub of the Year' award 2001.

Scarborough has plenty to interest young and old alike, and one of the most popular attractions, very close to the Ivanhoe, is the Sea Life Centre, whose occupants range from shrimps to sharks. There are several golf courses in the vicinity, and the Ivanhoe offers special rates for golfing parties.

Opening Hours: Mon-Sat 11.00-23.00; Sun, 12.00-22.30

Food: Bar meals served all day

Credit Cards: Access, Mastercard, Visa.

Accommodation: 12 en suite rooms.

Facilities: Car Park, children's amusements, milk shake machines, business area

Local Places of Interest/Activities: The sights of Scarborough, sandy beaches, golf courses.

70   Mallyan Spout Hotel

Goathland, Nr. Whitby,
North Yorkshire YO22 5AN
Tel: 01947 896206
Fax: 01947 896327

Directions:
From Pickering take the A169 towards Whitby; after about 12 miles tun left on to minor road signposted Mallyan Spout and Goathland.

Situated on the common of one of Yorkshire's prettiest villages, the **Mallyan Spout Hotel** takes its name from the waterfall that drops 70 feet into a wooded valley a short walk from the hotel. Built as a gentleman's residence in 1892, the hotel offers style, luxury and the best Yorkshire hospitality behind its ivy-clad facade. Open fires keep winter at bay in the three roomy lounges, which enjoy fine views of the garden, moors and valley, and in the cosy, convivial bar lively conversation accompanies a large selection of liquid refreshment, including real ales from local breweries. Seafood fresh from Whitby is a speciality in the dining room, where excellent work in the kitchen is matched by friendly, efficient service. The 22 bedrooms, mostly decorated in cottage style, all have bath or shower room en suite, tv and telephone. Two of the rooms in the converted coach house are on the ground floor, making them perhaps the preferred choice for guests who have difficulty with stairs.

After the pleasures of hospitality, comfort and fine food and wine, the great outdoors beckons, with marvellous walks through moorland and by rivers, taking in the ozone by the coast or exploring the many delightful villages and the historic towns in the area. And no stay here would be complete without a trip on the scenically unsurpassed North Yorkshire Moors Railway, which calls at the village on its steam-powered journey from Grosmont to Pickering. Judith and Peter Heslop, who have owned and run the hotel since the early 1970s, welcome guests for short or long stays and are happy to organise gourmet weekends and walking or sporting breaks. The hotel has unlimited parking space and a little shop selling local crafts and gifts.

Opening Hours: 08.00-23.00

Food: A la carte menus.

Credit Cards: Access, Amex, Mastercard, Visa

Accommodation: 22 en suite rooms.

Facilities: Car Park, Patio, Large garden

Local Places of Interest/Activities: Whitby 9 miles, North Yorkshire Moors National Park, Egton Bridge, Beck Hole.

Internet/Website:
e-mail: mallyan@ukgateway.net

Middleton Arms　　71

North Grimston,
Nr. Malton,
North Yorkshire YO18 8EW
Tel: 01944 768255

Directions:
5 miles southeast of Malton on the B1248

The Middleton Arms is an elegant country pub dating from the last part of the 19th century. It stands proudly in its own grounds, and behind the substantial frontage it's cosy and inviting but also very roomy, with plenty of floor space, attractively curtained windows and neatly placed dining tables - all adding up to a really warm and inviting country hostelry. The landlady, Kathleen Grayston, plays a hands-on role with the help of her super staff and takes great pride in the number of customers who have become regulars - many of them are from the racing fraternity, which is a very strong presence in this part of the world.

The Middleton Arms is very much a food-driven establishment, and just the thought of its marvellous steak pie brings people from far and wide. Fresh produce is always the order of the day, with locally sourced fish, game and vegetables to the fore on the mouthwatering menu; and well-kept cask ales take excellent care of thirsts. Food is not the only ace in the pack at this splendid free house, which also provides excellent overnight accommodation in three comfortably appointed bedrooms, one with full en suite facilities, the others with shower units and shared use of a private bathroom. Kathleen welcomes visitors of all ages, and the beer garden has a play area for small children. The Middleton Arms is a great place to come and relax, but he brain cells need to be in top form for the quiz nights, which take place every other Sunday. Car park.

Opening Hours: Mon-Sat; 10.30-15.00, 18.30-23.00; Sun 10.30-15.00, 19.00-22.30

Food: Bar meals and à la carte, restaurant open Mon-Sun 12.00-14.00, 19.00-21.00

Credit Cards: All except Amex

Accommodation: 3 bedrooms, 1 en suite.

Facilities: Function room (45 covers), Car Park front an back

Entertainment: Quiz night every second Sunday.

Local Places of Interest/Activities: Malton 5 miles, Castle Howard.

72   Netherby House

90 Coach Road,
Sleights,
Whitby,
North Yorkshire
YO22 5EQ
Tel/Fax:
 01947 810211

Directions:

From Whitby, take
the A171/A169 3
miles southwest of
Whitby.

'By the sea, the moors and the National Park'. The setting is one of the great assets of **Netherby House**, a delightful little hotel in the village of Sleights, three miles from Whitby. The house, built as a gentleman's residence in the last decade of Queen Victoria's reign, is owned and run by Barry and Lyn Truman, who welcome guests of all ages into a happy, relaxed atmosphere and a peaceful, attractive ambience. The house has 1½ acres of gardens - including a croquet lawn - overlooking the Esk Valley and the borders of the North York Moors National Park. They have 11 letting bedrooms, all with bath or shower en suite, tv, radio-alarm and tea-makers. One room has the added luxury of a Victorian four-poster bed. Hairdryers and irons are available on request, and there are facilities for drying out-door clothing and footwear.

Meals are take in the cosy candle-lit dining room, with local meat and fish and their own garden produce to the fore. Draught beers and a good selection of wines complement the fine cuisine. Picnic lunches and afternoon tea can be provided with notice. Residents have a comfortable for relaxing with a good book, and there's a car park with security lighting at the back of the hotel.

The countryside around Netherby House is particularly beautiful, and there are miles of moorland walks and heritage coastline for working up an appetite while enjoying the scenery. Whitby, with its Captain Cook and Dracula connections, is only three miles away, while attractions inland include the National Park and the villages of Goathland, Egton and Grosmont, northern terminus of the scenic, steam-hauled North York Moors Railway.

Opening Hours: Residents only.

Food: Evening menu.

Credit Cards: Mastercard, Visa.

Accommodation: 11 en suite rooms.

Facilities: Car Park.

Local Places of Interest/Activities: Whitby 3 miles, North York Moors National Park 1 mile, Grosmont 3 miles, Goathland 4 miles, Robin Hood Bay 7 miles.

The New Inn 73

Maltongate,
Thornton-le-Dale,
North Yorkshire
YO18 7LF
Tel: 01751 474226
Fax: 01751 477715

Directions:

Two miles east of
Pickering on the
A170 road to
Scarborough.

Occupying a prominent corner site on the A170 road to the coast at Scarborough, **the New Inn** is a grand old Georgian coaching house dating back to 1720. Recent alterations and refurbishment have enhanced the old-world charm and atmosphere, and the lounge is a roomy, inviting place to relax with a drink or settle down to a snack or a meal.

The inn prides itself on its variety of freshly prepared food - mainly locally sourced - that is served lunchtime and evening seven days a week. For guests staying overnight the New Inn has six letting bedrooms, all with tv and tea/coffee-making facilities. Standard rooms have double beds and en suite shower, WC and wash basin, while the larger rooms have a bath as well as a shower, and either king-size, four-poster or twin beds. Alternative accommodation is available behind the pub in a self-catering cottage that can sleep four. Parking space is plentiful in a large car park at the back of the pub.

Thornton-le-Dale (just Thornton Dale on some maps) is situated on the southern edge of the beautiful North Yorkshire Moors National Park. A beck runs along its main street, and the market cross and the old village stocks stand in the park in front of the pub. Pickering, just two miles along the A170, is a charming market town with many places of interest, including the parish church with its renowned 15th century wall paintings and a museum of local history. Also nearby, at Kirby Misperton, is Flamingo Land Zoo.

Opening Hours: Bar: Mon-Sat 12.00-14.30, 18.30-23.00: Sun 12.00-15.00, 18.30-22.30

Restaurant: 12.00-14.00, 18.30-21.00 daily

Food: A la carte.

Credit Cards: All except Amex or Diners

Accommodation: 6 en suite rooms + 1 self-catering cottage.

Facilities: Car Park.

Local Places of Interest/Activities: Pickering 2 miles, Scarborough 15 miles, Lastingham (church with Norman crypt), Whitby 20 miles, Castle Howard.

Internet/Website:
e-mail: newinntld@aol.com

74   The Ox Inn

Lebberston,
Nr. Scarborough,
North Yorkshire
YO11 3PB
Tel: 01723 582306

Directions:

From Scarborough
A64 to Eastfield
then left on to
B1261; 3 miles to
Lebberston.

The residents of the quaint little village of Lebberston, just off the main road from Scarborough to Bridlington, are lucky indeed to have such a splendid local as **the Ox Inn**. But it's not just the villagers who are attracted here, as people drive for many miles to enjoy the cheerful ambience and hospitality dispensed by engaging owners James Bloor and Jenny Marley. The small public bar and the oak-beamed lounge are kept in apple-pie order, the walls covered in prints with a horsy theme. Pool is played in a separate games room.

This is a super spot either for a quiet pub lunch or for an evening spent relaxing over a full meal. Sensible food at sensible prices keeps the crowds coming back for more, and the 30 covers soon fill up, so it's definitely best to book ahead, especially at the weekend. The printed menu is supplemented by daily specials, which often include seasonal game - venison and jugged hare were on a recent list. Food is served lunchtime and evening every day in summer, but not on Monday off season. Occasional quiz and blues/folk nights. The pub has excellent off-road parking.

The urban delights of Scarborough are a few minutes away, but there are also quieter places to head for. The nearest sandy beaches are at lovely Cayton Bay, a brisk walk to the north, or in the broad sweep of coast that runs from Filey to Reighton. A little further down are the 400' Bempton Cliffs, an RSPB sanctuary with a summer population of upwards of 200,000 seabirds. The constant battle between the land and the sea can be witnessed in dramatic style at Flamborough Head, where the rocky promontory is gradually being eroded.

Opening Hours: 12.00-15.00 and 18.00-23.00

Food: Bar meals. Restaurant open 12.00-14.00 and 18.00-20.30

Credit Cards: Access, Mastercard, Visa

Accommodation: None.

Entertainment: Occasional quiz nights and folk/blues nights

Facilities: Off-road parking.

Local Places of Interest/Activities:
Scarborough 3 miles, Filey, Cayton Bempton Cliffs.

The Postgate

75

Egton Bridge,
Nr. Whitby,
North Yorkshire
YO71 1UX
Tel: 01947 895241
Fax: 01947 895111

Directions:

From Whitby (8 miles)
or Guisborough (15
miles) take the A171
and turn on to minor
road signposted
Egton.

An exquisite little pub in the top corner of the North Yorkshire Moors National Park. **The Postgate** was built in 1860, and in the main lounge a feature stove that must be as old as the pub burns cheerfully. Diners come from all over Yorkshire and beyond to enjoy Jane King's hospitality, to sample the excellent food and maybe to spend the night in warm, comfortable surroundings. Local produce features strongly in the cooking, which combines the best traditional Yorkshire and time-honoured British recipes with a hint of modern European influences.

For visitors staying overnight the Postgate has five pleasantly appointed rooms with tv and tea-making facilities. Three are en suite, the other two share a bathroom. The pub has a nice beer garden and a good big car park. It's a very sociable place, and locals and tourists join in the regular special events, including charity nights, blues nights and karaoke sessions. The Postgate is something of a celebrity, but under its 'stage name' of the Black Dog Inn, which is how it appears in the popular television series *Heartbeat*. Its real name, Postgate, remembers the martyr Nicholas Postgate, who was born in the village in 1596. Ordained as a Roman Catholic priest in France, he returned to the Moors to minister to those still loyal to the outlawed faith. He was betrayed, and at the age of 81 was hung, drawn and quartered in York.

The village is dominated by the Roman Catholic St Hedda's Church, which has a dazzling blue roof with gold stars; inside, a notable feature is some fine Belgian terracotta work on the altar. Egton Bridge is the setting for a typical British happening, the annual Gooseberry Show, to which growers from all over the world bring their prize specimens. The village is a stop on the North Yorkshire Moors Railway (the station is next to the pub) on which steam-hauled trains ply the gloriously scenic route from Grosmont to Pickering.

Opening Hours: Mon-Sat, 11.00-23.00; Sun 11.00-22.30

Food: Bar meals, open for coffee from 9 am

Credit Cards: Access, Mastercard, Visa.

Accommodation: 5 rooms, 3 en suite.

Facilities: Car Park, Front Terrace

Entertainment: Blues and karaoke nights.

Local Places of Interest/Activities: North Yorkshire Moors National Park, Moors Centre at Danby 7 miles, Mallyan Spout, Whitby 7 miles.

76

The Red Lion

Cloughton,
Nr. Scarborough,
North Yorkshire
YO13 0AE
Tel:01723 870702

Directions:

From Scarborough
4 miles north on
the A171.

Window boxes and hanging baskets make a colourful sight in summer at the **Red Lion**, which is located in the village of Cloughton on the A171 between Scarborough and Whitby. But it doesn't need to be summer to feel the warmth of the welcome, and the open fires in the bar and lounge certainly play their part. The pub is run by the Whites (two brothers and their wives), and it attracts both local residents and visitors to the North Yorkshire coast, whether for a quiet drink and a chat - in the garden when the sun shines - or to take a longer break to enjoy a meal. The food is served all day, every day in good old-fashioned portions and represents excellent value for money, and the well-kept ales include some lesser known Yorkshire brews - Blacksheep and guest real ales.

There's plenty to keep visitors occupied in the neighbourhood, and the Red Lion can provide an economical base where families are welcome. It has four upstairs letting bedrooms, a single, a double, a twin and a family room that share a bathroom. All have washbasins, Sky tv and tea-makers. The bar has a separate games room with a pool table, and on Friday night all minds are focused on the weekly quiz.

Cloughton is less than a mile from the sea, at Cloughton Wyke, where in 1932 a huge whale beached itself and briefly generated national interest. Scarborough, Yorkshire's first seaside resort, is a few minutes' drive away, while inland there's great walking and great sightseeing: Forge Valley is a particularly attractive spot on a lovely stretch of the River Derwent. Close by the valley are the ruins of Ayton Castle, the most southerly of the many defences built against the threat of Scottish marauders.

Opening Hours: 11.00-23.00, Sun to 22.30.

Food: Bar meals.

Credit Cards: None.

Accommodation: 4 rooms sharing a bathroom.

Facilities: Car Park. Large garden

Entertainment: Quiz Friday.

Local Places of Interest/Activities:
Scarborough 4 miles, Forge Valley 4 miles.

The Rose Inn 77

Bridge Street,
Pickering,
North Yorkshire
YO18 8DT
Tel: 01751 475366

Directions:

Behind the bridge in
Pickering, which lies
at the junction of
the A169 and A170.

Living proof that good things come in small packages is provided by this delightful little inn tucked away behind the bridge in the charming town of Pickering. The pub could not be more relaxed and it could not be more friendly, and the father-and-son team of Fishers (Peter and Peter) guarantee that visitors will not find a warmer welcome in any of Pickering's many public houses. Some of the locals look on it almost as a second home, and with its huge open fire and comfortable bench-style seating, it also provides a welcome break for shoppers and sightseers.

The Rose Inn's bar food is every bit as unpretentious as the surroundings - simple, satisfying and easy on the pocket; snacks and light bites are served throughout the day, hot meals from 12 to 3 and from 5 to 8. Darts and pool are played in the games room, and the Fishers can always bank on a full house for the occasional jazz and folk nights.

Pickering is a town with a lot to offer the visitor, including the ruins of a medieval (mainly 14th century) castle and an absorbing museum of local and rural life. It is also the southern terminus of the North Yorkshire Moors Railway, a preserved steam-hauled line which runs north through glorious scenery to Grosmont. One of the many spectacular local sights is the Hole of Horcum, on the road to Whitby, a mile-wide natural amphitheatre gouged out of the moorland by spring water eroding the limestone - or, some say, by the Devil himself!

Opening Hours: 11.00-23.00; Sun 12.00-22.30

Food: Snacks and bar meals.

Credit Cards: None

Accommodation: None.

Facilities: Beer Garden, small car park

Entertainment: Jazz and Folk nights.

Local Places of Interest/Activities: North Yorkshire Moors Railway (Pickering-Grosmont), Flamingo Land Zoo at Kirby Misperton, Malton 8 miles, Scarborough 17 miles, Whitby 20 miles, Dalby Forest, Rievaulx Abbey & Terrace, Hutton-le-Hole (Ryedale Folk Museum).

78 The Tap & Spile

New Quay Road,
Whitby,
North Yorkshire
YO21 1DH
Tel: 01947 603937

Directions:

18 miles north of
Pickering on the A169.

Built as a cellar pub at
the end of the 19th cen-
tury, **the Tap & Spile**
was rebuilt much as it
looks today in 1937. It
enjoys a delightful set-
ting among the little
shops and restaurants on
the New Quay side of
town and attracts a regu-

lar clientele with its pleasant atmosphere and convivial surroundings. The present owners,
Peter and Sheree Fleming, have a wealth of pub management experience and took over the
tenancy of this pub 18 months ago, although they have been here for six years. They and
their staff engender a happy feeling at the pub, where evening entertainment five days a
week features music for all tastes. The Tap & Spile (two terms relating to a beer barrel) is well
known for its selection of cask ales and is also a popular choice for a meal - a quick snack
for those in a hurry or a leisurely two or three courses for those with time to relax and to
enjoy the entertainment later on.

The attractive seaside town of Whitby is perhaps known for its jet and its strong links
with early Christianity - the old town is dominated by the ruins of Whitby Abbey high up
on a cliff. Whitby was Captain Cook's home port, and the house where he lodged during
his apprenticeship is now the Captain Cook Memorial Museum. There's a Dracula connection, too, for Whitby was the place where, according to Bram Stoker's novel, Count
Dracula, in the form of a wolf, came ashore from a without a crew that had drifted into the
harbour. The classic 1931 film with Bela Lugosi as the Count was filmed in the original
locations at Whitby. Walk Whitby Way takes visitors on a walkabout that reveals all the
myths and legends associated with the port - if the Ghost Walk gets too scary, the Tap &
Spile is ready to bring visitors back to the present day with a smile and a song and a glass or
two of ale.

Opening Hours: Mon-Sat; 12.00-23.00; Sun
12.00-22.30 (Sundays in winter 12.00-16.00,
19.00-22.30) Late closing 1st June to 30th
September - Fri-Sat 12.00, Sun 23.00

Food: Bar meals

Credit Cards: None

Accommodation: None

Entertainment: Live music 5 nights a week.
Quiz night on Thursdays

Local Places of Interest/Activities: Whitby
Abbey, Egton Bridge (Gooseberry Show) 7
miles, Goathland (Mallyan Spout) 8 miles,
Beck Hole (World Quoits Championship) 7
miles.

The Wheeldale Hotel

North Promenade,
Whitby,
North Yorkshire
YO21 3JX
Tel: 01947 602365

Directions:

Whitby is on the A169 from Pickering, the A171 from Guisborough and Scarborough and the A174 from Redcar and Saltburn. On entering Whitby follow signs for West Cliff.

In a quiet location overlooking the sandy beach on Whitby's West Cliff, **the Wheeldale** has a relaxed atmosphere that immediately puts visitors at ease. Personally run by owners Liz and Ian Bouttell, the hotel has recently been refurbished throughout. All bedrooms are en suite, with a colour tv and tea-coffee trays. The premier suite comprises bedroom, en suite shower room and separate sitting room. A non-smoking policy operates in the bedrooms and in the seaview dining room. Smoking is permitted in the lounge-bar. The hotel is open from February to early November.

One of the most attractive and historic of all the towns in North Yorkshire, Whitby has much to offer the visitor. It was one of the earliest major centres of the Christian religion, and high on the cliff that towers above the old town stand the ruins of Whitby Abbey, where in AD664 leading church dignitaries were summoned to the Synod of Whitby to settle the question of when Easter should be celebrated. The influence of the sea is naturally very strong, and the sea and Christianity come together in St Mary's Church, whose interior was reputedly built by Whitby sailors. Robin Hood's Bay, renowned for its tales of smuggling, is five miles down the coast, while attractions inland include the annual Gooseberry Show at Egton Bridge, Beck Hole, scene of the annual World Quoits Championship, and Grosmont, northern terminus of the scenic North Yorkshire Moors Railway, constructed in the 1830s by none other than George Stephenson.

Opening Hours: Feb - Nov

Food: evening table d'hote.

Credit Cards: Access, Mastercard, Visa, Delta.

Accommodation: 9 en suite rooms.

Facilities: Car Park.

Local Places of Interest/Activities:
Scarborough 22 miles, Guisborough 20 miles, Saltburn 20 miles, Goathland (Aidensfield from the TV series Heartbeat) 3 miles

Internet/Website:
e-mail: wheeldale_hotel@lineone.net
website: www.wheeldale-hotel.co.uk

Ye Horseshoe Inn

**Egton, Whitby,
North Yorkshire
YO21 1TZ
Tel: 01947 895274**

Directions:

From Whitby A171; after about 5 miles, turn left on to minor road marked Egton and Glaisdale.

Resident landlord Andrew Hall offers something for everyone at **Ye Horseshoe Inn**, a fine old Yorkshire inn located in a village six miles inland from Whitby. Oak tables and chairs enhance the old-world effect in the bar, where snacks and meals are served lunchtime and evening seven days a week. The ploughman's platter and the home-made pies are always among the favourites. Coffee, tea and light bites are available from 11 in the morning. A full menu is served every evening in the 26-cover restaurant, where typical dishes run from breaded mushrooms or paté and toast to grilled lemon sole, chicken chasseur and pepper steak. Booking is advisable for the Saturday night and Sunday lunch carveries, and also for a room for the night. The accommodation, available for short or long stays throughout the year, comprises an attractive lounge, an en suite double bedroom, two twin bedrooms each with wash basin and sharing an adjacent bathroom. Access to the accommodation is direct from the garden - guests can come and go as they choose.

With the sea a few minutes away and a host of scenic delights all around, the inn is a fine base for coast and country holidays, and the beer garden is a most agreeable spot for enjoying a summer drink or a barbecue. Attractions within minutes of the inn include lovely walks through the Esk Valley, picturesque villages and the North Yorkshire Moors steam railway starting at Grosmont. Egton itself is a delightful village with many handsome old properties, and in nearby Egton Bridge stands the dazzling Church of St Hedda.

Opening Hours: 11.00-15.00, 18.00-23.00

Food: Bar meals 12.00-14.30, 18.00-21.30
Restaurant 18.00-21.30

Credit Cards: All the major cards.

Accommodation: 3 bedrooms, 1 en suite.

Facilities: Car Park. Children and dogs welcome

Entertainment: Darts, dominoes and quizes all year round.

Local Places of Interest/Activities: Whitby 6 miles, Egton Bridge 2 miles, Grosmont 1 mile, Goathland 6 miles.

3 The City of York and Central Yorkshire

PLACES OF INTEREST:

PUBS AND INNS:

The Hidden Inns of Yorkshire

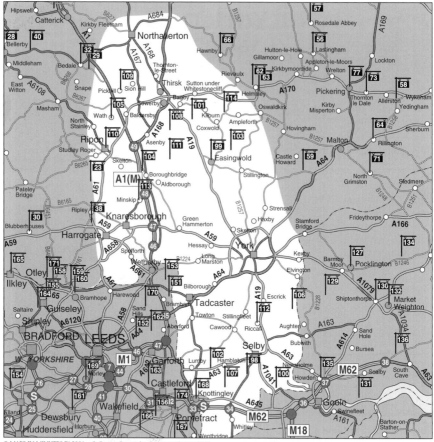

© MAPS IN MINUTES ™ 2001   © Crown Copyright, Ordnance Survey 2001

98 The Anchor Inn, Burn	**107** Kellington Manor, Kellington
99 The Angel Inn, Easingwold	**108** The Moon & Pheasant, Dalton
100 The Black Dog Inn, Camblesforth	**109** The Nags Head, Pickhill
101 The Carlton Inn, Carlton Husthwaite	**110** The Navigation Inn, Ripon
102 The Crown Inn, Monk Fryston	**111** The Oak Tree Inn, Helperby
103 The Durham Ox, Crayke	**112** Park View Hotel, Riccall
104 The Fox & Hounds, Langthorpe	**113** The White Swan, Minskip
105 The George Country Inn, Wath	**114** The Wombwell Arms, Wass
106 The Jefferson Arms, Thorganby	

Please note all references refer to page numbers

The City of York and Central Yorkshire

The Vale, or Plain as it's sometimes called, is rich, agricultural land that stretches some 60 miles northwards from York almost to the Tees. Although flat itself, there are almost always hills in view: the Hambleton and Cleveland Hills to the east, the Dales and the Pennines to the west. In between lies this fertile corridor of rich farmland and low-lying meadows, a vast plain bisected by the Great North Road linking London and Edinburgh. For most of its life the Great North Road has been a rocky, pot-holed and swampy obstacle course. The best stretches, by far, were those where it ran along the meticulously engineered course the Romans had built centuries earlier. It took more than 1,800 years for the English to realise the importance of constructing viable, all-weather roads. We were, one might say, slow learners. All the locations mentioned in this chapter are within a few miles of York itself.

PLACES OF INTEREST

ALDBOROUGH

The ancient Roman town of *Isurium Brigantum*, or Aldborough, as it is known today, was once the home of the 9th Legion, who wrested it from the Celtic Brigantian tribe. The modern-day focal point of the village is the tall maypole on the village green, around which traditional dances take place each May. At one end of the green is a raised platform - all that remains of the Old Court House and it bears an inscription recalling that, up to 150 years ago the election of members of Parliament was announced here. Below are some well-preserved stocks that are, in fact, only replicas of the originals. The **Aldborough Roman Museum** houses relics of the town's past. This was once a thriving Roman city of vital strategic importance; near the museum are some of the original walls and tessellated pavements of that city.

The **Church of St Andrew** was built in 1330 on the site of a Norman church that was burnt down by the Scots in 1318. This in turn had been built on the site of an ancient Temple of Mercury. Modern archaeologists no doubt reel in horror at the thought that parts of the present church were built with stones from the Temple's walls. One ancient relic that is still preserved in the church's grounds is an Anglo-Saxon sundial known as the Ulph Stone.

BOROUGHBRIDGE

This attractive and historic town dates from the reign of William the Conqueror, though it was once on a main thoroughfare used by both the Celts of Brigantia and, later, the Romans. The bridge over the River Ure, from which the village takes its name, was built in 1562 and it formed part of an important road link between

Devil's Arrows, Boroughbridge

84

Edinburgh and London. Busy throughout the coaching days with traffic passing from the West Riding of Yorkshire to the North, Boroughbridge has now returned to its former unassuming role of a small wayside town now bypassed by the A1(M) which takes most of the 21st century traffic from its streets.

The great **Devil's Arrows**, three massive Bronze Age monoliths, stand like guardians close to the new road and form Yorkshire's most famous ancient monument: thought to date from about 2000 BC, the tallest is 30 feet high. The monoliths stand in a line running north-south and are fashioned from millstone grit which has been seriously fluted by weathering. A local legend, however, attributes the great stones to the Devil, suggesting that they were, actually, crossbow bolts that he fired at nearby Aldborough which, at the time, was a Christian settlement.

COXWOLD

Coxwold enjoys a particularly lovely setting in the narrow valley that runs between the Hambleton and Howardian Hills. At the western end of the village stands the 500-year-old **Shandy Hall**, home of Laurence Sterne, vicar of Coxwold in the 1760s. Sterne was the author of *Tristram Shandy*, that wonderfully bizarre novel which opened a vein of English surreal comedy leading directly to The Goons and the Monty Python team. The architecture of the Hall, Tudor in origin, includes some appropriately eccentric features - strangely-shaped balustrades on the wooden staircases, a Heath Robinson kind of contraption in the bedroom powder-closet by which Sterne could draw up pails of water for his ablutions, and a tiny, eye-shaped window in the huge chimney stack opening from the study to the right of the entrance. A more conventional attraction is the priceless collection of Sterne's books and manuscripts.

The Revd Sterne much preferred the cosmopolitan diversions of London to the rustic pleasures of his Yorkshire parish, and rarely officiated at the imposing church nearby with its striking octagonal tower, three-decker pulpit and Fauconberg family tombs. A curiosity here is a floor brass in the nave recording the death of Sir John Manston in 1464. A space was left for his wife Elizabeth's name to be added at a later date. The space is still blank. Outside, against the wall of the nave, is Sterne's original tombstone, moved here from London's Bayswater when the churchyard there was deconsecrated in 1969.

Just to the south of Coxwold is **Newburgh Priory**, founded in 1145 as an Augustinian monastery and now a mostly Georgian country house with fine interiors and a beautiful water garden. Since 1538, the Priory has been the home of the Fauconberg family. An old tradition asserts that Oliver Cromwell's body is

Newburgh Priory, nr Coxwold

interred here. Cromwell's daughter, Mary, was married to Lord Fauconberg, and when Charles II had her father's corpse hanged at Tyburn and his head struck off, Lady Fauconberg claimed the decapitated body, brought it to Newburgh and, it is said, buried the remains under the floorboards of an attic room. The supposed tomb has never been opened, the Fauconbergs even resisting a royal appeal from Edward VII when, as Prince of Wales, he was a guest at the Priory. The house, which is still the home of the Earls of Fauconberg, and its extensive grounds are open to the public during the spring and summer months.

From Coxwold, follow the minor road northeastwards towards Ampleforth. After about 2 miles, you will see the lovely, cream-coloured ruins of **Byland Abbey**. The Cistercians began building their vast compound in 1177 and it grew to become the largest Cistercian church in Britain. Much of the damage to its fabric was caused by Scottish soldiers after the Battle of Byland in 1322. The English king, Edward II had been staying at the Abbey but fled after his defeat, abandoning vital stores and priceless treasures. In a frenzy of looting, the Scots made off with everything the king had left and ransacked the Abbey for good measure. The ruined west front of the Abbey, although only the lower arc of its great rose window is still in place, gives a vivid impression of how glorious this building once was.

EASINGWOLD

This agreeable market town was once surrounded by the Forest of Galtres, a vast hunting preserve of Norman kings. It lies at the foot of the Howardian Hills, an Area of Outstanding Natural Beauty covering 77 acres of woods, farmland and historic parkland. Easingwold's prosperity dates back to the 18th century when it flourished as a major stage coach post - at that period the town could offer a choice of some 26 public houses and inns. Until the recent construction of a bypass the old town was clogged with traffic but it is now a pleasure again to wander around the market place with its impressive **Market Cross** and, nearby, the outline of the old bull-baiting ring set in the cobbles. Easingwold used to enjoy the distinction of having its own private railway, a two and a half mile stretch of track along which it took all of ten minutes to reach the main east coast line at Alne. Older residents fondly remember the ancient, tall-chimneyed steam locomotive that plied this route until its deeply regretted closure to passenger traffic in 1948.

A little to the south of Easingwold, on the B1363, is **Sutton Park**, a noble early 18th century mansion, built in 1730 by Thomas Atkinson and containing some fine examples of Sheraton and Chippendale furniture, and much-admired decorative plasterwork by the

Market Cross, Easingwold

Italian maestro in this craft, Cortese. The ubiquitous "Capability" Brown designed the lovely gardens and parkland in which you'll find a Georgian ice-house, well-signposted woodland walks and a nature trail. There's also a gift shop and a cafe.

HARROGATE

One of England's most attractive towns and a frequent winner of Britain in Bloom, Harrogate features acres of gardens that offer an array of colour throughout the year, open spaces and broad tree-lined boulevards. However, until the 17th century Harrogate - or *"Haregate"* as it was then called - was just a collection of cottages close to the thriving market town of Knaresborough. It was William Slingsby, of Bilton Hall near Knaresborough, who, whilst out walking his dog, discovered a spring bubbling up out of the rock that was to found the fortunes of the town. Tasting the waters, Slingsby found them to be similar to those he had tasted at the fashionable wells of Spaw, in Belgium. Expert opinion was sought and, in 1596, Dr Timothy Bright confirmed the spring to be a chalybeate well and the waters to have medicinal powers - curing a wide variety of illness and ailments from gout to vertigo.

Slingsby's well became known as **Tewit Well**, after the local name for peewits, and it can still be seen today, covered by a dome on pillars. Other wells were also found in the area, St John's Well in 1631 and the **Old Sulphur Well** which went on to become the most famous of Harrogate's springs. Though this spring had been known, locally, for years it was not until 1656 that this sulphurous smelling well, nicknamed the "Stinking Spaw", began to attract attention.

During the mid-17th century bathing in the heated sulphurous waters became fashionable as well as a cure for various ailments and lodging houses were built around the sulphur well in Low Harrogate. Bathing took place in the evening and, each morning, the patients would drink a glass of the water with their breakfasts. The cupola seen over the well was erected in 1804.

In order to serve the growing number of people arriving at Harrogate seeking a cure for their ailments the Queen's Head Hotel was built and it is probably the oldest inn here as it dates from before 1687. When stagecoaches began to arrive in the 18th century the inn moved with

86

the times and it became the first at the spa to serve the needs of the coaches.

By the late 1700s it was one of the largest hotels in the fast growing town and, though the hotel changed its name to the Queen's Hotel in 1828 and underwent extensive renovation and remodelling in the mid-19th century, it did not survive the decline of the spa and, in 1951, it became the offices for the Regional Hospital Board. Many other hotels were built including the Crown Inn, next to the Old Sulphur Well, which too became a coaching inn in 1772 and hosted a visit by Lord Byron in 1806. However, one of the town's most famous hotels, The Majestic, a turn of the century red brick building, does survive and it was the place where Elgar stayed whilst visiting Harrogate.

The **Royal Pump Room Museum** was built in 1842 to enclose the Old Sulphur Well and this major watering place for spa visitors has been painstakingly restored to illustrate all the aspects of Harrogate's history. Beneath the building the sulphur water still rises to the surface and can be sampled.

There will be few Harrogate residents who have not heard of Betty Lupton, the almost legendary *"Queen of the Wells"* who, for over 50 years, dispensed the spa waters, dishing out cupfuls to paying visitors, who were then encouraged to walk off the dubious effects of the medicine by taking a trip around the Bogs Fields, known today as **Valley Gardens**. She conducted her business in the ostentatiously named **Royal Baths Assembly Rooms** which, in their heyday, were full of rich visitors sampling the waters. Today, the buildings have been restored to house the Turkish Baths where visitors can enjoy a sauna and solarium, and are

open to the public daily. The **Mercer Art Gallery** is housed in the oldest of the town's surviving spa buildings, originally built in 1806. The ``Promenade Room'' has been restored to its former glory and displays a superb collection of fine art.

By the late 18th century Harrogate had become one of Europe's most fashionable spa towns and it was not only serving the needs of those with acute and chronic ailments but also members of *"good society"*. Fuelled by competition from spa towns abroad, Harrogate sought to provide not only medical care for the sick but also to appeal to the needs of the fashionable. In 1858, Charles Dickens visited the town and described it as *"the queerest place, with the strangest people in it leading the oddest lives of dancing, newspaper reading, and table d'hôte''*. Though its status as a spa town has declined, it is still a fashionable place, a sought after conference location, home of the annual Northern Antiques Fair, and a town with much to offer the visitor.

As well as a spa, Harrogate developed into a centre for shopping for the well-to-do; the many old fashioned shops are typified by **Montpellier Parade**, a crescent of shops surrounded by trees and flowerbeds. Another attractive aspect of the town is **The Stray**, which is unique to Harrogate and virtually encircles the town centre. The 200 acres of open space are protected by ancient law to ensure that the residents of, and visitors to, the town always have access for sports, events, and walking. The spacious lawns are at their most picturesque during the spring when edged with crocus and daffodils. Originally part of the Forest of Knaresborough the land was, fortunately, not enclosed under the 1770 Act of Parliament. The large gritstone pillar, beside The Stray, marks the boundary of the Leeds and Ripon turnpike. On The Stray stands the Commemorative Oak Tree, planted in 1902 by Samson Fox to commemorate the ox roasting that took place here as part of the celebrations for Queen Victoria's Jubilee in 1887 and the end of the Boer War in 1902.

Perhaps the most well known tale associated with Harrogate is the disappearance of Agatha Christie in 1926. In a set of circumstances reminiscent of one of her novels, Agatha went missing in December of that year, possibly as a result of marital difficulties. Her crashed car was discovered near a chalk pit near her home, but the novelist was nowhere to be found and one of the largest police manhunts was put into

Royal Bath Assembly Rooms, Harrogate

operation. Agatha had, in fact, travelled to Harrogate, after abandoning her car, and booked into the Old Swan Hotel under the name of her husband's mistress, Theresa Neele. After 10 days she was spotted and her husband came to collect her, putting her disappearance down to loss of memory. However, this did not dispel rumours that the marriage was in trouble nor that the surprising event was nothing more than a publicity stunt. Whatever the truth, two years later the couple divorced and Colonel Christie married his long-time mistress Theresa.

One of Harrogate's major visitor attractions is **Harlow Carr Botanical Gardens**, just over a mile from the town centre. Established in 1948 by the Northern Horticultural Society and now covering some 68 acres, the gardens feature all manner of plants in a wide variety of landscapes which allows members of the public to see how they perform in the unsympathetic conditions of northern England. The society, as well as having their study centre here, has also opened a fascinating **Museum of Gardening**.

KNARESBOROUGH

This ancient town of pantiled cottages and Georgian houses is precariously balanced on a hillside by the River Nidd. A stately railway viaduct, 90 feet high and 338 feet long, completed in 1851, spans the gorge There are many unusual and attractive features in the town, among them a maze of steep stepped narrow streets leading down to the river and numerous alleyways. In addition to boating on the river, there are many enjoyable riverside walks.

The town is dominated by the ruins of **Knaresborough Castle**, built high on a crag overlooking the River Nidd by Serlo de Burgh, who had fought alongside William the Conqueror at Hastings. Throughout the Middle Ages, the castle was a favourite with the court and it was to Knaresborough that the murderers of Thomas à Becket fled in 1170. Queen Philippa, wife of Edward III, also enjoyed staying at Knaresborough and she and her family spent many summers here. However, following the Civil War, when the town and its castle had remained loyal to the king, Cromwell ordered its destruction.

Also in the town is the **Old Courthouse Museum** which tells the history of the town and houses a rare Tudor Courtroom. The nearby **Bebra Gardens** are named after Knaresborough's twin town in Germany and its attrac-

tive flower beds are complemented by luxurious lawns and a paddling pool. In the High Street, visitors should also keep an eye out for **Ye Oldest Chymists' Shoppe** in England which dates back to 1720. For the last century and more, it's been owned by the Pickles family which manufactures some 40 lotions, ointments and creams. Among their potions are *"Fiery Jack"*, a rubbing ointment, *"Snowfire"* for chapped hands, and *Snufflebabe Vapour Rub.*

However, Knaresborough is probably best known for **Mother Shipton's Cave**, the birthplace of the famous prophetess, and for its Petrifying Well which provides a constant source of curiosity to the visitor. The effects that the well's lime rich water has on objects are truly amazing and an array of paraphernalia, from old boots to bunches of grapes, are on view - seemingly turned to stone. It is little wonder that these were considered magical properties by the superstitious over the centuries or that the well was associated with witchcraft and various other interesting tales.

Knaresborough

88

The foremost tale concerns Mother Shipton, who was said to have been born in the cavern situated by the well on 6th July 1488 and who has the reputation of being England's most famous fortune-teller. The story says that she was born in the midst of a terrible storm and was soon found to have a strange ability to see the future. As she grew older her prophetic visions became more widely known and feared throughout England. However, the most singular feature about Mother Shipton has to be that she died peacefully in her bed, as opposed to being burnt at the stake as most witches were at that time.

She had been threatened with burning by, among others, Cardinal Wolsey, when she had warned him on a visit to York that he might see the city again but never enter. True to her prediction Wolsey never did enter York, for he was arrested on a charge of treason at Cawood. Among her many other prophesies she reputedly foretold the invasion and defeat of the Spanish Armada in 1588 and Samuel Pepys recorded that it was Mother Shipton who prophesied the disastrous Great Fire of London in 1666.

While in Knaresborough it is well worth taking the opportunity to visit the **House in the Rock** hewn out of solid rock by Thomas Hill, an eccentric weaver, between 1770 and 1786. It was Hill's son who renamed the house Fort Montagu and flew a flag and fired a gun salute on special occasions. On the banks of the River Nidd there is also the infamous **St Robert's Cave** which is an ancient hermitage. Robert was the son of a mayor of York who, at the time of his death in 1218, was so beloved that the people of Knaresborough would not allow the monks of Fountains Abbey to bury him. Instead they kept his bones and finally interred him in a place near the altar in the **Chapel of Our Lady of the Crag**. It is guarded by the statue of a larger than life-size figure of a knight in the act of drawing a sword.

In the tradition of this town's reputation for exceptional and odd characters is *"Blind Jack of Knaresborough"*. Jack Metcalfe was born in 1717 and lost his sight at the age of six, but went on the achieve fame as a roadmaker. He was a remarkable person who never allowed his blindness to bar him from any normal activities - he rode, climbed trees, swam, and was often employed to guide travellers through the wild Forest of Knaresborough. He was a talented fiddle player and one of his more roguish exploits was his elopement with Dolly Benson, the daughter of the innkeeper of the Royal Oak in Harrogate, on the night before she was due to marry another man. His most memorable achievement however, was the laying of roads over the surrounding bogs and marshes which he achieved by laying a foundation of bundles of heather, a feat which had never been done before.

Another of Knaresborough's attractive amenities is **Conyngham Hall**, a majestic old house enclosed within a loop of the River Nidd. Once the home of Lord Macintosh, the Halifax toffee magnate, the Hall itself is not open to the public but its landscaped grounds, stretching down to the river, are and provide tennis, putting and other activities.

A mile or so to the south of Knaresborough, **Plumpton Rocks** provide an ideal picnic spot. There's an idyllic lake surrounded by dramatic millstone grit rocks and woodland paths that were laid out in the 18th century. It has been declared a garden of special historic interest by English Heritage and is open every weekend and daily during July and August.

LONG MARSTON

Lying on the edge of the Vale of York and sheltered by a hill, this village is an ancient agricultural community. However, in July 1644, the peace of this tranquil village was shattered by the battle of Marston Moor, one of the most important encounters of the Civil War and one which the Royalists lost. The night before the battle, Oliver Cromwell and his chief officers stayed at **Long Marston Hall** and the bedroom they used is still called The Cromwell Room.

Each year the anniversary of the battle is commemorated by the members of the Sealed Knot and, it is said, that the ghosts of those who fell in battle haunt the site. Certainly, local farmers still, occasionally, unearth cannonballs from the battle when they are out ploughing the fields.

Less than 100 years later, Long Marston Hall saw the birth, in 1707, of the mother of General James Wolfe, the famous English soldier who scaled the Heights of Abraham to relieve the siege of Quebec.

NORTHALLERTON

The county town of North Yorkshire, Northallerton has the broad High Street, almost half a mile long, typical of the county's market towns. In stage coach days the town was an important stop on the route from Newcastle to London and several old coaching inns still stand along the High Street. The most ancient is **The Old Fleece**, a favoured drinking haunt of Charles Dickens during his several visits to the town. It's a truly Dickensian place with great oak beams and a charming olde-worlde atmosphere. The Old Fleece recalls the great days of the stage coach which came to an abrupt end with the arrival of the railway. One day in 1847, a coach called the Wellington made the whole of the 290 mile journey from Newcastle to London, via Northallerton, completely empty. The era of this romantic - if uncomfortable and extremely expensive - mode of transport was over.

Northallerton has many old buildings of interest, including an ancient **Grammar School** whose history goes back to at least 1322. The school was rebuilt in 1776 at the northern end of the High Street - a building that is now a solicitors' office. By the end of the 19th century the school had *"no great reputation"* and by 1902 only thirteen pupils were registered. Things went from bad to worse the next year when the headmaster was convicted of being drunk and disorderly. Fortunately the school, now Northallerton College and in new buildings, has recovered its reputation for academic excellence.

The town also boasts a grand medieval church, a 15th century almshouse and, of more recent provenance, a majestic County Hall built in 1906 and designed by the famous Yorkshire architect Walter Brierley. The oldest private house in Northallerton is Porch House which bears a carved inscription with the date "1584". According to tradition, Charles I came here as a guest in 1640 and returned seven years later as a prisoner.

Two miles north of the town, a stone obelisk beside the A167 commemorates the **Battle of the Standard**, fought here in 1138. It was one of the countless conflicts fought between the English and the Scots, and also one of the bloodiest with more than 12,000 of the Scots, led by King David, perishing under a rain of English arrows. The battle took its name from the unusual standard raised by the English: the mast of a ship mounted on a wagon and, crowning its top, a pyx containing the consecrated Host.

NORTH STAINLEY

89

Just over 100 years ago, in 1895, excavations in a field just outside the village revealed the site of a Roman villa called Castle Dykes though all that can be seen now are the grassed outlines of the foundations and the moat. However, the discovery does prove that there has been a settlement here for many centuries. The monks of Fountains Abbey also knew North Stainley. Slenningford Grange is thought to have been one of their many properties and a fishpond, dating from medieval times, is still in existence.

Just to the south of the village lies the **Lightwater Valley Theme Park** set in 175 acres of scenic grounds. The Park boasts "Ultimate" - the biggest roller coaster in the world (authenticated by the *Guinness Book of Records*), the Rat Ride, Falls of Terror, and the Viper to name just a few and there are also plenty of more appropriate activities for younger children. Also within the grounds is Lightwater Village (free) which offers a wide variety of retail and factory shops, a garden centre, restaurant and coffee shop.

RICCALL

The ancient village of Riccall is mentioned in the Domesday Book and has a church that was built not long after. The south doorway of the church dates back to about 1160 and its fine details have been well-preserved by a porch added in the 15th century. The village's great moment in history came in 1066 when the gigantic King Harold Hardrada of Norway and Earl Tostig sailed this far up the Ouse with some three hundred ships. They had come to claim Northumbria from Tostig's half-brother King Harold of England but they were comprehensively defeated at the Battle of Stamford Bridge.

Riccall is popular with walkers: from the village you can either go southwards alongside the River Ouse to Selby, or strike northwards towards Bishopthorpe on the outskirts of York following the track of the dismantled York to Selby railway. This latter path is part of the 150 mile long Trans Pennine Trail linking Liverpool and Hull.

Just to the south of Skipwith, the Yorkshire Wildlife Trust maintains the **Skipwith Common Nature Reserve.** This 500 acres of lowland heath is one of the last such areas remaining in the north of England and is regarded as

90

of national importance. The principal interest is the variety of insect and birdlife, but the reserve also contains a number of ancient burial sites.

RIPON

This attractive cathedral city, on the banks of the Rivers Ure, Skell, and Laver, dates from the 7th century when Alfrich, King of Northumbria granted an area of land here, surrounding a new monastery, to the Church. Later that century, in 672, St Wilfrid built a church on the high ground between the three rivers but, at the time of the demise of the Northern Kingdom in the mid-10th century, the monastery and church were destroyed, though the Saxon crypt survives to this day. By the time of the Norman Conquest, Ripon was a prosperous agricultural settlement under ecclesiastical rule and it was at this time that a second St Wilfrid's Church was erected on the site of the Saxon building. On Christmas Day 1132, monks from York worshipped here whilst they were making a journey to found Fountains Abbey and, traditionally, the people of Ripon follow this ancient route on Boxing Day.

A striking survival of the Saxon cathedral is the 1,300-year-old Crypt. At its northeast corner is a narrow passage known as The Needle. According to the 17th century antiquary Thomas Fuller, women whose chastity was suspect were made to pass through it. If they were unable to do so, their reputations were irretrievably tarnished. *"They pricked their credits"* Fuller wrote *"who could not thread the Needle"*.

The Crypt is all that remains of St Wilfrid's church but the magnificent **Cathedral of St Peter and St Wilfrid**, which now stands on the site, is certainly well worth visiting. Begun in the mid-12th century by Archbishop Roger of York, it was originally designed as a simple cruciform church; the west front was added in the mid-13th century and the east choir in 1286. Rebuilding work was begun in the 16th century but the disruption of the Dissolution of the Monasteries caused the work to be abandoned and it was only the intervention of James I in the early 1600s, that saved the building from ruin. Then established as a collegiate church, the diocese of Ripon was formed in 1836 and the church made a cathedral. Often referred to as the Cathedral of the Dales, the building, though one of the tallest cathedrals in England,

Ripon Cathedral

is also the smallest.

Throughout the Middle Ages, the town prospered: its market charter had been granted by King Alfred in the 9th century and, at one time, Ripon produced more woollen cloth than Halifax and Leeds. The collapse of the woollen industry saw a rise in spur manufacture in the 16th century and their fame was such that Ripon spurs were referred to in the old proverb: *"As true steel as a Ripon rowel."* As well as having three rivers, Ripon also had a canal. Built between 1767 and 1773 to improve the navigation of the River Ure: John Smeaton, builder of the Eddystone Lighthouse, was the designer. However, by 1820 the company running the canal had fallen into debt and it was little used after that time.

Fortunately for today's visitor, the Industrial Revolution, and all its associated implications, by-passed Ripon and it was not until the early 20th century that the town flourished, though briefly, as a spa. However, many ancient customs and festivals have survived down the centuries and perhaps the most famous is the sounding of the *"Wakeman's Horn"* each night at 9 p.m. in the market place. Dating back to the 9th century, the Wakeman was originally appointed to patrol the town after the nightly curfew had been blown and, in many ways, this was the first form of security patrol. The Wakeman was selected each year from the town's 12 aldermen and those choosing not to take office were fined heavily. Today, this old custom is revived in the Mayor-making Ceremony when the elected mayor shows great reluctance to take office and hides from his colleagues.

As might be expected, any walk around this ancient town reveals, in its buildings, its interesting and varied past. The heart of the town is the **Market Place** and here stands a tall obelisk which was erected in 1702 to replace the market cross. Restored in 1781, at its summit are a horn and a rowel spur, symbolizing Ripon's crafts and customs. Situated at the edge of the square are the 14th century **Wakeman's House** and the attractive **Georgian Town Hall**.

The Spa Baths building, opened in 1905 by the Princess of Battenberg, is a reminder of Ripon's attempt to become a fashionable spa resort. With no spring of its own, the town had to pipe in sulphur mineral water from Aldfield near Fountains Abbey. However, the scheme failed, though the baths building, which now houses the city's swimming pool, is a fine example of art nouveau architecture and the **Spa Gardens** are still a pleasant place for a stroll.

Near to the cathedral is Ripon's old Courthouse that was built in 1830 on the site of an earlier 17th century Common Hall, used for the Quarter Sessions and the Court Military. Adjacent to this fine Georgian courthouse is a Tudor building that was part of the Archbishop of York's summer palace.

Also not far from the cathedral is the House of Correction, built in 1686 which served as the local prison between 1816 and 1878 and then became the police station until the late 1950s. This austere building is now home to the **Ripon Prison and Police Museum**, established in 1984, which depicts the history of the police force as well as giving visitors a real insight into the life of a prisoner in Victorian times. Almost as unfortunate as those prisoners were the inmates of **Ripon Workhouse**, the city's newest museum. The restored vagrants' wards of 1877 provide a chilling insight into the treatment of paupers in Yorkshire workhouses and the displays include a "Victorian Hard Times Gallery".

Finally, horse racing at Ripon dates back to 1713 and the present course opened in 1900. Meetings are held between April and August and the course is widely regarded as one of the most beautiful in the country.

SELBY

In 1069 a young monk named Benedict, from Auxerre in France, had a vision. It's not known

exactly what the vision was but it inspired him to set sail for York. As his ship was sailing up the Ouse near Selby, three swans flew in formation across its bows. (Three swans, incidentally, still form part of the town's coat of arms). Interpreting this as a sign of the Holy Trinity, Benedict promptly went ashore and set up a preaching cross under a great oak called the *Stirhac*. The small religious community he established went from strength to strength, acquiring many grants of land and, in 1100, permission to build a monastery. Over the course of the next 120 years, the great **Selby Abbey** slowly took shape, the massively heavy Norman style of the earlier building gradually modulating into the much more delicate Early English style. All of the Abbey was built using a lovely cream-coloured stone. Over the centuries this sublime church has suffered more than most. During the Civil War it was severely damaged by Cromwell's troops who destroyed many of its statues and smashed much of its stained glass. Then in 1690 the central tower collapsed. For years after that the Abbey was neglected and by the middle of the 18th century a wall had been built across the chancel so that the nave could be used as a warehouse. That wall was removed during a major restoration during the 19th century but in 1906 there was another

Selby Abbey

calamity when a disastrous fire swept through the Abbey. Visiting this serene and peaceful church today it's difficult to believe that it has endured so many misfortunes and yet remains so beautiful. Throughout all the Abbey's misfortunes one particular feature survived intact - the famous Washington Window which depicts the coat of arms of John de Washington, Prior of the Abbey around 1415 and a direct ancestor of George Washington. Prominently displayed in this heraldic device is the stars and stripes motif later adapted for the national flag of the United States.

Devotees of railway history will want to pay their respects to Selby's old railway station. Built at the incredibly early date of 1834 it is the oldest surviving station in Britain.

SION HILL

Sion Hill Hall, about four miles northwest of Thirsk, is celebrated as the "last of the great country houses". Its light, airy and well-proportioned rooms, all facing south, are typical of the work of the celebrated Yorkshire architect, Walter Brierley - the "Lutyens of the North". He completed the building in 1913 for Percy Stancliffe and his wife Ethel, the wealthy daughter of a whisky distiller. The rooms

Fountains Abbey

haven't altered one bit since they were built, but the furniture and furnishings certainly have. In 1962, the Hall was bought by Herbert Mawer, a compulsive but highly discerning collector of antiques. During the twenty years he lived at Sion Hill, Herbert continued to add to what was already probably the best collection of Georgian, Victorian and Edwardian artefacts in the north of England. Furniture, paintings, porcelain, clocks (all working), ephemera, crowd the twenty richly furnished rooms and make Sion Hill a delight to visit. A recent addition to the many sumptuous displays is a charming exhibition of dolls from the early 1900s.

In the Hall's Victorian Walled Garden is another major visitor attraction - **Falconry U.K.'s Bird of Prey and Conservation Centre.** More than 80 birds from 34 different species have their home here: owls, hawks, falcons, buzzards, vultures and eagles from all around the world. At regular intervals throughout the day these fierce-eyed, sharp-beaked predators behave in a remarkably docile and co-operative way as they take part in fascinating flying demonstrations.

SKELTON

This charming little village has some surviving cottages, dating from 1540, which are built from small handmade bricks with pantiled roofs. A ferry used to cross the River Ure, at this point, to Bishop Monkton and, in 1869, it was the scene of a notorious hunting accident. Members of the York and Ainsty Hunt boarded the ferry in order to follow a fox that had swum across the river. Half way across the horses panicked, capsizing the boat, and the boatman, along with five hunt members, were drowned.

Hidden away just to the south of the village is one of the area's finest stately homes, **Newby Hall.** Built in the 18th century and designed by Robert Adam, much of the house is open to the public including the splendid Billiard Room with its fine portrait of Frederick Grantham Vyner; an ancestor of the family which has lived here from the mid-19th century, Frederick was murdered by Greek bandits after being kidnapped. The house, though is perhaps most famous for its superb tapestries and there is also a fine collection of Chippendale furniture.

It is, though, the award winning **Newby Hall Gardens** that draw most people to the house. Extensive and well designed, it was the present owner's father who transformed a 9-hole golf course into the 25 acres of award-winning gardens that offer something for everyone whatever the time of year. Also found here is a wonderful Woodland Discovery Walk, a miniature railway, plenty of other attractions specially designed for children, a Plant Stall, Shop and Restaurant.

SPOFFORTH

This ancient village, situated on the tiny River Crimple, is home to the splendid Palladian mansion, **Stockeld Park**, built between 1758 and 1763 by Paine. Containing some excellent furniture and a fine picture collection, the house is surrounded by extensive parkland which offers garden walks. Though privately owned, the house is open by appointment.

Spofforth Castle is another place of note, an historic building whose sight stirs the imagination, despite its ruined state. The powerful Percy family originally built the castle here in the 16th century to replace the manor house which had been repeatedly laid to waste. The castle itself is now a crumbling ruin after it too was destroyed during the Civil War. Among the many events which took place here it is said to have been the birthplace of Harry Hotspur. The ruins are now in the care of English Heritage.

STUDLEY ROGER

The magnificent **Studley Royal Gardens** were created in the early 18th century before they were merged with nearby Fountains Abbey in 1768. Started by John Aislabie, the disgraced Chancellor of the Exchequer and founder of the South Sea Company that spectacularly burst its bubble in 1720, the landscaping took some 14 years. It then took a further 10 years to complete the construction of the buildings and follies found within the gardens. With a network of paths and the River Skell flowing through the grounds, it is well worth exploring these superb gardens.

A National Trust property, like the adjoining gardens, **Fountains Abbey** is the pride of all the ecclesiastical ruins in Yorkshire and the only World Heritage Site in Yorkshire. The abbey was one of the wealthiest of the Cistercian houses and its remains are the most complete of any Cistercian abbey in Britain. Founded in 1132, with the help of Archbishop Thurstan of York, the first buildings housed just 12 monks

of the order and, over the centuries its size increased, even spreading across the River Skell itself. The abbey

93

reached its peak in the 15th century with the grandiose designs of Abbot Marmaduke Huby, whose beautiful tower still stands as a reminder of just how rich and powerful Fountains became. In fact, the abbey was run on such businesslike lines that, at its height, as well as owning extensive lands throughout Yorkshire, it had an income of about a thousand pounds a year, then a very substantial sum indeed.

It is commonly thought that one of the abbey's friars, renowned for his strength and skill as an archer, challenged Robin Hood to a sword fight. Forced to concede, the friar joined the Merry Men of Sherwood and became known as Friar Tuck. The Dissolution hit the abbey as it did all the powerful religious houses. The abbot was hanged, the monks scattered, and its treasures taken off or destroyed. The stonework, however, was left largely intact, possibly due to its remote location. In 1579, Sir Stephen Proctor pulled down some outbuildings, in order to construct **Fountains Hall**, a magnificent Elizabethan mansion which still stands in the abbey's grounds and part of which is open to the public.

SUTTON-UNDER-WHITESTONECLIFF

Boasting the longest place name in England, Sutton is more famous for the precipitous cliff that towers above it, **Sutton Bank**. For one of the grandest landscape views in England, go to the top of Sutton Bank and look across the vast expanse of the Vale of York to the Pennine hills far away to the west. James Herriot called it the *"finest view in England"*. He knew this area well since his large veterinary practice covered the farms from here right over to the Dales. A continuation of the Cleveland Hills, the Hambleton Hills themselves lead into the Howardian Hills: together they form the mighty southwest flank of the North York Moors.

There's a National Park Information Centre at the summit of Sutton Bank and a well-marked Nature Trail leads steeply down to, and around, **Lake Gormire**, an Ice Age lake trapped here by a landslip. Gormire is one of Yorkshire's only two natural lakes, the other being Semerwater in Wensleydale. Gormire is set in a large basin with no river running from it: any overflow disappears down a 'swallow hole' and emerges

94

beneath White Mare Cliffs. Sutton Bank used to be a graveyard for caravans because of its steep (1 in 3) climb and sharp bends. On one July Saturday in 1977, some 30 vehicles broke down on the ascent and five breakdown vehicles spent all day retrieving them. Caravans are now banned from this route. Sutton Bank may be tough on cars but its sheer-sided cliffs create powerful thermals making this a favoured spot for gliders and bright-winged hang-gliders.

TADCASTER

The lovely magnesian limestone used in so many fine Yorkshire churches came from the quarries established here in Roman times. Their name for Tadcaster was simply 'Calcaria' - limestone. By 1341, however brewing had become the town's major industry, using water from river Wharfe. Three major breweries are still based in Tadcaster: John Smiths whose bitter is the best selling ale in Britain, Samuel Smiths (established in 1758 and the oldest in Yorkshire), and the Tower Brewery, owned by Bass Charringtons. The distinctive brewery buildings dominate the town's skyline and provide the basis of its prosperity. Guided tours of the breweries are available by prior booking.

Also worth visiting is **The Ark**, the oldest building in Tadcaster dating back to the 1490s. During its long history, The Ark has served as a meeting place, a post office, an inn, a butcher's shop, and a museum. It now houses the Town Council offices and is open to the public in office hours. This appealing half-timbered building takes its name from the two carved heads on the first floor beams. They are thought to represent Noah and his wife, hence the name. Tadcaster also offers some attractive riverside walks, one of which takes you across the **Virgin Viaduct"** over the River Wharfe. Built in 1849 by the great railway entrepreneur George Hudson, the viaduct was intended to be part of a direct line from Leeds to York. Before the tracks were laid however Hudson was convicted of fraud on a stupendous scale and this route was never completed.

About 4 miles southwest of Tadcaster is **Hazelwood Castle**, now owned by the Carmelite Friars who use it as a retreat and conference centre. But for more than eight centuries it was the home of the Vavasour family who built it with the lovely white limestone from their quarry at Thevesdale - the same quarry that provided the stone for York Minster and King's College Chapel, Cambridge. The well-maintained gardens and nature trail are open every afternoon, (tea room and shop open on Sundays only), and guided tours of the Castle with its superb Great Hall and 13th century Chapel, can be arranged by telephoning 01937 832738.

THIRSK

Thirsk has become famous as the home of veterinary surgeon Alf Wight, better known as James Herriot, author of *All Creatures Great and Small*, who died in 1995. In his immensely popular books, Thirsk is clearly recognisable as "Darrowby". The Easter of 1999 saw the opening in Thirsk of a £1.4m tribute to the celebrated vet. **The World of James Herriot** is housed in the original surgery in Kirkgate and offers visitors a trip back in time to the 1940s, exploring the life and times of the world's most famous country vet. There's also the opportunity to take part in a TV production, and a "Visible Farm" exhibit where you can explore farm animals inside and out!

Just across the road from the surgery is the birthplace of another famous son of Thirsk. The building is now the town's museum and tourist office and a plaque outside records that Thomas Lord was born here in 1755: 30 years later he was to create the famous cricket ground in Marylebone that took his name. A more recent celebrity whose home is in Thirsk is Bill Foggitt, renowned for his weather forecasts based on precise observations of nature.

This pleasant small town of mellow brick houses has a sprawling Market Place and a magnificent 15th century **St Mary's Church** is generally regarded as the finest parish church in North Yorkshire. It was here that the real life "James Herriot" married his wife, Helen. Cod Beck, a tributary of the River Swale, wanders through the town, providing some delightful - and well-signposted riverside walks.

Thirsk appeared in the Domesday Book not long after William the Conqueror had granted the Manor of Thirsk to one of his barons, Robert de Mowbray. The Mowbrays became a powerful family in the area, a fact reflected in the naming of the area to the north and west of Thirsk as the Vale of Mowbray. In the early 1100s the family received permission to hold a market at Thirsk but then blotted their copy-book by rebelling against Henry II in 1173. The rebellion failed and their castle at Thirsk was burnt to the ground. Not a trace of it remains. The market however is still thriving, held twice-weekly on Mondays and Saturdays. An old market by-law used to stipulate that no butcher be allowed to kill a bull for sale in the market until the beast had been baited by the town dogs. That by-law was abandoned in the early 1800s and the bull-ring to which the animal was tethered has also disappeared.

On the edge of town, the **Trees to Treske Visitor Centre** is an imaginative exhibition exploring how trees grow, the character of different woods and examples of the cabinet maker's craft. Nearby is Thirsk Racecourse, known to devotees of the turf as the "Country Racecourse". There are around 12 race meetings each year, all well attended by visitors keen to experience this intrinsic feature of Yorkshire life. Travelling through the areas between the Dales and the North York Moors, one is constantly reminded of the great tradition of horse-breeding that the county is famous for. The tradition runs deep: even the long flat straight stretch of main railway line between York and Darlington is known as the "racecourse".

WATH

The stately home of **Norton Conyers** has been owned by the Graham family since 1624 though, undoubtedly, the house's main claim to fame is the visit made by Charlotte Brontë. During her stay here the novelist heard the story of Mad Mary, supposedly a Lady Graham. Apparently Lady Graham had been locked up in an attic room, now tantalisingly inaccessible to the public, and Charlotte eventually based the character of Mrs Rochester in her novel *Jane Eyre* on the unfortunate woman. Visitors to the hall will also see the famous painting of Sir Bellingham Graham on his bay horse, as Master of the Quorn hunt. It is rumoured that ownership of the painting was once decided on the throwing of a pair of dice. Other family pictures, furniture and costumes are on display and there's a lovely 18th-century walled garden within the grounds.

WETHERBY

Situated on the Great North Road, at a point midway between Edinburgh and London, Wetherby was renowned for its coaching inns, of which the two most famous were The Angel and The Swan & Talbot. It is rumoured that serving positions at these inns were considered so lucrative that employees had to pay for the privilege of employment in them! The town fortunately has remained unspoilt and has a quaint appearance with a central market place that was first granted to the Knights Templar. Many of the houses in the town are Georgian, Regency, or early Victorian. Apart from its shops, galleries, old pubs and cafés, there is also a popular racecourse nearby. Another feature is the renowned 18th-century bridge with a long weir which once provided power for Wetherby's corn mill and possibly dates from medieval times.

YORK

"The history of York is the history of England" said the Duke of York, later to become George VI. A bold claim, but well justified. For almost 2,000 years the city has been at the centre of great events and, better than any other city in England, it has preserved the evidence of its glorious past. One of the grandest cityscapes in the country opens up as you walk along the old city walls towards **York Minster,** a sublime expression of medieval faith.

The Minster stands on the site of an even older building, the headquarters of the Roman legions. The Imperial troops arrived here in AD71 when the governor, Quintus Petilius Cerealis, chose this strategic position astride the Rivers Ouse and Foss as his base for a campaign against the pesky tribe of the Brigantes. The settlement was named Eboracum. From this garrison, Hadrian directed the construction of

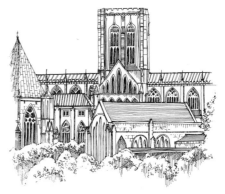

York Minster, York

96

his great wall and a later general, Constantine, was proclaimed Emperor here. The legions finally left the city around AD410, but the evidence of their three and a half centuries of occupation is manifest all around York in buildings like the **Multangular Tower**, in rich artefacts treasured in the city's museums and even in a pub: at the **Roman Bath Inn** you can see the remains of steam baths used by the garrison residents.

Little is known of York during the Dark Ages, but by the 8th century the city had been colonised by the Anglo-Saxons, who named it Eoferwic, and it was already an important Christian and academic centre. The Vikings put an end to that when they invaded in the 9th century and changed the name once again, this time to Jorvik. The story of York during those years of Danish rule is imaginatively told in the many displays at the **Jorvik Centre**.

After the Norman Conquest, the city suffered badly during the Harrowing of the North when William the Conqueror mounted a brutal campaign against his rebellious northern subjects. Vast tracts of Yorkshire and Northumberland were laid waste and some historians reckon that

it took more than 100 years for the area to recover from this wholesale devastation.

In later Norman times, however, York entered one of its most glorious periods. The Minster, the largest Gothic church in England, was begun around 1230 and the work was on such a scale that it would not be completed until two and a half centuries later. Its stained glass windows - there are more than 100 of them - cast a celestial light over the many treasures within. A guided tour of the Great Tower gives dizzying views across the city; a visit to the crypt reveals some of the relics from the Roman fortress that stood here nearly 2000 years ago.

This superb building has survived seemingly unscathed from three major fires. The first occurred in 1829 and was started by a madman, Jonathan Martin. Believing that God wanted him to destroy the church, he started a fire using prayer and hymn books. The fire was not discovered until the following morning by which time the east end of the Minster had been severely damaged. The second blaze, in 1840, was caused by a workman leaving a candle burning. As a result of his carelessness, the central part of the nave was destroyed. The most recent conflagration was in July 1984, shortly after a controversial Bishop of Durham had been installed. Some attributed the fire to God's wrath at the Bishop's appointment; the more prosaic view was that it had been caused by lightning. The subsequent restoration has allowed modern masons and craftsmen to demonstrate that they possess skills just as impressive as those of their medieval forebears.

The network of medieval streets around the Minster is one of the city's major delights. Narrow lanes are criss-crossed by even narrower footpaths - ginnels, snickets or "snickelways", which have survived as public rights of way despite being built over, above and around. Narrowest of all the snickelways is Pope's Head Alley, more than 100 feet long but only 31 inches wide. The alley was also known as Introduction Lane - if you wanted to know someone better, you simply timed your walk along it so as to meet the other party half-way. Whipma-Whop-ma-Gate, allegedly, is where felons used to be "whipped and whopped". Probably most famous of these ancient streets is **The Shambles**. Its name comes from 'Fleshammels', the street of butchers and slaughter houses. The houses here were deliberately built to keep the street out of direct sunlight, thus protecting the

Jorvik Centre

carcasses which were hung outside the houses on hooks. Many of the hooks are still in place.

During these years, York was the second largest city in England and it was then that the town walls and their "bars", or gates, were built. The trade guilds were also at their most powerful and in Fossgate one of them built the lovely black and white timbered **Merchant Adventurers Hall**. The Merchant Adventurers controlled the lucrative trade in all "goods bought and sold foreign" and they spared no expense in building their Great Hall where they conducted their affairs beneath a complex timbered roof displaying many colourful banners of York's medieval guilds. To this period too belong the **York Mystery Plays**, first performed in 1397 and subsequently every four years.

During Tudor times, York's importance steadily declined but re-emerged in the 18th century as a fashionable social centre. Many elegant Georgian houses, of which **Fairfax House** in Castlegate is perhaps the most splendid, were built at this time and they add another attractive architectural dimension to the city.

The following century saw York take on a completely different rôle as the hub of the railway system in the north. At the heart of this transformation was the charismatic entrepreneur George Hudson, founder of what became the Great Northern Railway, part visionary, part crook. His wheeler-dealing eventually led to his disgrace but even then the citizens of York twice elected him as Lord Mayor and he still has a pub named after him. It was thanks to Hudson that York's magnificent railway station, with its great curving roof of glass, was built, a tourist attraction in its own right. Nearby, in Leeman Street, is the **National Railway Museum**, the largest of its kind in the world. This fascinating exhibition covers some 200 years of railway history, from Stephenson's *Rocket* to the Channel Tunnel. Among the thousands of exhibits demonstrating the technical and social impact of the "Iron Horse" are Gresley's record-breaking locomotive, *Mallard*, Queen Victoria's royal carriage, and displays demonstrating the workings of the railway system. There's an extensive library and reading room (booking advised), and the "Brief Encounter" restaurant is themed on the classic movie.

Another aspect of railway history is on view at the **York Model Railway**, next door to the station, which has almost one third of a mile of track and up to 14 trains running at any one time. Machinery of a very different kind is on display at the **Museum of Automata**. Automata are "man made objects that imitate the movement of living things through a mechanism that is concealed, so as to make them appear to move spontaneously." The museum traces the history of automata, from the simple articulated figurines of ancient civilisations, through to displays of modern robotics: the Automata Shop sells contemporary pieces, music boxes, mechanical toys and craft kits suitable for all ages.

In Coppergate is the **Jorvik Centre**, a fairly recent innovation celebrating a 1,000-year-old story. Visitors step aboard a time-car for a journey through representations of real-life Viking Age Britain. You pass through a bustling market thronged with Danes bartering for chickens, corn and other provisions and wares, penetrate dark smoky houses, cross a busy wharf where goods transported along the rivers Ouse and Foss are being off-loaded. The experience comes complete with authentic sounds and even smells and for children in particular is both fun and educational.

In a beautifully restored church close to the Shambles is the **Archaeological Research Centre** (ARC), an award-winning hands-on exploration of archaeology for visitors of all ages. Here you can meet practising archaeologists who will demonstrate how to sort and identify genuine finds or to try out ancient crafts. For the more technically minded, there's a series of interactive computer displays which illustrate how modern technology helps to discover and interpret the past. Fascinating.

Very popular with those who have an interest in the more macabre aspects of York's long history is the **Original Ghostwalk of York** which starts at the King's Arms pub on Ouse Bridge and sets off at 8 p.m. every evening. At the last count, York was reckoned to have some 140 resident ghosts within its walls - on this guided walk you visit some of their haunts and hear dark tales, grim accounts of murder, torture, and intrigue. Prepare to have your blood chilled.

It's impossible here to list all York's museums, galleries and fine buildings, but you will find a wealth of additional information at the Tourist Information Centre close to one of the historic old gateways to the city, **Bootham Bar**.

98   The Anchor Inn

Doncaster Road, Burn, Selby,
East Yorkshire
YO8 8LA
Tel: 01757 270255

Directions:
From Selby 3 miles south on the A19; from the M62 leave at junction 34 and take A19 about 6 miles north.

Pete Chilton and Rosemary run this most sociable of pubs, which stands by the Selby Canal a few minutes south of Selby. Dating from the late 19th century, with a freshly painted roughcast facade and ornate windows, it has a really inviting interior with oak beams, open fires, copper-topped tables and row upon row of mugs, plates and ornamental brasses. Good straightforward bar food is served lunchtime and evening seven days a week. Monday night is fish 'n' chips night, with a guaranteed healthy turn-out of regulars. Thursday night is quiz night, jazz nights are every fortnight, alternating with Country & Western, live music is performed on Saturday nights, Friday night sees a singalong session and there are regular theme nights (murder mysteries etc) with food included. Barbecues by the Canal (DIY if you like) are a popular summer feature, and children can romp to their hearts' content in a play area in the garden.

With so much going, the evenings in Burn are largely taken care of, but in the daytime visitors will find plenty to occupy themselves in the vicinity: Selby with its magnificent Abbey and the oldest railway station in the land; the extraordinary stately home Carlton Towers near Camblesforth; historic churches at Snaith and Hemingbrough; and the vast cooling towers of Drax dominating the low-lying ground between the Ouse and the Aire.

Opening Hours: 12.00-23.00, Sun to 22.30

Food: Bar meals.

Credit Cards: None.

Accommodation: None.

Facilities: Car Park.

Entertainment: Regular music and quiz nights.

Local Places of Interest/Activities: Selby 3 miles, Carlton Towers.

The Angel Inn

99

Market Place,
Easingwold,
North Yorkshire
YO61 3AA
Tel: 01347 821605

Directions:

Easingwold is
signposted off the
A19 at a roundabout
12 miles north of
York.

The Angel Inn, just minutes from the busy A19, is a favourite with both local residents and with motorists looking for somewhere congenial to take a break in their journey. Mine hosts John and Margaret McKenzie have a no-nonsense approach to their business that works admirably - a genuine welcome, a relaxed ambience and a range of food and drink to that should please any visitor. Even from the outside the inn has a cheerful, inviting look, with masses of flowers and plants adorning the shuttered facade, while inside the hunt provides the decorative inspiration. There are sporting prints everywhere, and most of the remaining hanging space is filled with literally hundreds of copper and brass ornaments - pots and pans, horse brasses, horns, bugles.

This is a favourite spot with the racing fraternity, too, and aficionados of the turf will encounter more than the occasional familiar face. Open fires, oak beams, sturdy iron chairs and copper-topped tables complete the rustic picture. Cask ales do a good job in quenching thirsts, while appetites large and small are taken care of on a menu of freshly prepared home-cooked food - home made pies are a speciality - straightforward dishes at sensible prices - a quick bite for anyone in a hurry or a full meal with one the many specials if there's time to relax. Live music takes the stage here every other Sunday - Country & Western is just one of several themes for the evenings. There's plenty of car parking space, and for summertime sipping and nibbling picnic-style benches are set out under parasols in the front garden.

Opening Hours: Mon-Sat, 11.00-23.00; Sun 12.00-22.30

Food: Bar meals and snacks.

Credit Cards: None

Accommodation: None

Facilities: Car Park.

Entertainment: Live music every second Sunday.

Local Places of Interest/Activities: York 12 miles, Thirsk 15 miles, Ampleforth College, Beningborough Hall (NT), Rievaulx Abbey & Terrace.

100 The Black Dog Inn

Selby Road,
Camblesforth, Selby,
North Yorkshire
YO8 8HX
Tel: 01757 618247

Directions:

4 miles south of Selby
on the A1041.

A late 19th century inn by the road that runs south from Selby to Snaith. The owner of the **Black Dog Inn** is Martin Petch, a hard-working, go-ahead young man who believes in the virtues of good service and value for money. Behind the neat, freshly painted frontage, the interior is equally well cared for, with the look of a well-furnished home. Traditional pub games are played in the bar, where there is always a choice of cask ales and guest real ales. In the 40-cover restaurant, with pristine linen on pretty little tables, good home cooking presents a choice of favourite Yorkshire recipes and ideas from all around the world. The pub has no accommodation on the premises but owns an adjacent caravan site with five pitches.

Selby, with its great Abbey, is a must for visitors to the region, but much closer to the Black Dog is another attraction that should on account be missed. Carlton Towers, which has been described as 'something between the Houses of Parliament and St Pancras Station', was created in the 1870s by two young English eccentrics, Henry, 9th Lord Beaumont, and Edward Welby Pugin, son of the famous architect. Together they transformed a traditional Jacobean house into an exuberant mock medieval fantasy abounding in turrets, towers, gargoyles and heraldic shields. The richly decorated High Victorian interior, modelled on medieval banqueting halls, contains a minstrels' gallery and a vast Venetian-style drawing room. Carlton Towers is the Yorkshire home of the Duke of Norfolk and is open for visits during the summer months.

In stark contrast, a couple of miles to the east is the village of Drax, which as well as providing Ian Fleming with an appropriately sinister name for one of James Bond's enemies also provides the National Grid with 10% of all the electricity used in England and Wales. The vast cooling towers of Europe's largest coal-fired power station can be seen for miles.

Opening Hours: 11.00-23.00, Sunday to 22.30.

Food: Bar meals.

Credit Cards: None

Accommodation: None.

Facilities: Car Park.

Entertainment: Traditional pub games

Local Places of Interest/Activities: Selby 4 miles, Drax 2 miles.

The Carlton Inn　101

Main Street,
Carlton Husthwaite,
Nr. Thirsk,
North Yorkshire
YO7 2BW
Tel/Fax:
01845 501265

Directions:

Carlton Husthwaite
is located 18 miles
north of York, 6 miles
south of Thirsk, on a
minor road off the
A19.

Built as long ago as the 17th century, **The Carlton** was at one time the home of makers of woollen garments, who started selling drinks as a sideline and thus established the building as an ale house. It has also seen service as a coaching inn, and in the last three years has been splendidly renovated and refurbished to bring back all the original charm and character.

The public bar is a convivial meeting place for enjoying a drink and a chat, and there is a separate bar and lounge that is used mainly by diners before they settle down for a meal in the 80-cover restaurant. Two rooms are offered for dining - smoking and non-smoking, both with original timbers, pine floors, stone walls and distinctive and unusual decor and furnishings. The cooking does full justice to the lovely setting: classically trained chefs bring modern touches to a mouthwatering menu that ranks with the best of Yorkshire pubs. The food is complemented by a well-balanced wine list. On sunny days the beer garden beckons with boules and quoits, and there's also a large patio for alfresco dining.

Another major attraction in the picturesque village of Carlton Husthwaite is Fox Furniture in the Old Hall Workshop, where master craftsman Malcolm Pipes makes traditional furniture from English oak and other hardwoods. All the oak furniture is adzed, pegged, mason-jointed and finished with wax polish. A fox's mask is carved by hand on every item. Visitors are allowed to wander around the workshop and watch the work in progress - should thirst get the better of them, the Carlton is just a few steps along the road!

Opening Hours: Mon-Sat 12.00-15.00, 18.30-23.30; Sun 12.00-22.30

Food: A la carte, table d'hôte

Credit Cards: Switch, Access, Visa
Accommodation: None

Facilities: Car Park, Beer Garden, Quoits and Boules pitches outside, wheelchair friendly

Entertainment: None.

Local Places of Interest/Activities: Thirsk (horseracing) 6 miles, York 18 miles, Sutton Bank, Rievaulx Abbey & Terrace, Herriott Museum at Thirsk. The Carlton is the starting point for a well known circular walk.

Internet/Website:
e-mail: mel@thecarlton.fsbusiness.co.uk

102 The Crown Inn

Main Street, Monk Fryston, Nr. Leeds,
North Yorkshire LS25 5DU
Tel: 01977 682468

Directions:

A63 from Leeds, join A1 to roundabout at Lumby, cross A162, A63 again 1 mile to Monk Fryston. From Selby 10 miles west along A63.

New owners have completely refurbished the large, L-shaped **Crown Inn**, which is thought to have been the temporary home of the monks who built the village church in the mid-18th century. Partners Marianne, Tonu and Sally, along with Marianne and Tonu's son William (the chef) and daughter Kate(the restaurant manageress) bring in a strong following of local residents and a growing number of tourists with their special blend of charm, hospitality and good food.

The roomy bar areas feature ceiling and wall timbers and fires in massive stone surrounds, and upstairs, under the heavily timbered eaves, is the 40-seat Crows restaurant. The bars offer a wide variety of light snacks and quick meals, while the restaurant puts the spotlight on Traditional English dishes prepared with care from prime ingredients. Hot sandwiches - roast pork with stuffing, beef & onion, Cajun chicken - are popular snack items, and the main dishes include sausage and mash with onion gravy, bacon-wrapped lamb's liver, filo-wrapped salmon with beurre blanc and beef stew with dumplings. Something that's definitely not English but is becoming quite a favourite is crispy duck drizzled in hoisin sauce and served on a bed of noodles. It's advisable to book for a table in the restaurant. Food is served every lunchtime and evening except Sunday after 5 o'clock. The inn has a beer garden, a large courtyard and plenty of off-road parking space. Quiz night is Tuesday.

Local places of interest include the historic town of Selby, which has a beautiful abbey and the oldest railway station in the country (1834).

Opening Hours: Mon-Fri 11.30-15.00 and 17.30-23.00; Sat 11.30-23.00; Sun 12.00-22.30

Food: Bar meals and à la carte.

Credit Cards: Access, Mastercard, Visa, Switch.

Accommodation: None.

Facilities: Car Park, Function Room

Entertainment: Quiz night Tuesday.

Local Places of Interest/Activities: Leeds 10 miles, Selby 8 miles.

The Durham Ox

Westway, Crayke,
North Yorkshire
YO61 4TE
Tel: 01347 821506
Fax: 01347 823326

Directions:

From York take the A19 to Easingwold. In Easingwold main street, turn right through market place and straight up the hill to Crayke. Or take the B1363 and turn left at Stillington then first right to Crayke.

The Ibbotson family's **Durham Ox** (managed by son Michael), 300 years old and situated on the hill of 'The Grand Old Duke of York' fame, is located in a delightful village with redbrick houses and a church and castle that both date from the 15th century. The pub is one of the very best in North Yorkshire, and for many reasons - the charm and character, the great views over the Vale of York, the superb food and the luxuriously comfortable Bed & Breakfast accommodation. two huge open fires in ancient stone fireplaces, flagstone floors, oak panelling and antique furniture - all this adds up to a marvellously atmospheric setting for relaxing and enjoying top-quality, freshly prepared dishes using the pick of the local produce. Food is served seven days a week, lunchtime and evening: bar meals in the Pub and Tap Room, or à la carte, with starched linen, fresh flowers and fine wines, in the restaurant.

The bedrooms are housed in charming converted farm buildings offering standards that many a hotel would be proud of; there are four self-contained suites and two cottages with the option of self-catering. Touches of luxury include jacuzzis, extra-comfortable wrought-iron beds, fresh fruit, chocolates and a library of tapes for the video tv. Golf, shooting, fishing and riding can be arranged, along with car hire and transport to and from airport or station. The Durham Ox is very much at the heart of social life hereabouts.

Opening Hours: 12.00-15.00 and from 18.00 daily

Food: Bar meals and à la carte. Last orders for food 14.30 and 21.30

Credit Cards: Visa, Amex

Accommodation: 6 en suite rooms.

Facilities: Function room, Car Park.

Local Places of Interest/Activities: York 12 miles, Easingwold 4 miles, Sutton Park (Georgian House, Capability Brown garden), Newburgh Priory, Castle Howard

Internet/Website:
www. thedurhamox.com

104   The Fox & Hounds

Langthorpe, Boroughbridge,
North Yorkshire YO51 9RZ
Tel/Fax: 01423 322717

Directions:
From the A1, going north, leave at J48;
going south leave at Boroughbridge.

Originally a cottage with an adjacent granary, the **Fox & Hounds** stands invitingly in the village of Langthorpe very close to the A1(M). The pristine white facade gives way to an equally spotless interior with a cosy public bar, lounge bar and non-smoking restaurant.

The fox and hounds theme runs through the decor in the bar, where a good selection of beers is served. The pub is run by the husband and wife team of Joe and June Flynn - Joe is an ex-Metropolitan policeman, June a talented cook. Honest, no-frills Yorkshire fare is her speciality, and her steak and ale pie is spoken of in hushed tones for miles around! On Saturday night, entertainment is provided by tasteful live music. With the A1 so close, access to the north and south is quick and easy, but there are several very good reasons for staying in the vicinity.

Aldborough, a couple of miles away, was once a thriving Roman city and home of the 9th Legion; its museum houses many fascinating local finds. Even closer is Boroughbridge, where the massive monolithic Devil's Arrows are one of the county's best-known ancient monuments. Just outside the neighbouring village of Skelton-on-Ure is one of the area's finest stately homes, the Robert Adam-designed Newby Hall with superb tapestries, a collection of Chippendale furniture and award-winning gardens.

Opening Hours: 11.00-15.00, 18.30-23.00.

Food: Bar meals.

Credit Cards: Amex, Mastercard, Visa.

Accommodation: None.

Facilities: Car Park.

Entertainment: Live music Saturday.

Local Places of Interest/Activities: Ripon 5 miles, Boroughbridge, Newby Hall

The George Country Inn | 105

Main Street, Wath,
Ripon,
North Yorkshire
HG4 5EN
Tel: 01765 640202
Fax: 01765 640632

Directions:

From Ripon take the A61; after about 1 mile turn left on to minor road signposted Wath, or turn left 1 mile further along the A61 and reach Wath through Melmerby.

On the main street of a village a short drive north of Ripon, the **George Country Inn** is a handsome brick building dating from the latter part of the 19th century. It was bought by Karen and Tony Coupe in the autumn of 2000, since when they have spent much time, energy and money in a total refurbishment that has left the whole place as neat as a new pin. Karen and Tony are both trained chefs, and their splendid home cooking of the pick of the local suppliers keeps the restaurant busy. The area around Wath is rich in history and visitor attractions, and the George is a perfect base for exploring the region. The six letting bedrooms, including two able to accommodate families, all have en suite facilities, tvs and tea-makers. On Wednesday nights good prizes are offered in the sponsored quiz, and other entertainment includes regular live music sessions.

The historic town of Ripon is only minutes away, and several other places of interest are even closer. In Wath itself, the stately home of Norton Conyers has been owned by the Graham family since 1624, but its main claim to fame is the visit made by Charlotte Brontë. During her stay she heard the story of Mad Mary, apparently a Lady Graham, who was kept locked up in an attic room. It is said that Charlotte used this unfortunate woman as the basis of the character of Mrs Rochester in her novel *Jane Eyre*. Graham family pictures, furniture and costume are on display, and there's a lovely 18th century walled garden in the grounds. Near the village of North Stainley, the Lightwater Theme Park set in 175 acres of scenic grounds boasts the biggest roller coaster in the world and several other exhilarating (or should that be terrifying?) rides. It's probably best to visit this place *before* one of the George's splendid meals rather than just after!

Opening Hours: 11.30-23.00

Food: A la carte.

Credit Cards: Access, Mastercard, Visa.

Accommodation: 6 en suite rooms.

Facilities: Car Park.

Entertainment: Quiz night Wednesday, regular live music

Local Places of Interest: Ripon, North Stainley.

106   The Jefferson Arms

Thorganby,
North Yorkshire
YO19 6DA
Tel/Fax:
 01904 448316

Directions:

From Selby, A19 to
Barlby, right on to
A163, left on minor
road signposted
Skipwith and
Thorganby; from
York A19 south to
Crockley Hill then
left on to minor road
to Wheldrake and

The Jefferson Arms is a substantial redbrick pub in classic style, located in a tranquil village hidden away down country roads between Selby and York. The lounge was made for relaxation, with plenty of comfortable armchairs to sink into, and there are two areas for diners.

Outside, the pub is surrounded by lovely gardens, both paved and lawned. The owners of the pub are a Swiss-born couple, Margaret and Adolf Rapp; he is a classically trained chef, and his menus offer a combination of traditional Yorkshire fare and dishes from Switzerland and Germany. The fine food is complemented by a long and varied wine list that caters for all tastes and pockets. Food is served from 12 to 2.30 and from 6 to 9, with the exception of Monday and Tuesday lunchtimes. The Jefferson Arms is situated in an area that is scenically attractive and very peaceful, and a stay here will provide a real tonic for anyone needing a break from the bustle of the city. The pub has two letting bedrooms, both with en suite facilities, tv and tea/coffee-making tray.

The River Derwent flows past the village, and there is a nature reserve close by. It's an easy drive to Selby, with its beautiful, serene Abbey, and to York, about which the Duke of York, later to become King George VI, said: 'The history of York is the history of England'. Its almost endless attractions include the wonderful Minster, the Jorvik Viking Centre and the best railway museum in the world.

Opening Hours: 18.00-23.00 Tues; 12.00-15.00, 18.00-23.00 Wed-Sat; 12.00-22.30 Sun; closed Monday

Food: Bar meals, à la carte.

Credit Cards: Mastercard, Visa.

Accommodation: 2 en suite rooms.

Facilities: Car Park.

Entertainment: Quiz Tuesday.

Local Places of Interest/Activities: Selby 10 miles, York 10 miles.

Kellington Manor 107

Whales Lane,
Kellington,
East Yorkshire
DN14 0SB
Tel: 01977 661000

Directions:

Leave M62 at J34 then north on A19 towards Selby; Kellington is signposted on the left after about 2 miles.

Built as a gentleman's residence towards the end of the 19th century, the handsome red-brick **Kellington Manor** remained a private dwelling until about 20 years ago. Largely unaltered, it is a fine example of the architecture of the period and the lofty bars with open log fires are roomy, comfortable places to meet for a drink or a meal. Alan Lawrence runs the bar, while his wife Molly is in charge in the kitchen. She has built up quite a reputation with her no-nonsense, good-value dishes served every lunchtime and evening, and the huge chalkboard offers plenty of variety - her steaks in particular are always in demand. Cask ales and good wines accompany the food. Pool and darts are played in the games room, while outside, children can keep themselves amused in their special area of the garden. The pub has a very large car park.

Kellington enjoys a peaceful location just below the Aire Valley. It's a short drive north to Selby, where the three-towered Abbey built of cream-coloured stone is a beautiful monument to the builders' skills of 900 years ago. One of its most famous features is the Washington Window, which depicts the coat-of-arms of John Washington, Prior of the Abbey around 1415 and a direct ancestor of George Washington. This heraldic device with a stars and stripes motif was later adapted for the national flag of the United States of America. In the other direction, Pontefract is famous for its 11th century castle, where Richard ll was murdered, and for being the home of Pontefract Cakes. Licorice root has been grown here since monastic times and there's even a small planting of the root in the local park. Country roads to the east lead to the magnificent Carlton Towers, a mock medieval fantasy in stone that is the Yorkshire home of the Duke of Norfolk.

Opening Hours: 11.00-16.00, 17.30-23.00

Food: Bar meals.

Credit Cards: Visa, Mastercard, Switch, Delta

Accommodation: None.

Facilities: Car Park.

Local Places of Interest/Activities: Selby 6 miles, Pontefract 8 miles, Carlton Towers 8 miles.

108   The Moon & Pheasant

Dalton, Nr. Thirsk,
North Yorkshire
YO7 3JD
Tel: 01845 577268

Directions:
From Thirsk (6 miles) take A168 and turn left at Topcliffe on to minor road signposted Dalton or A19 turn left after 2 miles on to minor road signposted Dalton.

Behind an unassuming facade the 150-year-old **Moon & Pheasant** has a particularly warm and friendly atmosphere. The lounge and public bar are both well-appointed and spotlessly clean, and the staff dispense a great selection of real ales, beers and lagers with a smile. Bar meals - straightforward dishes freshly prepared and generously served - are available from 12 till 4 and from 6.30 to 9.30 all sessions except Sunday evening. This is very much a place for the whole family. Children have their own menu, and outside in the beer garden is a children's play area with a bouncy castle; inside is a games room where pool and darts keep the grown-ups amused. Saturday night calls for a sharpening not of the arrows but of the brains, as it's quiz night.

Owners Paul and Susan arrived quite recently with ambitious plans for making the pub even more appealing - a new conservatory is due to come on stream for the summer of 2001. Adjacent to the pub is a caravan site where touring vans are welcome to drop anchor; alternatively, two static vans are available for letting. The location links well with several main roads: the A19 connecting York and Newcastle; the A1(the old Great North Road); and the A170 that runs to the coast at Scarborough. The nearest towns are Thirsk (6 miles), which is Darrowby in *All Creatures Great and Small*, and Ripon (11 miles) with its magnificent cathedral. Both towns have racecourses with many summer fixtures in the Flat season.

Opening Hours: 12.00-23.00 Mon-Sat; 12.00-22.30 Sun

Food: Bar meals.

Credit Cards: None

Accommodation: Caravan park.

Facilities: Beer garden, children's play area

with free bouncy castle.

Entertainment: Quiz night Saturday

Local Places of Interest/Activities: Thirsk 6 miles, Ripon 11 miles, Fountains Abbey, Rievaulx Abbey and Terrace.

The Nags Head — 109

Pickhill, Nr. Thirsk,
North Yorkshire
YO7 4JG
Tel: 01845 567391
Fax: 01845 567212

Directions:

Leave the A1 approx 25 miles north of Wetherby at the B6267 junction and follow the minor road through Sinderby to Pickhill.

The Nags Head, one of the many 17th century coaching inns that served the London-Edinburgh route, is a splendid, genuine country inn at the heart of a tiny village a few minutes' drive from the A1. Brothers Edward and Raymond Boynton, here since 1972, offer all that is best in the tradition of country coaching inns - a warm welcome, genuine hospitality, traditional decor, food and a warm bed for the weary traveller.

On the accommodation side the Nags Head has 17 well-appointed modern bedrooms, all en suite, with tv, telephone and modem; two rooms on the ground floor are accessible by guests in wheelchairs. Also available is a self-contained two-bedroom cottage for either self-catering or fully serviced accommodation - an ideal option for families who would like a less formal arrangement but with the benefit of the hotel's facilities to hand. The Nags Head has built up a great reputation for the quality of its cuisine, backed up by a range of fine wines and real ales. The same menu is served in the restaurant, the choice for a more formal occasion, the Lounge Bar and the Tap Room - let your mood decide where you settle in to enjoy the best of traditional and modern cooking, from the simplest bar snack to a feast of three or four courses.

The brothers have always moved with the times and will tailor individual packages for business meetings or conferences, as well as sporting breaks. Activities include hunting, shooting, fishing, golf (the brothers and their families are keen golfers) and horseracing - Thirsk (Flat), Ripon (Flat) and Catterick (Flat and National Hunt) are all within 15 minutes' drive. The little village of Pickhill has a very interesting church, and further afield the whole region is filled with scenic delights and historic sights.

Opening Hours: All day

Food: Bar snacks and à la carte 12.00-14.00 and 18.00-22.00

Credit Cards: Barclaycard, Mastercard, Switch, Delta

Accommodation: 17 en suite rooms.

Facilities: Putting green, boules, quoits, function room, Car park

Local Places of Interest/Activities: Thirsk 8 miles, Ripon 9 miles, Catterick 12 miles, many sports and leisure activities at Camp Hill 3 miles. Wetherby Races

Internet/Website:
enquiries@nagsheadpickhill.freeserve.co.uk
website: www.nagsheadpickhill.co.uk

110 The Navigation Inn

1 Canal Road,
Ripon,
North Yorkshire
HG4 1QN
Tel: 01765 605676

Directions:

The cathedral city of Ripon lies 11 miles north of Harrogate on the A61.

A great favourite with the locals, the **Navigation Inn** is one of the social hubs of Ripon, and in Adam Stanton it has one of the most sociable landlords. The inn, which dates back to the middle of the 18th century, is located by a canal at a point which was the most northerly on the English Canal System. The canal was built between 1767 and 1773 to improve the navigation of the River Ure; the designer was John Smeaton, who was also responsible for the Eddystone Lighthouse.

The Navigation is a winner of the 'Ripon in Bloom' competition, and the summer season sees a riot of colour in the window boxes and hanging baskets that adorn the front of the inn. There's also a lovely show of colour in the partly- covered beer garden. Inside, the scene is no less appealing - an inviting blend of roomy open spaces and lots of cosy little corners, all in apple pie order. The inn has 50 covers for doing what a lot of the regulars do, settling down with a good glass of beer and something from the well-priced, varied menu of satisfying home-cooked fare. But eating and drinking are not the only activities at this splendid place, where the quiz nights, live music, karaoke, theme nights and barbecue parties are all occasions to look forward to. Adam is an enthusiastic supporter of charities and is rightly proud of the amount of money that he raises for good causes through all the special events.

If you make yourself so comfortable for the evening that you don't feel like leaving, you don't have to, as the pub has three rooms for overnight accommodation. One is a family room with en suite facilities, the other two share a bathroom; all three have tvs and tea-makers. There are many things to see and do in this attractive cathedral city. Horseracing on a picturesque course that opened in 1900 takes place during the Flat season between April and August.

Opening Hours: Mon-Sat 12.00-23.00; Sun 12.00-22.30

Food: Home cooked

Credit Cards: None

Accommodation: 3 bedrooms, 1 en suite.

Facilities: Beer garden

Entertainment: Live music, karaoke, quiz nights

Local Places of Interest/Activities: Historic Ripon, Thirsk 12 miles, Harrogate 11 miles.

The Oak Tree Inn

Raskelf Road,
Helperby,
North Yorkshire
YO61 2PH
Tel: 01423 360268

Directions:

Helperby lies 12 miles south of Thirsk off the A19; or leave the A1(M) at junction 4 and take the minor road after Boroughbridge marked Brafferton and Helperby.

Helperby is a small village on the River Swale, rich in history, with some very old buildings holding their own against the new. **The Oak Tree**, a listed stone building, dates from the middle of the 18th century, its cream-painted, shuttered and tiled facade standing square on the main road through the village. Bright, fresh and well appointed within, it is furnished in homely, unpretentious style, its walls covered in old prints and pictures of the village. The bar is a great place to enjoy a fine glass of cask ale and a chat or a game of darts with the regulars, who are as friendly a bunch as you'll meet anywhere. There's also a little games room with a pool table, a beer garden and a 24-cover eating area.

This is the first venture into the licensed trade for the tenants Paul Weetman and his partner Tracey, who arrived here only recently and are already making their mark. Food is beginning to play a greater part with a roast Sunday Lunch from 12.00-14.00. this is proving very popular so it is advisable to book. A limited selection of bar snacks are available at present but the menu is being extended very shortly.

The nearest town of any size is Boroughbridge on the River Ure, once an important stop on the London-Edinburgh coaching route and now bypassed by the A1. A notable nearby landmark is the Devil's Arrows, three great Bronze Age monoliths thought to be about 3,000 years old; the tallest is 30 feet high. A mile or so east of Boroughbridge off the B6265 stands Aldborough, the ancient Roman garrison town of Isurium Brigantum. The museum houses relics from the town's past. A tall maypole stands on the village green around which traditional dances take place each May. RAF Dishforth is near Helperby, alongside the A1, and many visitors stop awhile to watch the planes take off.

Opening Hours: 12.00-23.00 Mon-Sat; 12.00-22.30 Sun

Food: Bar Meals.

Credit Cards: None

Accommodation: None.

Facilities: Car Park.

Entertainment: Occasional karaoke and quiz nights.

Local Places of Interest: Thirsk 12 miles, Ripon 10 miles, Boroughbridge 6 miles.

Internet/Website:
e-mail: tprice1967@aol.com

Park View Hotel

Nor..
YO19 6PX
Tel: 01757 248458
Fax: 01757 249211

Directions:
From Selby, 4 miles
north on the A19.

Built in 1827 as a residence for a wealthy farmer, **Park View Hotel** stands in its own grounds in the village of Riccall, bypassed by the A19 Selby-York road. The hotel has recently been taken over by the partnership of Geoff Antlett and Sue Taylor, and refurbishment has put the place in apple pie order. Behind the cream-painted frontage the interior is cosy and homely, and the seven double bedrooms are notably warm, comfortable and well equipped. All have private bathroom with bath and/or shower, tv, direct-dial phone, radio-alarm, trouser press and tea-making facilities, and guests start the day with a hearty English breakfast. Sue is the cook, and will provide dinner by prior arrangement. Guests can relax with a drink and a snack in the bar lounge, whose French windows open on to a patio garden. The hotel has ample car parking space.

Selby, which is less than ten minutes away by car, is a town steeped in history, reputedly the birthplace of Henry 1, and its spectacular Abbey is one of the sights that should not be missed on a visit to Yorkshire. Begun in the 11th century, the Abbey has survived Civil War damage, the collapse of its tower and a disastrous fire in 1906, and today it stands serene and beautiful, a tribute to the skills of architects and builders of almost 1,000 years ago. In the other direction, York has been at the centre of British history since Roman times and offers the visitor a host of attractions, from the sublime Minster to the Jorvik Viking Centre and the superb National Railway Museum.

Opening Hours: Residents only.

Food: Dinner for Residents.

Credit Cards: Mastercard, Visa.

Accommodation: 7 en suite rooms.

Facilities: Car Park.

Local Places of Interest/Activities: Selby 4 miles, York 15 miles.

Internet/Website:
e-mail: geoffandsue@hotel-park-view.co.uk
website: www. hotel-park-view.co.uk

The White Swan 113

Minskip,
Nr. Boroughbridge,
North Yorkshire
YO51 9JF
Tel: 01423 322598

Directions:

From the north leave the A1(M) at Boroughbridge. From the south leave the A1(M) at J48. From Knaresborough/ Harrogate take the A6055 about 7 miles to Minskip.

The White Swan Stands proudly at the top of a village a few miles north of Harrogate and very close to the A1(M). It dates from 1743, and its facade is adorned in summer with colourful hanging baskets. Inside, it's old-fashioned and very inviting, comfortably cluttered, with the rural side of life reflected in the decor. Stan Megson, the tenant for the past year, keeps local residents and visitors from further afield happy with a combination of the welcoming, unpretentious ambience, some good cask ales and home-cooked food served in generous helpings at extremely reasonable prices; the steaks are particularly popular. Sunday night is quiz night at this agreeable spot, where in the summer tables and chairs are set out under parasols in the garden.

Minskip is well placed for touring a very interesting part of the county, and the White Swan offers low-price accommodation in two bedrooms with a shared bathroom. Among the many places to visit is the spa town of Harrogate, one of Britain's most attractive towns, with broad streets, many open spaces and a very visible legacy of its days as a leading health resort, including the Old Sulphur Well and the Royal Pump Room Museum.

Even closer to the pub is Knaresborough, an ancient town perched on a hillside by the River Nidd and dominated by the ruins of its castle. In the other direction, across the A1(M), stands Boroughbridge, where the county's most famous ancient monument attracts visitors by the thousand. This is the Devil's Arrows, three massive Bronze Age monoliths which local legend insists are bolts fired by the Devil.

Opening Hours: 12.00-15.00, 18.00-23.00 (Sun to 22.30).

Food: Bar meals.

Credit Cards: None.

Accommodation: Two bedrooms sharing a bathroom.

Facilities: Car Park.

Entertainment: Quiz Sunday.

Local Places of Interest/Activities:
Boroughbridge 2 miles, Knaresborough 7 miles, Harrogate 8 miles.

114   The Wombwell Arms

Wass, Nr. Helmsley,
North Yorkshire YO61 4BE
Tel: 01347 868280 Fax: 01347 868039

Directions:
6 miles southwest of Helmsley off the A170.

New owners Andy and Sue Cole have ambitious plans for the **Wombwell Arms**, a white-washed village inn dating from the 17th century. The first step, already completed, was the upgrading of the accommodation, and the four letting bedrooms - double-bedded - offer impressively high levels of comfort, decor and furnishings. The bar is uncluttered, with an open fire to warm the visitor and plenty of space to unwind. Ampleforth College, is only a short drive away.

Food is a very serious subject at this outstanding pub, where a highly skilled team of chefs have built up a reputation that is recognised far beyond the borders of Yorkshire. Connoisseurs of good food fill the three dining areas (one is reserved for non-smokers) to enjoy the finest British and international dishes featuring prime local produce whenever possible. A lounge provides diners with a pleasant place to enjoy an aperitif before the meal. The eclectic wine list offers a good selection by the glass as well as by the bottle, and the bar stocks some well-kept real ales.

The inn occupies a corner site in a village that nestles at the foot of the Hambleton Hills. A famous landmark in the hills at Kilburn is the Kilburn White Horse, a gigantic figure carved in 1857 by a local schoolmaster. Kilburn was the home of the renowned furniture-maker Robert 'Mouseman' Thompson. The area is particularly rich in historic buildings, the closest of which - literally just along the road - is Byland Abbey, founded by monks from Furness.

Opening Hours: Mon-Sat: 11.00-23.00: Sun: 12.00-22.30

Food: A la carte.

Credit Cards: All except Amex or Diners

Accommodation: 4 en suite rooms.

Facilities: Car Park.

Entertainment: None.

Local Places of Interest/Activities: Helmsley 6 miles, Rievaulx Abbey & Terrace, Byland Abbey, Thirsk (horseracing) 12 miles, Coxwold (church with octagonal tower and Fauconberg monuments).

4 The East Riding and North Humberside

The Hidden Inns of Yorkshire

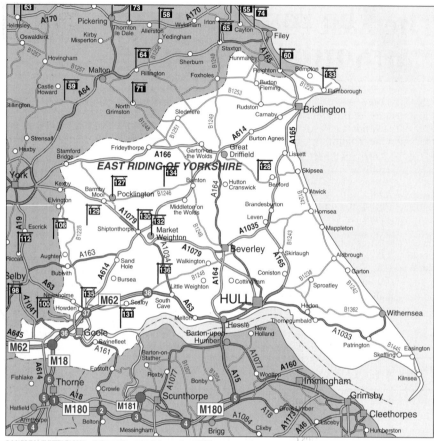

© MAPS IN MINUTES ™ 2001   © Crown Copyright, Ordnance Survey 2001

127 **The Black Bull**, Pocklington

128 **Blue Post Inn**, North Frodingham

129 **The Cross Keys Inn**, Melbourne

130 **The Crown**, Shiptonthorpe

131 **The Hope & Anchor**, Blacktoft

132 **The Red Lion**, Market Weighton

133 **The Royal Dog & Duck**, Flamborough

134 **The Star Inn**, North Dalton

135 **The Wheatsheaf**, Howden

136 **The White Hart**, North Cave

Please note all references refer to page numbers

The East Riding and North Humberside

"Fold upon fold of encircling hills, piled rich and golden" - such was the author Winifred Holtby's fond memory of the Wolds landscape. She was born in 1898 in Rudston on the northern edge of the Wolds, a village dominated by the prehistoric **Rudston Monolith.** This colossal block of stone, a daunting symbol of some misty pagan belief, stands challengingly close to Rudston's Christian parish church. Twenty-five feet high, it is the tallest standing stone in Britain. Winifred Holtby left the village and became a leading figure in London literary circles, editor of the influential magazine *Time and Tide*, but in her own books it was those *"rich and golden"* hills that still enthralled her. In her most successful novel, *South Riding*, the fictional Riding is unmistakably recognisable as the Wolds among whose gently rolling acres she had spent her childhood.

The Wolds are a great crescent of chalk hills that sweep round from the coast near Flamborough Head to the outskirts of Hull. There were settlers here some 10,000 years ago - but never very many. In the early 1700s, Daniel Defoe described the area as *"very thin of towns and people"* and also noted the *"great number of sheep"*. Little has changed: the Wolds remain an unspoilt tract of scattered farmsteads and somnolent villages with one of the lowest population densities in the country. Artists remark on the striking quality of the light and air, and on the long views that open up, perhaps across undulating hills to the twin towers of Beverley Minster or to the great towers of the Minster at York. The Wolds never rise above 800 feet, but the open landscape makes them particularly vulnerable to winter snowstorms: children may be marooned in their schools, the dipping and twisting country roads can be blocked for weeks at a time.

"Lordings, there is in Yorkshire, as I guess / A marshy country called Holdernesse". With these words Chaucer begins the Summoner's story in the Canterbury Tales. It's not surprising that this area was then largely marshland since most of the land lies at less than 30 feet above sea level. The name ``Holderness'' comes from Viking times: a ``hold'' was a man of high rank in the Danelaw, ``ness'' has stayed in the language with its meaning of promontory. The precise boundaries of the Land of Holderness are clear enough to the east where it runs to the coast, and to the south where Holderness ends with Yorkshire itself at Spurn Point. They are less well-defined to the north and west where they run somewhere close to the great crescent of the Wolds.

PLACES OF INTEREST

BEMPTON

Bempton Cliffs, 400 feet high, mark the northernmost tip of the great belt of chalk that runs diagonally across England from the Isle of Wight to Flamborough Head. The sheer cliffs at Bempton provide an ideal nesting place for huge colonies of fulmars, guillemots, puffins and Britain's largest seabird, the gannet, with a wingspan 6 feet wide. In Victorian times a popular holiday sport was to shoot the birds from boats. Above them, crowds gathered to watch gangs of "climmers" make a hair-raising descent by rope down the cliffs to gather the birds' eggs. Most were sold for food, but many went to egg collectors. The climmers also massacred kittiwakes in their thousands: kittiwake feathers were highly prized as accessories for hats and for stuffing mattresses. The first Bird Protection Act of 1869 was specifically designed to protect the kittiwakes at Bempton: a ban on collecting eggs here didn't come into force until

118 1954. Bempton Cliffs are now an RSPB bird sanctuary, a refuge during the April to August breeding season for more than 200,000 seabirds making this the largest colony in Britain.

BEVERLEY

This southeastern corner of Yorkshire tends to be overlooked by many visitors. If only they knew what they were missing. Beverley is one of the most beguiling of Yorkshire towns and its Minster one of the greatest glories of Gothic architecture. Its parish church, built by a medieval guild, rivals the Minster in its grandeur and in its colourful interior. The whole town has the indefinable dignity you might expect from a community that was a capital of the East Riding in former days when Hull, just six miles to the south, was still a rather scruffy little port.

To the east and south of Beverley lies the old Land of Holderness, its character quite different from anywhere else in Yorkshire. A wide plain, it stretches to the coast where for aeons the land has been fighting an incessant, and losing, battle against the onslaught of North Sea billows. The whole length of the Holderness coast is being eroded at an average rate of three inches a year, but in some locations up to three feet or more gets gnawn away. At its southernmost tip, **Spurn Point** curls around the mouth of the Humber estuary, a cruelly exposed tip of land whose contours get re-arranged after every winter storm. The coastal towns and villages have a bleached and scoured look to them, perhaps a little forbidding at first. It doesn't take long however for visitors to succumb to the appeal of this region of wide vistas, secluded villages and lonely shores.

"For those who do not know this town, there is a great surprise in store ... Beverley is made for walking and living in." Such was the considered opinion of the late Poet Laureate, John Betjeman. In medieval times, Beverley was one of England's most prosperous towns and it remains one of the most gracious. Its greatest glory is the **Minster** whose twin towers, built in glowing magnesian limestone, soar above this, the oldest town in East Yorkshire. More than two centuries in the making, from around 1220 to 1450, the Minster provides a textbook demonstration of the evolving architectural styles of those years. Among its many treasures are superb, fine wood carvings from the Ripon school,

and a thousand year old *fridstol*, or sanctuary seat. Carved from a single block of stone, the fridstol is a relic from the earlier Saxon church on this site. Under Saxon law, the fridstol provided refuge for any offender who managed to reach it. The canons would then try to resolve the dispute between the fugitive and his pursuer. If after 30 days no solution had been found, the seeker of sanctuary was then given safe escort to the county boundary or the nearest port. The custom survived right up until Henry VIII's closure of the monasteries.

Unlike the plain-cut fridstol, the canopy of the 14th-century Percy Shrine is prodigal in its ornamentation - *"the finest piece of work of the finest craftsmen of the finest period in British building"*. The behaviour of some visitors to this glorious Shrine was not, it seems, always as reverent as it might have been. When Celia Fiennes toured the Minster in 1697 she recorded that the tomb of *"Great Percy, Earle of Northumberland was a little fallen in and a hole so bigg as many put their hands in and touch'd the body which was much of it entire."* Great Percy's remains are now decently concealed once again.

As well as the incomparable stone carvings on the shrine, the Minster also has a wealth of wonderful carvings in wood. Seek out those representing Stomach Ache, Toothache, Sciatica and Lumbago - four afflictions probably almost as fearsome to medieval people as the Four Riders of the Apocalypse.

Close by is the **North Bar,** the only one of the town's five medieval gatehouses to have survived. Unlike many towns in the Middle Ages, Beverley did not have an encircling wall. Instead, the town fathers had a deep ditch excavated around it so that all goods had to pass through one of the gates and pay a toll. North Bar was built in 1409 and, with headroom of little more than ten feet, is something of a traffic hazard, albeit a very attractive one. Next door is Bar House, in which Charles I and his sons stayed in the 1630s. Another visitor to the town, famous for very different reasons, was the highwayman Dick Turpin who, in 1739, was brought before a magistrates' hearing conducted at one of the town's inns. That inn has long since gone and its site is now occupied by the Beverley Arms.

St Mary's Church, just across the road from the Beverley Arms, tends to be overshadowed by the glories of Beverley Minster. But this is another superb medieval building, richly en-

St Mary's Church, Beverley

holding a pair of scales. Unusually, she is not wearing a blindfold. When an 18th century town clerk was asked the reason for this departure from tradition, he replied *"In Beverley, Justice is not blind."*

Beverley can boast three separate museums. The **Beverley Art Gallery and Museum** contains a variety of local antiquities, Victorian bygones and works by the noted local artist, F.W. Elwell RA; the **East Yorkshire Regimental Museum** has six rooms of exhibits chronicling the area's long association with the regiment, and the **Museum of Army Transport** in Flamingate includes an intriguing variety of vehicles. They range from the wagon in which Lord Roberts travelled during the Boer War, to a Beaver military aircraft; from the Rolls Royce used by Field Marshal Montgomery as a staff car in France and Germany, to the only example of a three-wheels-in-a-row motorcycle.

From Beverley, serious walkers might care to follow some or all of the 15 mile **Hudson Way**, a level route that follows the track of the old railway from Beverley to Market Weighton. The Hudson Way wanders through the Wolds, sometimes deep in a cutting, sometimes high on an embankment, past an old windmill near Etton and through eerily abandoned stations.

dowed with fine carvings - many brightly coloured - and striking sculptures. A series of ceiling panels depicts all the Kings of England from Sigebert (623-37) to Henry VI. Originally, four legendary kings were also included, but one of them was replaced in recent times by a portrait of George VI. Lewis Carroll visited St Mary's when he stayed with friends in the town and was very taken with a stone carving of a rabbit - the inspiration, it is believed, for the March Hare in Alice in Wonderland. Certainly the carving bears an uncanny resemblance to Tenniel's famous drawing of the Mad Hatter.

Tucked away in the historic Wednesday Market area of Beverley, within sight of the famous Minster, **Artlynk Gallery** is a small treasure-house displaying the best of British decorative art, past and present. Housed in an attractive Georgian listed building, the gallery presents an outstanding array of

The wide market square in the heart of the town is graced by an elegant Market Cross, a circular pillared building rather like a small Greek temple. It bears the arms of Queen Anne in whose reign it was built at the expense of the town's two Members of Parliament. At that time of course parliamentary elections were flagrantly corrupt but at Beverley the tradition continued longer than in most places - in 1868 the author Anthony Trollope stood as a candidate here but was defeated in what was acknowledged as a breathtakingly fraudulent election.

The Guildhall nearby was built in 1762, is still used as a courtroom and also houses the town's Tourist Information Centre. The impressive courtroom has an ornate plasterwork ceiling on which there is an imposing Royal Coat of Arms and also the familiar figure of Justice

BRIDLINGTON

Bridlington lies at the northern tip of the crescent of hills that form the Wolds. The old town lies a mile inland from the bustling seaside resort with its manifold visitor amusements and attractions that has been understandably popular since early Victorian times. The attractions of a vast, ten mile stretch of sandy beach distract most visitors from the less obvious beauties of **Bridlington Priory** in the old town. The Priory was once one of the wealthiest in England but it was ruthlessly pillaged during the Reformation. Externally it is somewhat unprepossessing, but step inside and the majestic 13th century nave is unforgettably impressive. A corner of the Priory churchyard recalls one of the most tragic days in the town's history. During a fearsome gale in January 1871, a whole fleet of ships foundered along the coast. Bridlington's lifeboat was launched but within minutes it was *"smashed to matchwood"*: most of its crew perished. Twenty bodies were washed ashore and later buried in the Priory churchyard: it was estimated that ten times as many souls found only a watery grave. This awesome tragedy is still recalled each year with a solemn service of remembrance when the lifeboat is drawn through the town.

Queen Henrietta Maria's visit to Bridlington was not as tragic, but it was certainly quite exciting. In February 1643, she landed here from a Dutch ship laden with arms and aid for her beleaguered husband, Charles I. Parliamentary naval vessels were in hot pursuit and having failed to capture their quarry, bombarded the town. Their cannonballs actually hit the Queen's lodging. Henrietta was forced to take cover in a ditch where, as she reported in a letter to her husband, *"the balls sang merrily over our heads, and a sergeant was killed not 20 paces from me."* At this point Her Majesty deemed it prudent to retreat to the safety of Boynton Hall, three miles inland and well beyond the range of the Parliamentary cannon.

These stirring events, and many others in the long history of Bridlington and its people, are vividly brought to life with the help of evocative old paintings, photographs and artefacts in the **Bayle Museum**. Quite apart from its fascinating exhibits the museum is well worth visiting for its setting inside the old gatehouse to the town, built around 1390.

A more recent attraction, opened at Easter 1999, is **Beside the Seaside**, an all-weather venue where visitors can take a promenade through Bridlington's heyday as a resort, sampling the sights, sounds and characters of a seaside town. Film shows and period amusements such as antique coin-in-the-slot games and a Punch & Judy Show, displays reconstructing a 1950s boarding house as well as the town's maritime history - the museum provides a satisfying experience for both the nostalgic and those with a general curiosity about the town's past.

On the northern outskirts of Bridlington is **Sewerby Hall**, a monumental mansion built on the cusp of the Queen Anne and early Georgian years, between 1714 and 1720. Set in 50 acres of garden and parkland (where there's also a small zoo), the house was first opened to the public in 1936 by Amy Johnson, the dashing, Yorkshire-born pilot who had captured the public imagination by her daring solo flights to South Africa and Australia. The Museum here houses some fascinating memorabilia of Amy's

pioneering feats along with displays of motor vehicles, archaeological finds and some remarkable paintings amongst which is perhaps the most famous portrait of Queen Henrietta Maria, wife of Charles I. Queen Henrietta loved this romantic image of herself as a young, carefree woman, but during the dark days of the Civil War she felt compelled to sell it to raise funds for the doomed Royalist cause which ended with her husband's execution. After passing through several hands, this haunting portrait of a queen touched by tragedy found its last resting place at Sewerby Hall.

Close by is **Bondville Miniature Village**, one of the finest model villages in the country. The display includes more than 1,000 hand-made and painted characters, over 200 individual and unique villages, and carefully crafted scenes of everyday life, all set in a beautifully landscaped 1-acre site. The Village is naturally popular with children who are fascinated by features such as the steam train crossing the tiny river and passing the harbour with its fishing boats and cruisers.

BURTON AGNES

The overwhelming attraction in this unspoilt village is the sublime Elizabethan mansion, Burton Agnes Hall, but visitors should not ignore **Burton Agnes Manor House** (English Heritage), a rare example of a Norman house: a building of great historical importance but burdened with a grimly functional architecture, almost 800 years old, that chills one's soul. As Lloyd Grossman might say, "How could anyone live in a house like this?"

Burton Agnes Hall is much more appealing: an outstanding Elizabethan house, built between 1598 and 1610 and little altered, Burton Agnes is particularly famous for its splendid Jacobean gatehouse, wondrously decorated ceil-

Burton Agnes Hall

ings and overmantels carved in oak, plaster and alabaster. It also has a valuable collection of paintings and furniture from between the 17th and 19th centuries - including a portrait of Oliver Cromwell "warts and all" - and a large collection of Impressionist paintings. The gardens are extensive with over 2,000 plants, a maze and giant board games in the Coloured Gardens. Other visitor facilities include a new ice cream parlour, a dried-flower and herb shop, a children's animal corner, and an artists' studio. A very popular addition is the plant sales where numerous uncommon varieties can be obtained. "The Impressionist Cafe", open throughout the Hall's season. It is licensed and offers only the very best in home cooking.

FLAMBOROUGH HEAD

At **Flamborough Head**, sea and land are locked in an unremitting battle. At the North Landing, huge, foam-spumed waves roll in between gigantic cliffs, slowly but remorselessly washing away the shoreline. Paradoxically, the outcome of this elemental conflict is to produce one of the most picturesque locations on the Yorkshire coast, much visited and much photographed.

Victorian travel writers loved Flamborough. Not just because of its dramatic scenery, but what about the people! They were so clannish and believed in such strange superstitions! No boat would ever set sail on a Sunday, wool could not be wound in lamplight, anyone who mentioned a hare or pig while baiting the fishing lines was inviting doom. No fisherman would leave harbour unless he was wearing a navy-blue jersey, knitted by his wife in a cable, diamond mesh peculiar to the village and still worn today. Every year the villagers would slash their way through Flamborough in a sword-dancing frenzy introduced here in the 8th century by the Vikings. Eventually, local fishermen grew weary of this primitive role so although the sword dance still takes place it is now performed by boys from the primary school, accoutred in white trousers, red caps and the traditional navy-blue jerseys.

Flamborough's parish church contains two particularly interesting monuments. One is the tomb of Sir Marmaduke Constable which shows him with his chest cut open to reveal his heart being devoured by a toad. The knight's death in 1518 had been caused, the story goes, by his swallowing the toad which had been drowsing in Sir Marmaduke's lunchtime pint of ale, apparently. The creature then devoured his heart. The other notable monument is a statue of St Oswald, patron saint of fishermen. This fishing connection is renewed every year, on the second Sunday in October, by a service dedicated to the **Harvest of the Sea,** when the area's seafarers gather together in a church decorated with crab pots and fishing nets.

Flamborough Head's first, and England's oldest surviving **lighthouse,** is the octagonal chalk tower on the landward side of the present lighthouse. Built in 1674, its beacon was a basket of burning coal. The lighthouse that is still in use was built in 1806. Originally signalling four

Flamborough Head

white flashes, developments over the years have included a fog horn in 1859 and in more recent years, a signal of radio bleeps. Until it was automated in 1995, it was the last manned lighthouse on the east coast.

Just to the north of Flamborough is **Danes Dyke,** a huge rampart four miles long designed to cut off the headland from hostile invaders. The Danes had nothing to do with it, the dyke was in place long before they arrived. Sometime during the Bronze or Stone Age, early Britons constructed this extraordinary defensive ditch. A mile and a quarter of its southern length is open to the public as a Nature Trail.

HESSLE

At Hessle the River Humber narrows and it was here that the Romans maintained a ferry, the *Transitus Maximus,* a vital link in the route between Lincoln and York. The ferry remained in operation for almost 2,000 years until it was replaced in 1981 by the Humber Bridge, whose mighty pylons soar more than 800 feet above the village. The great bridge dwarfs Cliff Mill, built in 1810 to mill the local chalk. It remained wind-driven until 1925 when a gas engine was installed. Although it is no longer working the mill provides a scenic feature within the **Humber Bridge Country Park**. This well laid out park gives visitors a true back-to-nature tour a short distance from one of modern man's greatest feats of engineering. The former chalk quarry has been attractively landscaped, providing a nature trail, extensive walks through woodlands and meadows, picnic and play areas, and picturesque water features.

HORNSEA

This small coastal town can boast not only the most popular visitor attraction in Humberside, Hornsea Pottery, but also Yorkshire's largest freshwater lake, Hornsea Mere. **Hornsea Pottery** is an extensive complex which includes the famous pottery where you can watch craftsmen at work and buy their wares, a factory viewing area, a collection of vintage cars, factory shops, a country park, and **Butterfly World** where more than 200 species of colourful butterflies flutter around a tropical greenhouse.

Hornsea Mere, two miles long and one mile wide, provides a refuge for over 170 species of birds and a peaceful setting for many varieties of rare flowers. Human visitors are well provided for, too, with facilities for fishing, boating and sailing. Hornsea is also the home of the **North Holderness Museum of Village Life.** Here, in a converted 18th-century farmhouse, period rooms have been recreated, and there are collections of agricultural equipment and the tools of long gone local tradesmen. Excellent sands, a church built with cobbles gathered from the shore, well-tended public gardens and a breezy, mile-long promenade all add to the town's popularity.

The excellent **Hornsea Museum**, established in 1978, has won numerous national awards over the years as well as being featured several times on television. The museum occupies a Grade II listed building, a former farmhouse where successive generations of the Burn family lived for 300 years up until 1952. Their way of life, the personalities and characters who influenced the development of the town or found fame in other ways, are explored in me-

ticulously restored rooms brimming with furniture, decorations, utensils and tools of the Victorian period. The kitchen, parlour, bedroom, have fascinating displays of authentic contemporary artefacts, and the museum complex also includes a laundry, workshop, blacksmith's shop and a barn stocked with vintage agricultural implements. In Swallow Cottage next door, children can undergo the Victorian school experience under the tutelage of "Miss Grim" - writing on slates, having good deportment instilled and, above all, observing the maxim *"Silence is Golden."* The cottage also houses a comprehensive and varied display of early Hornsea pottery, various temporary exhibitions, and, in summer, a refreshment room for visitors. Remarkably, this outstanding museum is staffed entirely by volunteers.

HOWDEN

Despite the fact that its chancel collapsed in 1696 and has not been used for worship ever since, **Howden Minster** is still one of the largest parish churches in East Yorkshire and also one of its most impressive, cathedral-like in size. From the top of its soaring tower, 135 feet high, there are wonderful views of the surrounding countryside - but it's not for the faint-hearted! The ruined chapter house, lavishly decorated with a wealth of carved mouldings, has been

Howden Minster

described as one of the most exquisite small buildings in England.

When the medieval Prince-Bishops of Durham held sway over most of northern England, they built a palace at Howden which they used as a pied-à-terre during their semi-royal progresses and as a summer residence. The Hall of that 14th century palace still stands, although much altered now.

Howden town is a pleasing jumble of narrow, flagged and setted streets with a picturesque stone and brick Market Hall in the market place. The celebrated aircraft designer Barnes Wallis knew Howden well: he lived here while working on the R100 airship which was built at Hedon airfield nearby. It made its maiden flight in 1929 and successfully crossed the Atlantic.

About 4 miles northwest of Howden are the striking remains of **Wressle Castle**, built in 1380 for Sir Henry Percy and the only surviving example in East Yorkshire of a medieval fortified house. At the end of the Civil War, three of the castle's sides were pulled down and much of the rest was destroyed by fire in 1796. But two massive towers with walls 6ft thick, the hall and kitchens remain. The castle is not open to the public but there are excellent views from the village road and from a footpath that runs alongside the River Derwent. A fine old windmill nearby provides an extra visual bonus.

HULL

During World War II Hull was mercilessly battered by the Luftwaffe: 7,000 of its people were killed and 92 per cent of its houses suffered bomb damage. Hull has risen phoenix-like from those ashes and is today the fastest-growing port in England. The port area extends for 7 miles along the Humber with 10 miles of quays servicing a constant flow of commercial traffic arriving from, or departing for, every quarter of the globe. Every day, a succession of vehicle ferries link the city to the European gateways of Zeebrugge and Rotterdam. Hull is unmistakably part of Yorkshire but it also has the free-wheeling, open-minded character of a cosmopolitan port.

Hull's history as an important port goes back to 1293 when Edward I, travelling north on his way to hammer the Scots, stopped off here and immediately recognized the potential of the muddy junction where the River Hull flows into the Humber. The king bought the land from

the monks of Meaux Abbey (at the usual royal discount) and the settlement thenceforth was known as "Kinges town upon Hull".

123

The port grew steadily through the centuries and at one time had the largest fishing fleet of any port in the country with more than 300 trawlers on its register. The port's rather primitive facilities were greatly improved by the construction of a state-of-the-art dock in 1778. Now superseded, that dock has been converted into the handsome Queen's Gardens, one of the

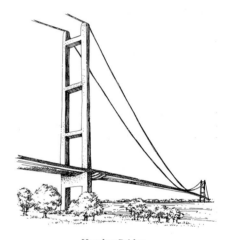

Humber Bridge

many attractive open spaces created by this flower-conscious city which also loves lining its streets with trees, setting up fountains here and there, and planting flower beds in any available space. And waymarked walks such as the Maritime Heritage Trail and the Fish Pavement Trail make the most of the city's dramatic waterfront.

A visit to Hull is an exhilarating experience at any time of the year, but especially so in October. Back in the late 1200s the city was granted a charter to hold an autumn fair. This began as a fairly modest cattle and sheep mart but over the centuries it burgeoned into the largest gathering of its kind in Europe. Hull Fair is now a 9-day extravaganza occupying a 14-acre site and offering every imaginable variety of entertainment.

124

That takes care of October, but Hull also hosts an Easter Festival, an International Festival (some 300 events from mid-June to late July), a Jazz on the Waterfront celebration (August), an International Sea Shanty Festival (September) and a Literature Festival in November.

Throughout the rest of the year, Hull's tourism office modestly suggests you explore its "Magnificent Seven" - a quite remarkable collection of historic houses, art galleries and museums. Perhaps the most evocative is the **Wilberforce House Museum** in the old High Street. William Wilberforce was born here in 1759 and, later, it was from here that he and his father lavished thousands of pounds in bribes to get William elected as Hull's Member of Parliament. Nothing unusual about that kind of corruption at the time, but William then redeemed himself by his resolute opposition to slavery. His campaign took more than 30 years and William was already on his deathbed before a reluctant Parliament finally outlawed the despicable trade. The museum presents a shaming history of the slave trade along with a more uplifting story of Wilberforce's efforts to eliminate it for ever.

Other stars of the "Magnificent Seven" are **The Ferens Art Gallery** which houses a sumptuous collection of paintings and sculpture that ranges from European Old Masters (including some Canalettos and works by Franz Hals) to challenging contemporary art; the **Town Docks Museum** which celebrates seven centuries of Hull's maritime heritage and includes a fine collection of scrimshaw. A more unusual museum is the **Spurn Lightship**. Once stationed on active duty 4.5 miles east of Spurn Point, the 200-ton, 33 metre long craft is now moored in Hull's vibrant Marina. Visitors can explore the 75-year-old vessel with the help of its knowledgeable crew. The city's noisiest museum is the **Streetlife Transport Museum** which traces 200 years of transport history. Visitors are transported back to the days of horse-drawn carriages, steam trains, trams and penny-farthing cycles. There are curiosities such as the "Velocipede", the Automobile à Vapeur (an early steam-driven car), and Lady Chesterfield's ornamental sleigh, caparisoned with a swan, rearing unicorn and a panoply of bells to herald her approach.

You will encounter a marvel of a different kind if you come by road to Hull from the south and drive over one of the most impressive bridges on earth - and also one of the least used. It's been described as the least likely place in Britain to find a traffic jam. Opened in 1981, the **Humber Bridge** is one of the world's longest single-span bridges with an overall length of 2,428 yards. That means that for more than a third of a mile only four concrete pillars, two at each end, are saving you from a watery death. From these huge pylons, 510 feet high, gossamer cables of thin-wired steel support a gently curving roadway. Both sets of pylons rise vertically, but because of the curvature of the earth they actually lean away from each other by several inches. The bridge is particularly striking at night when the vast structure is floodlit. Before leaving the city, one should mention two of its more unusual features. First, visitors to Hull soon become aware of its unique public telephones. They are still the traditional, curvy-topped, heavily-barred boxes but with the distinctive difference that Hull's are all painted a gleaming white. What isn't apparent is that by some bureaucratic quirk, Hull remained the only municipally owned telephone company in Britain until it was floated on the Stock Exchange early in 2000. The sale brought the City Council a huge windfall. The second unusual feature of Hull: in Nelson Street you can avail yourself of award-winning loos. These spotless conveniences, complete with hanging baskets of flowers, have become a tourist attraction in their own right.

PATRINGTON

Shortly after it was built, **St Patrick's Church** at Patrington was dubbed *"Queen of Holderness"*, and Queen it remains. This sublime church took more than a hundred years to build, from around 1310 to 1420, and it is one of the most glorious examples of the eye-pleasing style known as English Decorated. Its spire soars almost 180 feet into the sky making it the most distinctive feature in the flat plains of Holderness. St Patrick's has the presence and proportions of a cathedral although only enjoying the status of a parish church; a parish church, nevertheless, which experts consider among the finest dozen churches in Britain for architectural beauty. Patrington's parish council go further: a notice displayed inside St Patrick's states unequivocally *"This is England's finest village Church."* Clustering around it, picturesque Dutch style cottages complete an entrancing picture and just to the east of the village the Dutch theme continues in a fine old windmill.

POCKLINGTON

Set amid rich agricultural land with the Wolds rising to the east, Pocklington is a lively market town with an unusual layout of twisting alleys running off the market place. Its splendid church, mostly 15th century but with fragments of an earlier Norman building, certainly justifies its title as the Cathedral of the Wolds (although strictly speaking Pocklington is just outside the Wolds). William Wilberforce went to the old grammar school here and, a more dubious claim to fame, the last burning of a witch in England took place in Pocklington. Founded in Anglo-Saxon times by "Pocela's people", by the time the Domesday Book was compiled Pocklington was recorded as one of the only two boroughs in the East Riding. A market followed in the 13th century, but it was the building in 1815 of a canal linking the town to the River Ouse, and the later arrival of the railway, that set the seal on the town's prosperity.

A popular and unusual attraction in Pocklington is the **Penny Arcadia** housed in the Ritz Cinema in the market place. "Not so much a museum as a fun palace" it contains a wonderful collection of penny-in-the-slot amusement machines ranging from "What the Butler Saw" to fortune telling and pinball machines.

The people of Pocklington have good reason to be grateful to Major P.M. Stewart who, on his death in 1962, bequeathed **Burnby Hall and Gardens** to the town. The eight acres of gardens are world-famous for the rare collection of water-lilies planted in the two large lakes. There are some 50 varieties and in the main flowering season from July to early September they present a dazzling spectacle. The Major and his wife had travelled extensively before settling down at Burnby and there's a small museum in the Hall displaying his collection of sporting trophies.

A few miles to the south of Pocklington is **Londesborough Park**, a 400 acre estate which was once owned by the legendary railway entrepreneur, George Hudson. He had the York to Market Weighton railway diverted here so that he could build himself a comfortable private station. The railway has now disappeared but part of its route is included in the popular long distance footpath, the Wolds Way.

About 8 miles west of Pocklington, on the B1228 near Elvington, is the **Yorkshire Air Museum**. A memorial to the Allied Air Forces who flew from the area in World War II, the museum celebrates the history of aviation in Yorkshire and Humberside. Housed in the original wartime buildings, the museum has recreated the authentic atmosphere of the 1940s. Aircraft on display include a rebuilt Halifax and Mosquito, and one of the last surviving Lightnings.

SLEDMERE

Sledmere House is a noble Georgian mansion built by the Sykes family in the 1750s when this area was still a wilderness infested with packs of marauding wolves. Inside, there is fine furniture by Chippendale and Sheraton, and decorated plasterwork by Joseph Rose. The copy of a naked, and well-endowed, Apollo Belvedere in the landing alcove must have caused many a maidenly blush in Victorian times, and the Turkish Room - inspired by the Sultan's salon in Istanbul's Valideh Mosque - is a dazzling example of oriental opulence. Outside, the gardens and the 220 acres of parkland were landscaped, of course, by "Capability" Brown.

The Sykes family set a shining example to other landowners in the Wolds by agricultural improvements that transformed a *"blank and barren tract of land"* into one of the most productive and best cultivated districts in the county. They founded the famous Sledmere Stud, and the second Sir Tatton Sykes spent nearly two million pounds on building and restoring churches in the area. Sledmere House itself was ravaged by fire in 1911. Sir Tatton was enjoying his favourite lunchtime dessert of rice pudding when a servant rushed in with news of the fire and urged him to leave the house.

Sledmere House

"First, I must finish my pudding, finish my pudding" he declared, and did so. An armchair was set up for him on the lawn and Sir Tatton, then 85 years old, "followed the progress of the conflagration" as the household staff laboured to rescue the house's many treasures. After the fire, Sledmere was quickly restored and the Sykes family is still in residence. The house is open to the public and music lovers should make sure they visit between 2 and 4 p.m. when the enormous pipe organ is being played.

Across the road from Sledmere House are two remarkable, elaborately detailed, monuments. The **Eleanor Cross** - modelled on those set up by Edward I in memory of his Queen, was erected by Sir Tatton Sykes in 1900; the **Waggoners Memorial** designed by Sir Mark Sykes, commemorates the 1,000-strong company of men he raised from the Wolds during the First World War. Their knowledge of horses was invaluable in their role as members of the Army Service Corps. The finely-carved monument is like a "storyboard", its panels depicting the Waggoners' varied duties during the war.

SPROATLEY

A couple of miles north of Sproatley is **Burton Constable Hall,** named after Sir John Constable who in 1570 built a stately mansion here which incorporated parts of an even older house, dating back to the reign of King Stephen in the 1100s. The Hall was again remodelled, on Jacobean lines, in the 18th century and contains some fine work by Chippendale, Adam and James Wyatt. In the famous Long Gallery with its 15th-century Flemish stained glass, hangs a remarkable collection of paintings, among them Holbein's portraits of Sir Thomas Cranmer and Sir Thomas More, and Zucchero's *Mary, Queen of Scots.* Dragons abound in the dazzling Chinese Room, an exercise in oriental exotica that long pre-dates the Prince Regent's similar extravaganza at the Brighton Pavilion. Thomas Chippendale himself designed the fantastical Dragon Chair, fit for a Ming Emperor. Outside, there are extensive parklands designed by - who else could it be? - "Capability" Brown, and apparently inspired by the gardens at Versailles. Perhaps it was this connection that motivated the Constable family to suggest loaning the Hall to Louis XVIII of France during his years of exile after the Revolution. (Louis po-

litely declined the offer, preferring to settle rather closer to London, at Hartwell in Buckinghamshire.) Also in the grounds of the Hall are collections of agricultural machinery, horse-drawn carriages and 18th-century scientific apparatus.

The descendants of the Constable family still bear the title "Lords of Holderness" and along with it the rights to any flotsam and jetsam washed ashore on the Holderness peninsula. Many years ago, when the late Brigadier Chichester Constable was congratulated on enjoying such a privilege, he retorted, *"I also have to pay for burying, or otherwise disposing of, any whale grounded on the Holderness shore - and it costs me about £20 a time!"* The huge bones of one such whale are still on show in the grounds of the Hall.

WITHERNSEA

The next place of interest down the Holderness coast is Withernsea. Long, golden sandy beaches stretch for miles both north and south, albeit a mile further inland than they were in the days of William the Conqueror. The old lighthouse is a striking feature of the town and those energetic enough to climb the 127-foot tower are rewarded by some marvellous views from the lamproom. The lighthouse was decommissioned in 1976 and now houses two small museums. One is dedicated to the history of the Royal National Lifeboat Institution; the other to the actress Kay Kendall. Her grandfather helped build the lighthouse in 1892 and was the last coxswain of the deep sea lifeboat. Kay was born in Withernsea and later achieved great success in the London theatre as a sophisticated comedienne but she is probably best remembered for the rousing trumpet solo she delivered in the Ealing Studios hit film *Genevieve.*

South of Withernsea stretches a desolate spit of flat windswept dunes. This is **Spurn Point** which leads to Spurn Head, the narrow hook of ever-shifting sands that curls around the mouth of the Humber estuary. This bleak but curiously invigorating tag end of Yorkshire is nevertheless heavily populated - by hundreds of species of rare and solitary wild fowl, by playful seals, and also by the small contingent of lifeboatmen who operate the only permanently manned lifeboat station in Britain. Please note that a toll is payable beyond the village of Kilnsea, and there is no car park. Access to Spurn Head is only on foot.

The Black Bull | 127

18 Market Place,
Pocklington,
East Riding
YO42 2AR
Tel: 01759 302649

Directions:

From York (12 miles) take the A64 to A1079, turn left at Barnby Moor on to B1246 signposted Pocklington.

Rod and Ann Hodgson make a great team at the **Black Bull**, which enjoys a prime site in the historic town of Pocklington. The pristine white-painted facade invites the visitor inside, and the bars are equally well groomed, with plenty of comfortable seating and old prints of Pocklington on the walls. Traditional pub food caters for appetites large and small on a varied, well-balanced menu, and the cask-conditioned ales make an excellent accompaniment.

Pocklington is a town that merits much more than a quick trip, and the Black Bull makes an ideal base for exploring the town. The Cottage, at the end of the car park, offers five Bed & Breakfast rooms - three twins, a double and a single, all with tv and tea/coffee-makers; they share two bathrooms. Visitors of all ages are welcome, and in the beer garden is a children's area complete with an aviary. Wednesday night is disco night.

Pocklington is a lively market town with an unusual layout of twisting alleys running off the market place. Among the many attractions are places as diverse as the splendid 12th century church, some times known as the Cathedral of the Wolds, and the Oak House, Pocklington's civic arts centre which offers a varied programme of theatre, music, exhibitions and up to date cinema. Burnby Hall and Gardens are world famous for the collection of water lilies. Sport is widely catered for with a sports centre and swimming pool, 3 golf courses and numerous beautiful walks in the wolds.

Opening Hours: Mon-Sat 11.00-23.00; Sun 12.00-22.30

Food: Bar meals.

Credit Cards: None.

Accommodation: 5 rooms sharing 2 bathrooms

Facilities: Car Park.

Entertainment: Disco Wednesday.

Local Places of Interest/Activities: York 12 miles, Driffield 12 miles, Elvington (Yorkshire Air Museum) 10 miles.

Internet/Website:
rod@bullpocklington.freeserve.co.uk

128

Blue Post Inn

North Frodingham,
North Yorkshire
YO25 8LG
Tel: 01262 488300
Fax: 01262 481073

Directions:

From Driffield (8 miles) take the B1249 towards Skipsea.

Smartly painted in white and blue, the **Blue Post Inn** is easy to spot on the B1249 midway between Driffield and Skipsea. Wendy and Ray Jackson are the hands-on proprietors, Wendy behind the bar and Ray in the kitchen. A former chef in the RAF, Ray puts food high on the agenda at this friendly, family-oriented pub, and his tempting menus are really taking off - booking is advisable. Fresh local produce is used whenever possible, and the favourites with the regulars include scrumptious savoury pies and juicy steaks. Bar snacks cater for lighter appetites, and among other offerings are teatime specials and a traditional Sunday roast. The pub has a separate games room, a beer garden and a very large car park. Entertainment includes charity-based quiz nights and occasional live music events.

It's only a short drive from the Blue Post to Skipsea, while further down the coast there's plenty to see and do in the small town of Hornsea. Hornsea Pottery attracts visitors from far and wide, and after watching the potters at work they can flit across to Butterfly World, where more than 200 species of butterflies fly free in a tropical greenhouse. Hornsea Mere, Yorkshire's largest freshwater lake, provides a refuge for over 170 species of birds. At Feston-on-the-Wolds, just north of the Blue Post Inn, is another popular attraction in Cruckley Animal Farm, a 60-acre working farm with a large resident population of farm animals.

Opening Hours: Mon-Tue 19.00-23.30; Wed-Sat 12.00-23.30; Sun 12.00-23.00

Food: Bar meals and à la carte.

Credit Cards: Access, Mastercard, Visa.

Accommodation: None.

Facilities: Car Park.

Entertainment: Quiz and live music nights.

Local Places of Interest/Activities: Driffield 8 miles, Skipsea, Hornsea 12 miles.

The Cross Keys Inn

129

Melbourne,
Nr. York,
East Riding
YO42 4QJ
Tel: 01759 318257

Directions:

A64 east of York to junction with A1079; turn right on to B1228, follow road through Elvington and Sutton to junction with minor road signposted Melbourne.

Cream-painted and red-tiled, the **Cross Keys Inn** stands prominently in the middle of the delightful village of Melbourne, which is situated in open countryside about ten miles south-east of York, on the bank of the River Derwent. The bar is neat, trim and inviting, with little chairs arranged at polished tables on thick carpet. Victoria Worthington, owner and chef, is always delighted to welcome new faces into her pub, and those new faces are equally delighted with the warm atmosphere, the choice of cask ales and the excellent food. Fresh fish and prime steaks are cooked simply to highlight their quality and flavour, and when lobster is on the menu, it definitely should not be missed. Children can keep themselves amused in their special area in the garden. Live music sessions are held monthly. The Pocklington Canal runs past the back of the pub, and in the summer the long boats, converted from their working role into pleasure craft, make a pretty sight. Pocklington itself, some six miles to the east of Melbourne, across the A1079, has several attractions for the visitor, including the Penny Arcadia, with its wonderful collection of old amusement machines, and Burnby Hall and Gardens with their world-famous water lilies. Even closer to the Cross Keys, just outside Elvington on the road to York, is the Yorkshire Air Museum, a memorial to the Allied Air Forces who flew from the area in World War ll. Aircraft on display include a Halifax, a Mosquito and one of the last surviving Lightnings.

Opening Hours: 18.00-23.00 Mon-Thur; 12.30-14.30, 18.00-23.00 Fri; 12.30-15.00, 19.00-23.00 Sat; all day Sunday; 12.30-15.00, 18.00-23.00 bank holiday Mondays

Food: Bar meals/ evening restaurant

Credit Cards: None

Accommodation: None.

Facilities: Wheel chair access, beer garden

Entertainment: Live music once a month, pool, darts, dominoes

Local Places of Interest/Activities: York 11 miles, Pocklington 6 miles, Elvington (Yorkshire Air Museum) 5 miles.

130 The Crown

York Road,
Shiptonthorpe,
Nr. Market Weighton,
North Yorkshire
Y043 3PF
Tel: 01430 873310

Directions:

2 miles northwest of Market Weighton on the A1079 Hull to York road

A 19th century coaching in standing proud and pretty on the main road to York. Behind the white-painted facade it's all bright and fresh, and the atmosphere in the bar is genuinely friendly and relaxed. Holding the reins are the husband and wife team of Colin Medd and Beverly Lacksey, Colin behind the bar and Beverly in charge of the kitchen. The bar food is a major draw here, and the home-cooked dishes span both British and foreign cuisines. The owners have really put this grand little place on the map, and their plans for the future include the possibility of adding overnight accommodation. That would indeed be a great asset, as **The Crown** is well placed for touring an area that is rich in both history and scenic splendour. It's great walking country - the popular long-distance footpath the Wolds Way runs close by - and motorists have easy access to the city of York.

Only two miles away, Market Weighton is a busy little town where mellow 18th century houses cluster round an early Norman church. The best-known figure buried in the churchyard is William Bradley, who was born at Market Weighton in 1787 and grew up to become the tallest man in England at 7 feet 8 inches. Attractions at Pocklington include Burnby Hall and Gardens, with their unique collection of water lilies; and Penny Arcadia, with a wonderful line-up of end-of-pier penny-in-the-slot machines. A few miles south of Pocklington is Londesborough Park, a 400-acre estate which was once owned by the railway entrepreneur George Hudson. he had the YorkMarket Weighton railway diverted here so that he could build himself a private station. The railway is long gone, but part of its route is included in the Wolds Way.

Opening Hours: 12.00-15.00, 17.00-19.00.

Food: Bar meals.

Credit Cards: None.

Accommodation: None

Facilities: Car Park.

Local Places of Interest/Activities: Market Weighton 2 miles, Beverley 12miles, York 10 miles, Pocklington.

The Hope & Anchor | 131

*Main Street,
Blacktoft, East
Yorkshire
DN14 7YW
Tel: 01430 440441*

Directions:

From Goole B1228 to junction with A63, then B1230; turn right at Gilberdyke on minor road to Blacktoft. From Hull A63 to junction with M62 then B1230 to Gilberdyke, minor road on left to Blacktoft.

The hamlet of Blacktoft is well off the beaten track, but the detour to the banks of the Ouse is certainly worth while, as the **Hope & Anchor** has a great deal to offer the visitor. Owners Liz and Eddie Payne are rightly proud of their pub, which is quaint and cosy behind its smart cream-painted exterior. In the matter of food, freshness comes first, and as far as possible everything on the well-balanced menu is sourced locally. Sunday lunch is always a big occasion, so it's best to book. Fine cask conditioned ales are also available . Outside are a garden with a children's playground and a small caravan park; but the crowning glory of the Hope & Anchor has to be riverside setting, and the views from the garden are quite superb.

The location is just west of the point where the River Ouse meets the River Trent before flowing into the Humber. On the far bank of the Ouse is Blacktoft Sands, a nature reserve for waterfowl, and between this point and the metropolis of Hull are the breathtaking Humber Bridge, one of the world's longest single-span bridges, and the Humber Bridge Country Park with walks through woodland and meadows, nature trails and picnic and play areas.

Opening Hours: Mon-Tue 16.00-23.00; Wed-Sat 12.00-23.00; Sun 12.00-22.30

Food: Bar meals.

Credit Cards: Access, Mastercard, Visa.

Accommodation: None.

Facilities: Car Park, caravan park.

Local Places of Interest/Activities: Goole 8 miles, Hull 12 miles. On the Penine Trail Route

132 The Red Lion

High Street, Market Weighton,
East Riding YO43 3AH
Tel: 01430 872452

Directions:
From York A1079 20 miles; from Beverley A1079 10 miles.

In spring and summer the front of the **Red Lion** is almost hidden behind a wonderful blaze of colour in flowerpots, hanging baskets and window boxes. The promise of the exterior is amply fulfilled within, where the bars are bright, spotless, warm and very inviting, with lots of oak beams and gleaming brassware: inside and out are a tribute to the care and attention lavished on the place by hands-on owners Christine and Jim Bytheway. Easy-to-read menus offer a good selection of wholesome home cooking to suit all tastes (no food Tuesday evening) and there is always a choice of real ales. The locals play pool and darts and dominoes, and on Wednesday night brains are sharpened and memories jogged for the popular weekly quiz.

The pub stands by a roundabout at the centre of the busy little town of Market Weighton, where mellow 18th century houses cluster round an early Norman church. Buried in the churchyard is William Bradley, who was born in the town in 1787 and grew up to become the tallest man in England, standing 7 feet 8 inches. He was received at Court by George lll, who gave him a huge gold watch to wear across his chest. For walkers, the long-distance Wolds Way passes close to the inn, and motorists can reach Beverley, Hull and York in next to no time. Very close to Market Weighton is the village of Home upon Spalding Moor, where a splendid medieval church with an eight-pinnacled tower is a landmark that can be seen for miles around.

Opening Hours: 11.00-15.00, 18.00-23.00; Friday, Saturday and Sunday 11.00-23.00.

Food: Bar meals.

Credit Cards: None.

Accommodation: None.

Facilities: Car Park.

Entertainment: Quiz night Wednesday.

Local Places of Interest/Activities: Beverley 10 miles, York 20 miles, Wolds Way.

The Royal Dog & Duck

133

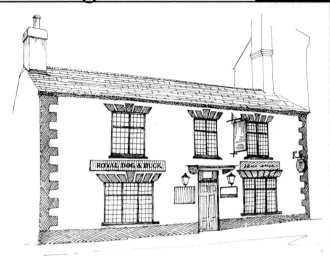

Dog & Duck Square,
Flamborough,
North Yorkshire
YO15 1NB
Tel: 01262 850206
Fax: 01262 851040

Directions:

5 miles Northeast of
Bridlington on the
B1255.

Behind an immaculate black-and-white frontage the **Royal Dog & Duck** has abundant character and individuality. Its origins are in the 17th century and the bars have an inviting, uncluttered charm - oak tables and chairs, open fires, dimly lit narrow corridors. Good wholesome Yorkshire food is on offer every lunchtime and every evening in the bars and in the 80-seat restaurant, with giant haddock and sizzling steaks among the favourite dishes. There's always a good selection of real ales and cask ales to enjoy at this convivial inn, and when the weather is kind the beer garden is the place to be. Beyond the good cheer and the good conversation, entertainment takes the form of folk, karaoke and quiz nights, which vary according to the seasons.

Kim and Jake and Pat and Barry are the partners in the Royal Dog & Duck, which an ancient sign board announces as the headquarters of Flamborough Association Football Club and Flamborough Cricket Club. Flamborough's parish church has an interesting monument with a lesson for all beer-drinkers. It shows Sir Marmaduke Constable with his chest cut open to reveal a toad eating his heart. The good knight had been drowsing over his lunchtime pint and did not notice that a toad had hopped into his glass. He swallowed the toad, which promptly devoured his heart.

Flamborough Head is an amazing place to visit, and the constant battle between the sea and the land is a stirring sight to behold. Flamborough's first lighthouse, and the oldest in England, is an octagonal chalk tower which in its working life was lit by a beacon of burning coals. It stands on the landward side of the present lighthouse, which until being automated in 1995 was the last manned lighthouse on the east coast.

Opening Hours: 11.00-23.00.

Food: bar meals, 2 restaurants

Credit Cards: None

Accommodation: None.

Facilities: Childrens arcade

Entertainment: karaoke and quiz nights

Local Places of Interest/Activities:
Flamborough Head, Bridlington 5 miles, Filey, Bempton Cliffs (RSPB sanctuary).

134

The Star Inn

North Dalton,
East Riding of
Yorkshire
YO25 9UX
Tel: 01377 217688
Fax: 01377 217791

Directions:

North Dalton is situated midway between Pocklington and Driffield on the B1246.

Keith and Joanne Kirk, he in the kitchen, she front of house, make a fine team at this splendid country hostelry in the heart of the Yorkshire Wolds. Once the main staging stop between York and Beverley on the Minster Way, the **Star Inn** continues to welcome travellers with the very best of Yorkshire hospitality. Often known as 'The Inn on the Pond', it nestles beside the village pond, and the promise of the idyllic location is more than fulfilled inside, where heavy oak beams and sturdy exposed brickwork take the eye. Dining in the Poolside Lounge is an enjoyably relaxed occasion, and the frequently changing menu and daily specials board offer a wide choice of dishes both traditional - fish & chips with mushy peas, steak & ale pie - and a little bit out of the ordinary such as boned lamb cutlets in a rich marmalade and mint jus or Thai tofu curry. Seven well-appointed en suite bedrooms provide peace and comfort for guests staying overnight; all are equipped with direct-dial phone, tv, hairdryer and tea/coffee-making facilities. The pondside rooms enjoy a pleasant view of the village church. Children and pets are welcome, and the Star can cater for private parties and functions in a separate meeting room. Walking is a good way to build up an appetite while taking in the lovely local scenery, and for motorists there are many places of interest in the area. Pocklington is a lively market town with a noble church that is sometimes called the Cathedral of the Wolds, and the renowned Burnby Hall and Gardens with a collection of rare water lilies is also nearby. Another famous church is at South Dalton, where the 200ft spire of St Mary's is an unmistakable landmark that can be seen for miles around.

Opening Hours: 12.00-14.00, 18.00-21.30; closed Monday lunchtime.

Food: A la carte and bar meals.

Credit Cards: Access, Mastercard, Visa.

Accommodation: 7 en suite rooms.

Facilities: Car Park, function room.

Entertainment: On special occasions

Local Places of Interest/Activities:
Pocklington 5 miles, Driffield 5 miles, Wolds Way Walk. Beverley Minster

Internet/Website:
website: www.innonthepond.co.uk

The Wheatsheaf

Hailgate,
Howden,
East Yorkshire
DN14 7SX
Tel: 01430 432334
Fax: 01430 431789

Directions:

11 miles east of Selby
on the A63.

The Wheatsheaf is a late 19th century pub in the centre of a little town with a long and rich history. The pub is very much a one-man show, with a go-ahead owner in Robert Colman, who clearly loves the place and is always pleased to welcome visitors. Behind the standard frontage with brass lamps and overhanging entrance the public space is a single open-plan area, all dark oak and gleaming brass, with an open fire at each end. The locals come here to enjoy a glass of cask ale and bar food at its best - a simple, straightforward menu of popular dishes at popular prices. The Wheatsheaf is still developing under Robert, who is finalising plans for theme nights and could soon expand the amenities of the pub by adding overnight accommodation.

Howden is a small market town, a pleasing jumble of narrow streets with a picturesque stone and brick Market Hall in the market place. The celebrated aircraft designer and inventor of the Bouncing Bomb Barnes Wallis knew the place well: he lived here while working on the R100 airship, which was built at nearby Hedon airfield. It made its maiden flight in 1929 and successfully crossed the Atlantic. Howden Minster is one of the largest parish churches in East Yorkshire, with wonderful views from the top of its tower. It has not been used for worship since its chancel collapsed in 1696. There are several other interesting churches nearby, notably at Eastington and at Hemingborough, where the Church of St Mary has an elegant 190ft spire and what is thought to be the oldest misericord (a hinged wooden choir seat) in Britain. Four miles northwest of Howden are the striking remains of 14th century Wressle Castle and, close to it, a fine old windmill.

Opening Hours: Mon, Tues, Wed 16.00-23.00; Thurs -Sat 11.00-23.00; Sunday 11.00-22.30.

Food: Bar meals.

Credit Cards: Access, Mastercard, Visa, Delta.

Accommodation: None

Facilities: Car Park.

Local Places of Interest/Activities: Selby 11 miles, Hemingborough, Wressle Castle 4 miles.

136 | The White Hart

Westgate,
North Cave,
East Yorkshire
HU15 2NJ
Tel: 01430 422432

Directions:

From the M62 junction 38 take B1230 for about 2 miles. From Beverley take B1230, crossing A1034, about 8 miles.

Chris Wilson and Melissa Payne took over the **White Hart** with their minds set on success, and success is indeed the reward for their labours. The late 19th century building presents a big, bold face to the world, and inside there's a choice between the superbly furnished lounge-dining room and the lovely little public bar with its intimate lighting and cosy alcoves. Everything on the menu is freshly made and most of it is locally sourced, offering a variety of good, wholesome dishes with daily specials adding to the written menu and a good selection of cask ales to wash it all down. Food is served at lunchtime from 12 till 2 and in the evening from 5 until 8 o'clock. On Wednesday and Saturday evenings the place bounces to live music and in summer the scene shifts to the beer garden. The pub has a very large car park.

With the M62 close by, the pub is well placed for easy access to the west, but there are also plenty of attractions and places on interest in the vicinity. The village of South Cave, only a couple of miles away, is officially a town, with its own town hall in the market place. The name is said to be a corruption of South Cove, since the southern end of the parish is set around a backwater of the Humber. The nearby village of Brantingham, just off the A63, has a remarkable war memorial, one described as 'lovingly awful'. Conceived on a monumental scale, it was built using masonry recycled from Hull's old Guildhall when that building was being reconstructed in 1914. In the pretty village of Welton, a little further south, a stream flows past the green, under bridges and into a tree-encircled duck pond. The Norman church is notable for its striking 13th century doorway and Pre-Raphaelite windows made by William Morris' craftsmen.

Opening Hours: 12.00-15.00, 17.00-23.00; Sunday open all day.

Food: Bar meals.

Credit Cards: None

Accommodation: None.

Facilities: Car Park

Entertainment: Live music Wednesday and Saturday.

Local Places of Interest/Activities: Beverley 8 miles, South Cave 2 miles, Brough.

5 West Yorkshire

PLACES OF INTEREST:

PUBS AND INNS:

The Hidden Inns of Yorkshire

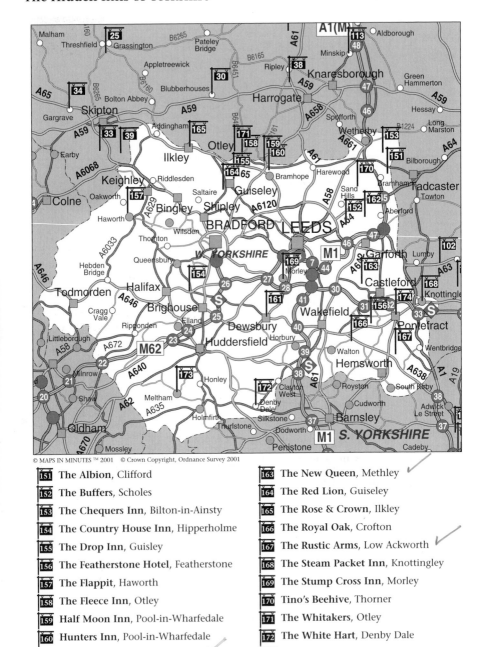

© MAPS IN MINUTES ™ 2001   © Crown Copyright, Ordnance Survey 2001

Please note all references refer to page numbers

West Yorkshire

The area of West Yorkshire surrounding the Brontë family home at Haworth is dominated by the textile towns and villages along the valley bottom and the wild and bleak moorland above. The land has been farmed, mainly with sheep, since the Middle Ages and, in order to supplement their wages, the cottagers took to hand loom-weaving in a room of their homes. The advances in technology, beginning in the 18th century, replaced the single man powered looms with water powered machinery that were housed in the large mill buildings in the valley bottom and close to the source of power.

During the 19th century there was an explosion of building and the quiet riverside villages grew into towns and the South Pennine textile boom was in full flow. At first the conditions in the mills were grim as, indeed, were the living conditions for the mill workers but, with the reduction in the hours of the working day, people were able to take the opportunity to discover, and in some cases rediscover, the beauty of the surrounding moorland.

Not all the villages were completely taken over by the mills and, in many, the old stone built weavers cottages, with their deep windows to let in light for the worker within, survive. This, then, was the landscape of the area to which the Brontë family moved in 1820 when their father, Patrick, took up the position of rector. In the first five years of the family living in Haworth, both Maria Brontë (the mother) and two of the five girls died; the harsh climate having begun to take its toll. Though all the remaining children did receive an education it was in a somewhat haphazard way and they spent much of their time with each other isolated at the parsonage. After various attempts at working, generally as teachers, the girls, and their brother Branwell, all returned to the parsonage in the mid-1840s - this is when their writing began in earnest.

PLACES OF INTEREST

BRADFORD

Bradford is a city with much to offer the visitor. In terms of numbers, the most popular attraction is undoubtedly the **National Museum of Photography, Film and Television** which houses IMAX, one of the largest cinema screens in the world. If you suffer from vertigo you'll need to close your eyes on the huge, wraparound screen shows such heart-stopping scenes as roller-coaster rides and Alpine mountaineering. There's plenty to keep you occupied here for hours, - virtual reality exhibits, the Kodak Gallery which leads you on a journey through the history of popular photography, an extensive television display which ranges from the world's first TV pictures to the very latest, and much, much more.

A recent addition is a vast new space presenting world-class exhibitions on photography, film, television and new media. Of related interest is Britain's only **Museum of Colour**. 'The World of Colour' gallery looks at the concept of colour, how it is perceived and its importance. Visitors can see how the world looks to other animals, mix coloured lights and experience strange colour illusions. In the ``Colour and Textiles'' gallery you can discover the fascinating story of dyeing and textile printing from Ancient Egypt to the present day. Computerised technology allows you to take charge of a dye making factory and decorate a room. While both these museums look to the future, the **Bradford Industrial Museum and Horses at Work** celebrates the city's industrial heritage. It is housed in an original worsted spinning mill complex built in 1875 and recreates life in Bradford in late Victorian times. Open all year, the museum offers horse-bus and tram rides, a Shire Horse centre, a reconstructed mill owner's house and the workingmen's back to back cottages. The complex also includes a café, shop and picnic area.

140

Architecturally, the most striking building in Bradford must be **Lister's Mill**. Its huge ornate chimney dominates the city skyline and its claimed that it is wide enough at the top to drive a horse and cart around. The mill fell silent some years ago though its exterior has been cleared up and there are plans to use to house a museum to the industry that brought the city its wealth - wool. A rather quirkier sign of the city's former riches is **Undercliffe Cemetery**. Here the wool barons were buried, each in a more opulent Gothic mausoleum than the last. It is easy to spend an hour here admiring the Victorian funereal art on show with the cityscape laid out before you. The fact that the city has a **Cathedral** is an indication of its importance. The first evidence of worship on the site is provided by the remains of a Saxon preaching cross. Today the Cathedral contains many items of interest, including beautiful stained glass windows, some of which were designed by William Morris, carvings and statuary.

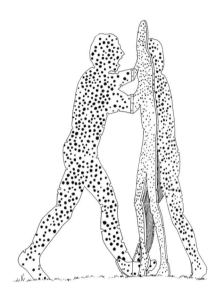

Yorkshire Sculpture Park

CLAYTON WEST

A popular attraction at Clayton West is the **Kirklees Light Railway**, a 15" gauge steam railway which runs along the old Lancashire & Yorkshire Clayton West branch line. The track runs through gently rolling farmland for about 4 miles with a quarter-mile long tunnel adding to the thrill. The large station/visitor centre at Clayton West provides passengers with comfortable, spacious surroundings to await their train or take advantage of the light refreshment café and the souvenir shop. The railway operates daily during the season and every weekend throughout the year. For train times and other information, telephone 01484 865727.

One of the leading attractions of the area is found about 3 miles northeast of Clayton West, conveniently close to Junction 38 of the M1. The **Yorkshire Sculpture Park** draws in some 200,000 visitors a year and since you only pay a small charge for parking it represents amazing value for money. Changing exhibitions of sculpture are set in the beautiful 18th-century parkland of Bretton Hall, 200 acres of historic landscape providing a wonderful setting for some of the best sculpture to be seen in Britain today by artists from around the world. Alongside the programme of indoor and outdoor exhibitions, more permanent features include the

YSP collection of works in many different styles, (from 19th-century bronzes by Rodin to contemporary sculptures), and a display of monumental bronzes by Henry Moore sited within the adjacent 100 acre Bretton Country Park.

DEWSBURY

Dewsbury is an extremely old town which once had considerable influence. It has one of the region's oldest town centres with an imposing Town Hall designed by Henry Ashton and George Fox. It also has a number of other notable public and commercial buildings, a substantial shopping area (with some 443,500 square feet of retail floorspace) and a famous open market.

According to legend, **Dewsbury Minster** is situated at the very spot where, in 627AD, St Paulinus baptised converts to Christianity in the River Calder. The church dates from the 12th century although the tower was erected in 1767 to a design by the eminent York architect, John Carr. The interior has some interesting features, amongst them fragments of an Anglo-Saxon cross and coffin lids. The Minster is perhaps best known for its custom of tolling the "Devil's Knell" on Christmas Eve to ward off evil spirits with a bell known as Black Tom. There are Brontë connections here. Patrick

Brontë was curate of Dewsbury between 1809-11, and Charlotte taught at Wealds House School nearby. The school was run by a Miss Wooler who later gave her away when she was married.

HALIFAX

Halifax boasts one of Yorkshire's most impressive examples of municipal architecture, the glorious 18th-century **Piece Hall**. It possesses a large quadrangle where regular markets are held on Fridays and Saturdays, surrounded by colonnades and balconies behind which are some forty specialist shops. On Thursdays a flea market is held here and there's a lively and varied programme of events for all the family throughout the season. There's also an art gallery with a varied programme of contemporary exhibitions and workshops, a museum and tea room.

The **Town Hall** is another notable building, designed by Sir Charles Barry, architect of the Houses of Parliament, and there's an attractive Borough Market, constructed in cast iron and glass with an ornate central clock. In Gibbet Street stands a grisly reminder of the past - a replica of a guillotine, the original blade being kept in the Piece Hall Museum. There are many hidden places in old Halifax to explore: from Shear's Inn, an old weavers' inn near the town centre, one can walk up the cobbled **Boy's Lane**, very little changed from Victorian times, or trace out the ancient *Magna Via*, a medieval path to the summit of Breacon Hill.

Halifax also boasts the largest parish church in England. Of almost cathedral sized proportions, it dates from the 12th and 13th centuries. It has a lovely wooden ceiling, constructed in 1635, and visitors should look out for *"Old Tristram"*, a life-sized wooden effigy of a beggar, reputedly based on a local character, which served as the church poor box - and still does.

Right next door to Piece Hall, the **Calderdale Industrial Museum** houses still-working looms and mill machinery, hand textile demonstrations and amongst the many displays one celebrating the town's greatest contribution to modern travel, the cat's-eye! From the Great Wheel to the Spinning Jenny, from mining to moquette, from steam engines (in live steam) to toffee, the museum provides a riveting insight into Halifax's industrial heritage.

Situated next to Halifax railway station, **Eureka!** is Britain's first and only interactive museum designed especially for children between 3 and 12 years old. With more than 400 larger than life exhibits and exciting activities available, Eureka! opens up a fascinating world of hands-on exploration. A team of "Enablers" help children make the most of their visit, there are regular temporary exhibitions, and the complex includes a café and gift shop.

Shibden Hall and Park, about a mile out of town, is somewhere very special that should not be missed. The Old Hall itself lies in a valley on the outskirts of the town and is situated in 90 acres of parkland. The distinctive timber framed house dates from 1420 and has been carefully furnished to reflect the various periods of its history. The 17th-century barn behind the Hall houses a fine collection of horse-drawn vehicles and the original buildings have been transformed into a 19th-century village centre with a pub, estate worker's cottage, saddler's, blacksmith's, wheelwright's and potter's workshop.

Also on the outskirts of the town is the **Bankfield Museum**, the home between 1837 and 1886 of Edward Akroyd, the largest wool

Piece Hall, Halifax

manufacturer in Britain. He lavished money and attention on the building, transforming it from a modest town house into a magnificent Italianate mansion with elaborate ceilings, staircases and plasterwork. After his death, his sumptuous home became a museum and now houses an internationally important collection of textiles and costumes from around the world. Contemporary crafts are also featured and the museum hosts an interesting programme of temporary exhibitions, workshops, seminars, master classes and gallery demonstrations.

HAREWOOD

One of the grandest stately homes in the country, **Harewood House** was built at a time when many of the most illustrious names in the history of English architecture, interior decoration, furniture making and landscape gardening were all at the peak of their powers. For the creation of Harewood in the mid-1700s, Edwin Lascelles was able to employ the dazzling talents of Robert Adam, John Carr, Thomas Chippendale and "Capability" Brown.

Edwin's son, Edward, was one of the first to patronise a young artist named JMW Turner, and many of Turner's paintings are still here along with hundreds of other distinguished painters collected by later generations of the family. Many of the finest of them are displayed in a superb Gallery that extends along the whole west end of the house, 76 feet long, 24 feet wide, 21 feet high. Amongst the masterpieces on show are works by Bellini, Titian, Veronese, El Greco and Tintoretto, while family portraits by Reynolds, Hoppner and Gainsborough look down from the silk-covered walls of the opulent drawing rooms.

Along with superb gardens, charming walks,

Harewood House

a Bird Garden which is home to some 120 exotic species, an Adventure Playground, boat trips on the lake, and an extensive events and exhibitions programme, Harewood House is indisputably one of Yorkshire's "must-see" visitor attractions.

HAWORTH

Once a bleak, moorland town in a dramatic setting that fired the romantic imaginations of the Brontë sisters, Haworth has been transformed into a lively, attractive place, with wonderful tea houses, street theatre, and antique and craft shops, very different to how it must have been in the Brontë's days. It was then a thriving industrial town, squalid amid the smoke from its chimneys, filled with the noise of the clattering looms, which were rarely still. It is, however, worth exploring the ginnels and back roads off the steeply rising high street, to get a feeling of what the place was like in the days of the Brontës.

The Parsonage, built in 1777, is the focus of most Brontë pilgrimages and is now given over to the **Brontë Parsonage Museum**. The Brontë Society have restored the interior to be as close as possible to the house in which the sisters lived with their father and brother. There are exhibitions and displays of contemporary material, personal belongings, letters, and portraits, as well as a priceless collection of manuscripts, first editions, and memorabilia in the newer

Brontë Parsonage Museum

extension. The Brontë family moved to the fine Georgian house in 1820 when Patrick Brontë, the sisters' father, became the local parson.

Taking their inspiration from the surrounding bleak and lonely Haworth Moor and from the stories they made up as children the three sisters, Anne, Charlotte, and Emily, under their male pen names, all became published authors whilst Branwell, though by all accounts a scholar, sought refuge in the beer at the local inn. Then the tuberculosis that had attacked the family earlier returned and, one by one, Patrick Brontë's children succumbed to the terrible disease. The story of the Brontë family is one of tragedy but the circumstances of their deaths were all too common in the 19th century and graphically illustrates the harshness of life just 150 years ago.

Many visitors are drawn to the area by the story of the family and the **Brontë Way**, a 40-mile linear footpath with a series of four guided walks, links the places which provided inspiration to the sisters. The most exhilarating and popular excursion is that to **Top Withins**, a favourite place of Emily's and the inspiration for the 'Wuthering Heights' of the novel. The route also takes into account a great variety of scenery, from the wild moorlands to pastoral countryside.

Brontë enthusiasts can also sit in the Black Bull, where Branwell sent himself to an early grave on a mixture of strong Yorkshire ale, opium, and despair (although the last two are not available here these days). The Post Office, from where the sisters sent their manuscripts to London publishers, is still as it was, as is the Sunday School at which they all taught. Sadly the church which they all attended no longer exists, although Charlotte, Emily, and Branwell (Anne is buried in Scarborough) all lie in a vault in the new church which dates from 1879.

As well as devotees of the Brontë legend, Haworth is popular with devotees of steam railways. The town is the headquarters of the **Keighley & Worth Valley Railway**, a thriving volunteer-run railway which serves 6 stations (most of them gas-lit) in the course of its 4¾ mile length. The railway owns an extensive and varied collection of locomotives and everything combines to re-create the atmosphere of the days of steam. There are daily services during July and August and intermittent services throughout the rest of the year. To listen to the talking timetable, telephone 01535 643629.

The countryside around Haworth inspires the modern visitor as much as it did the Brontës. This is excellent walking country and it is worth taking a trip via the Penistone Hill Country Park, following the rough track by old moorland farms to the Brontë Falls and stone footbridge. For the energetic, the path eventually leads to the deserted ruins of Top Withins Farm, said to

have been the inspiration for the setting of *Wuthering Heights*. It is said that the ghost of Emily Brontë has been seen walking, with her head bowed, between the Parsonage and Top Withins Farm.

143

HEBDEN BRIDGE

This mill town is characterised by the stepped formation of its houses which were stacked one on top of the other up the steep sides of the Calder valley. There has been a village here for many years centred around the crossing point of the River Calder. When the first bridge was built is not known but as early as the beginning of the 16th century its state of repair was causing concern and, in a style typical of this area of Yorkshire, a stone bridge was erected close by.

The **Rochdale Canal**, which flows through the town, was completed in 1798. It was constructed to link the Calder and Hebble Navigation with the Bridgwater and Ashton canals from Lancashire. Used by commercial traffic since 1939, the canal has been repaired and sec-

Hebden Bridge

tions of it, including that between Hebden Bridge and Todmorden, are now open to traffic though, now, it consists mainly of pleasure craft. Horse drawn or motor boat cruises are available from the marina.

One of the first purpose built industrial towns in the world, Hebden Bridge grew rapidly as the demand for textiles boomed. Over the years, the town has seen many changes of fortune and, today, though textiles have now gone, it is a place of bookshops, antique shops, restaurants, and a market.

144

HOLMFIRTH

BBC-TV's longest running situation comedy, *Last of the Summer Wine*, has made the little Pennine town of Holmfirth familiar to viewers around the world. Visitors can enjoy an authentic bacon buttie in the real "Sid's Café", gaze at Nora Batty's cottage and sit in the famous pub. The rest of the town offers a network of side lanes, courts and alleyways while the terraces of weavers' cottages are typical of a town famous for its production of wool textiles.

As with so many of these moorland villages, there is a lot of surrounding water and in its time Holmfirth has suffered three major floods. The worse occurred in 1852 when the nearby Bilbury Reservoir burst its banks, destroying mills, cottages and farms, and killing 81 people. A pillar near the church records the height the waters reached. Holmfirth has a lovely Georgian church, built in 1777-8 in neo-classical style to the designs of Joseph Jagger. The gable faces the street and the tower is constructed at the eastern end against a steep hillside.

A popular attraction in the town is the **Holmfirth Postcard Museum** which has a comprehensive collection of the traditional saucy seaside postcard produced by Bamfords of Holmfirth in the first half of the 20th century. The company also produced hymn sheets and, rather surprisingly, many early silent movies. The museum displays also include other vintage postcards, including patriotic cards from the First World War, less sentimental ones from the Second World War, and a moving audio-visual documentary presentation of the 1852 flood.

HONLEY

The centre of this delightful little Pennine village has been designated as a site of historic interest. There are charming terraces of weavers' cottages and lots of interesting alleyways, and the old village stocks still stand in the churchyard of St Mary's. The Coach and Horses Inn has strong connections with the Luddite movement of the early 1800s. It was here, in 1812, that two Luddites, Benjamin Walker and Thomas Smith, spent the night drinking after murdering a mill owner at nearby Marsden. They were later arrested, convicted and executed at York. Not far from the inn is another interesting feature - an old well dated 1796 whose date stone warns passers-by they will be fined 10 shillings (50p) for "defouling" the water.

Located in a beautifully renovated 18th-century house in the centre of the village, the **Lupton Square Gallery** offers the opportunity to view a wide range of original quality works of art in a friendly and informal setting.

HUDDERSFIELD

With its steep, often cobbled streets, millstone grit cottages and larger Victorian dwellings, Huddersfield has a very distinctive character all its own. The town flourished in Victorian times and its most impressive buildings date from that era. The stately railway station was designed by James Pigott of York and built between 1846-50. It was followed by the Italianate Town Hall and culminated in the lofty **Jubilee Tower**, built in 1897 to celebrate Queen Victoria's Diamond Jubilee, which crowns the summit of **Castle Hill** on the outskirts of the town. Inside the tower there's a museum which traces the hill's 4,000 years of history. One thousand feet high, **Castle Hill** has been occupied as a place of defence since Stone Age times. Simple tools, flints, bone needles, combs and pottery dating back to 2000 BC have been unearthed here. The much later ramparts of an Iron Age fort, built here around 600 BC can still be seen. In 1147 the Normans repaired the earthworks and built a motte and

Castle Hill and Jubilee Tower

bailey castle which was apparently used as a base for hunting. The hill was also used as a beacon when England was threatened by the Spanish Armada, and again during the Napoleonic wars.

Back in the town, the **Tolson Memorial Museum** has displays that range from the tools of the earliest settlers in the area to modern day collections contributed by local people. One of the most popular exhibits is the collection of vintage vehicles and motoring memorabilia in the 'Going Places' collection. Other displays trace the story of the Industrial Revolution, so important to the growth of the town, and the political protests it engendered.

ILKLEY

Originally an Iron Age settlement, Ilkley was eventually occupied by the Romans, who built a camp here to protect their crossing of the River Wharfe. They named their town Olicana, so giving rise to the present name with the addition of the familiar ley (Anglo-Saxon for "pasture"). Behind the medieval church is a grassy mound where a little fort was built, and in the town's Museum are altars carved in gritstone, dedicated to the Roman gods. The spring at **White Wells** brought more visitors to the town in the 18th century. A small bath house was built where genteel and elderly patients were encouraged to take a dip in the healing waters. Early Victorian times saw the development of the Hydros - hydropathic treatment hotels - providing hot and cold treatments based on the idea of Dr Preissnitz of Austria who, in 1843, became the director of Britain's first Hydro at nearby Ben Rhydding. The coming of the railways from Leeds and Bradford in the 1860s and 1870s, during a period of growth in the Yorkshire woollen industry, saw the town take on a new rôle as a fashionable commuter town. Wool manufacturers and their better-paid employees came, not only to enjoy the superb amenities, but to build handsome villas. If Bradford and Leeds were where people made their brass, so it was said at the time, then it was usually at Ilkley that it was spent. Even today, Ilkley sports some remarkable and opulent Victorian architecture as proof of this. Ilkley's patrons and well-to-do citizens gave the town a splendid Town Hall, Library, Winter Gardens and King's Hall, and a sense of elegance is still present along The Grove. It is still a delight to have morning coffee in the famous Betty's coffee house, and dis-

cerning shoppers will find a wealth of choice, some in a perfectly preserved Victorian arcade complete with beautiful potted palms and balconies.

One of the most famous West Yorkshire attractions has to be **Ilkley Moor**, immortalised in the well-known song. A visit is a must. Like any of the Yorkshire moors, Ilkley Moor can look inviting and attractive on a sunny day, but ominous and forbidding when the weather takes a turn for the worse. The River Wharfe runs along the edge of the moor and through the town of Ilkley, which is clustered within a narrow section of the valley in the midst of

Ilkley Moor

heather moorland, craggy gritstone and wooded hillside. Few places in the north can equal Ilkley Moor or, more correctly, Rombalds Moor. The moorland, much of it still covered in heather, is also an area of national importance for its archaeology. There is a series of mysteriously marked cup and ring stones dating from the Bronze Age. Almost in the centre of the moor is an ancient stone circle, no doubt a site of some religious importance. Only the keen walker is likely to find these, located high up on the moor, but there is a fine example of a cup and ring stone in the lower part of St Margaret's churchyard in Queen's Road.

Looking at a map of the area, many people's attention is drawn to the curiously named **Cow and Calf Rocks** which form a striking moor-edge landmark above Ben Rhydding. The Cow is a great gritstone outcrop concealing an old quarry, popular with climbers, while the freestanding Calf is a giant boulder.

Some 6 miles further southeast of Ilkley, in the village of Otley, an unusual memorial can be found. It is a stone model of **Bramhope Railway Tunnel** with its impressive crenellated en-

146

trance portals. The original was built in the 1830s on the Leeds-Thirsk railway line, and more than 30 labourers died during its construction - a tragic loss of life which the model commemorates. Another attractive feature of the town is The Chevin Forest Park, a forested ridge above the town which can be reached by a delightful walk that starts alongside the River Wharfe.

KEIGHLEY

Lying at the junction of the Rivers Worth and Aire, this bustling textile and engineering town, despite its modern redevelopment, still retains a strangely nostalgic air of the Victorian Industrial Revolution. It was that era of rapid growth that created the town seen today, beginning at Low Mill in 1780, when cotton spinning on a factory scale was first introduced. Reminders of hardship endured by the many factory workers of that time can be seen in the labyrinth of ginnels and terraces which lie amid the many elaborately decorated mills. There are delightful carvings, and on one early mill chimney are three heads, one wearing a top hat; in contrast is the classical French-styled **Dalton Mill** in Dalton Lane with its ornate viewing gallery.

The centre of Keighley is dominated by impressive Victorian civic buildings and a beautifully set out covered shopping precinct, where the statue of legendary local giant, Rombald, stands. The parish church, also in the centre, is famous as the site where Patrick Brontë often officiated at marriages. The graveyard contains 15th century headstones, as well as a crude cross made from four carved heads which is believed to be Saxon in origin. Above the town, by way of escaping the industrial past, one might enjoy a walk in Park Woods, taking the cobbled path to Thwaites Brow, which affords magnificent views of the town below.

Outside the town centre is **Cliffe Castle** which, despite its deceptive name, is in fact a grand late-19th century mansion complete with a tower, battlements and parkland, which once belonged to local mill owners, the Butterfields. It now houses **Keighley Museum**, which concentrates on the fascinating local topography and geology of Airedale as well as the history of the town. Also housed in the museum is the hand loom, complete with unfinished cloth, that was used by Timmy Feather, the last handloom weaver in England. Part of the building is still furnished and decorated in the lavish style of the 1880s.

LEEDS

In recent years, the city of Leeds has seen something of a renaissance. Its waterfront, neglected and derelict for so long, is now buzzing with new developments. Abandoned warehouses have been imaginatively transformed into fashionable bars, restaurants and tourist attractions, all less than 15 minutes walk from the shopping centre. Debenhams has recently opened a new flagship store in the heart of the city and other high profile stores are also flocking to the city. Perhaps the most talked about store is Harvey Nichols, whose Knightsbridge emporium enjoyed a heightened reputation in the 1990s thanks to the BBC series *Absolutely Fabulous*. In parallel with these developments Aire and Calder Navigation, which is set to celebrate its 300th birthday, is being transformed to enable leisure traffic to use the waterway as well as freight.

The city is also a major European cultural centre with its own opera and ballet companies, Northern Ballet Theatre and Opera North, while the West Yorkshire Playhouse, regarded as the "National Theatre of the North", is a showcase for classic British and European drama as well as work by new Yorkshire writers. The Leeds International Film Festival, held every October since 1986, has provided major world premieres for films such as *Brassed Off*. The city also boasts some outstanding galleries and museums. Located right next to the monumental City Hall, the **Leeds City Art Gallery** boasts an exceptional collection of Victorian and French Post-Impressionist paintings along with major works by Courbet, Lowry, Sickert, Stanley Spencer and Bridget Riley. Linked to the gallery is the Henry Moore Institute, the first centre in Europe devoted to the display and study of sculpture of all periods. There's also a Craft & Design shop selling cards, jewellery and pottery, and an art library.

The **Thackray Medical Museum**, one of the largest museums of its kind in Europe, possesses more than 25,000 extraordinary objects in its collection. They range from a surgical chainsaw and Prince Albert's Medical Chest through to a 17th-century Correction Frame. Visitors can listen in to the thoughts and feelings of a surgeon, his assistants and Hannah Dyson, an 11-year-old girl whose leg has been crushed in a factory accident, as they prepare for the amputation of Hannah's leg. Or you might prefer to walk through a giant gut in Bodyworks and find out exactly why your tummy rumbles.

Opened by the Queen in 1998, the **Royal Armouries** traces the development of arms and armour from the 5th century BC to modern times. The museum utilises interactive computer displays, videos, films, music and poetry to tell the story of arms and armour in battle, self-defence, sport and fashion. Outside, the Tiltyard features jousting and hunting tournaments daily from April to September, while a bustling Menagerie Court includes displays of falcons, hunting dogs and horses.

Lovers of real ale may well want to take advantage of a joint ticket which gives admission to both the Royal Armouries and **Tetley's Brewery Wharf**. Here you can learn how Joshua Tetley founded his great empire and learn the secret of his famous brew. Costumed actors depict how the English pub has played an important part in British life throughout the centuries and the centre also includes traditional pub games, working Shire horses, a shop and café.

To the northwest of the city, **Kirkstall Abbey** is one of the most complete ruins in this part of Yorkshire. Building started in 1152 by the Cistercians and was completed within a generation, so Kirkstall is regarded by many as representing Cistercian architecture at its most monumental. It was executed with the typical early Cistercian austerity as can be seen in the simplicity of the outer domestic buildings. The bell tower, a 16th century addition, was in contravention of the rule of the Order that there were to be no stone bell towers as they were considered an unnecessary vanity.

A few miles north of Leeds city centre is one of the UK's most popular garden tourist attractions and home to the largest collection of tropical plants outside Kew Gardens - **Tropical World**. Visitors can follow the "Tropical Trail" into the Amazon rain forest, for example, where waterfalls tumble into jungle pools and birds of every hue fly through the trees. There's also a "Desert World" and a Nocturnal House where fruit bats, monkeys, bush babies and rock cavies reside - animals that can normally only be seen during twilight hours.

About 8 miles to the northeast, **Bramham Park** is one of Yorkshire's most exquisite country houses and is special for a number of reasons. The house itself dates from the Queen

Anne era, built by Robert Benson, Lord Bingley, between 1698 and 1710, and superbly proportioned in an elegant and restrained classical style. The final effect is more French than English and indeed the gardens were modelled on Louis XIV's Versailles, with ornamental canals and ponds, beech groves, statues, long avenues and a superb arboretum with a collection of rare and unusual trees. The interior contains elegant furniture and paintings by artists such as Kneller and Sir Joshua Reynolds.

A couple of miles southwest of the city is **Temple Newsam House**, known as the Hampton Court of the North. Set in 1200 acres of parkland (entry to which is free), this Tudor-Jacobean gem boasts extensive collections of decorative arts displayed in their original room settings. Among them is one of the largest collections of Chippendale furniture in the country. Adjacent to Temple Newsam House is the country's largest approved Rare Breeds Centre - **Home Farm**. Visitors to this working farm will see pigs, goats, horses and poultry alongside interesting displays of vintage farm machinery and past farming methods.

OAKWORTH

Those visiting Oakworth may find its Edwardian station, on the Keighley and Worth Valley Railway line, somewhat familiar. In fact, not only did it feature in the classic children's film, *The Railway Children*, but also in episodes of the television series *Sherlock Holmes*. There are some delightful walks to be had in the area, one of which takes in places used in the classic film between Oakworth and Haworth.

PONTEFRACT

Shakespeare alluded to the town in his plays as "Pomfret" - a place of influence and power, often visited by kings and their retinues. The great shattered towers of **Pontefract Castle** stand on a crag to the east of the town. Built by Ilbert de Lacy in the 11th century it was one of the most formidable fortresses in Norman England. In medieval times it passed to the House of Lancaster and became a Royal Castle. Richard II was imprisoned here and tragically murdered in its dungeons on the orders of Henry Bolingbroke who then assumed the crown as Henry IV.

The castle was a major Royalist stronghold during the Civil War, after which it was de-

148

stroyed by Cromwell's troops. Today it remains as a gaunt ruin with only sections of the inner bailey and the lower part of the keep surviving intact. There is an underground chamber, part of the dungeons where prisoners carved their names so that they might not be utterly forgotten. Perhaps the unfortunate Richard II may have been incarcerated in this very chamber.

Many of the streets of Pontefract evoke memories of its medieval past with names such as Micklegate, Beast Fair, Shoe Market, Salter Row and Ropergate. Modern development has masked much of old Pontefract but there are still many old Georgian buildings and winding streets.

The town's most famous products, of course, are Pontefract Cakes. Liquorice root has been grown here since monastic times and there's even a small planting of liquorice in the local park. The town celebrates this unique heritage with the 5-day **Pontefract Liquorice Fayre** in mid-August which includes two days of jousting, archery and battle re-enactments at Pontefract Castle.

RIDDLESDEN

Parts of **East Riddlesden Hall**, now a National Trust property, date back to Saxon times. The main building, however, was constructed in the 1630s by James Murgatroyd, a wealthy Halifax clothier and merchant. A fine example of a 17th century manor house, the gabled hall is built of dark stone with mullioned windows, and it retains its original centre hall, superb period fireplaces, oak panelling, and plaster ceilings. The house is furnished in Jacobean style, which is complemented by carved likenesses of Charles Stuart and Henrietta Maria. East Riddlesden Hall also has one of the largest and most impressive timber framed barns in the North of England, and now houses a collection of farm waggons and agricultural equipment.

SALTAIRE

Saltaire is the model village created by Titus Salt for the workers at his mill. Salt was a very benevolent employer and determined to provide his workers with everything essential for a decent standard of living. Built between 1851 and 1876, the facilities in the village were designed to cater for all their needs - health, leisure and education, but there were no public

houses. The spiritual needs of the work force were attended to by the elegant Congregational church which has been described as the most beautiful Free Church in the north of England. A statue of Titus Salt stands in nearby Robert's Park (where swearing and gambling were banned) above the figures of a llama and an alpaca whose wool he imported for spinning in his mills.

The **Victoria Boat House** was built in 1871 and has been beautifully restored, with an open fire, pianola and wind-up gramophone, all recreating a traditional parlour atmosphere where you can enjoy cream teas and attend special Victorian Evenings in the dress of that time. Also in Saltaire is the **Museum of Victorian Reed Organs** which has a collection of more than 45 instruments, including harmonicas and an American organ, which are demonstrated from time to time, and some of which are available for visitors to try. Saltaire isn't completely locked in the past. The former Salt's Mill has been converted into the **1853 David Hockney Gallery** which displays the world's largest collection of paintings by the internationally acclaimed artist who was born in Bradford in 1937.

THORNTON

Thornton is an essential stopping place on the Brontë trail for it was here that the three sisters were born, at No. 74 Market Street, now open to the public as the **Brontë Birthplace**. Their father was the vicar of Thornton and one of the treasures of his parish church is a font, inscribed with the date 1687, in which Charlotte, Emily and Anne were all baptised. Charlotte was only 4 years old, her two sisters still toddlers, when the family moved a few miles northwest to Haworth where their father had been appointed Rector.

TODMORDEN

This is another typical mill town that grew with the expansion of the textile industry. Before the 19th century, Todmorden had been a spartan place with many of the villagers eking out frugal lives by hand loom-weaving. Following the building of the first mill here Todmorden began to grow and the highly ornate and flamboyant public buildings were, in the main, built by the mill owners. Though many towns which owe their existence to industry also bear the scars, Todmorden has retained all its charm and

Todmorden Town Hall

character and is an excellent place to visit for those interested in architecture. It boasts a magnificent **Town Hall** designed by John Gibson and opened in 1875. One of the finest municipal buildings of its size in the country, the grand old building stands half in Yorkshire and half in Lancashire. So the ornate carving in the pediment represents the farming and iron trades of Yorkshire in the right panel; the cotton trade of Lancashire in the left.

WAKEFIELD

One of the oldest towns in Yorkshire, Wakefield stands on a hill guarding an important crossing of the River Calder. Its defensive position has always been important and it was the Battle of Wakefield in 1460, when the Duke of York was defeated, that gave rise to the mocking song *The Grand Old Duke of York*.

Many students of the Robin Hood legends claim that the famous outlaw had his origins in Wakefield. As evidence they cite the Court Rolls in which one "Robin Hode" is noted as living here in the 14th century with his wife Matilda before fleeing to the woods of Sherwood Forest. Also medieval in origin are the Wakefield Miracle Plays which explore Old and New Testament stories in vivid language. The 600-year-old cycle is performed in the Cathedral precincts as part of the city's annual Festival.

There are four main streets in the city: Westgate, Northgate, Warrengate and Kirkgate, which still preserve the medieval city plan. One of the most striking surviving buildings of that time is the tiny Chantry Chapel on Chantry Bridge which dates from the mid-1300s and is the best of only four such examples of bridge

chapels in England. It is believed to have been built by Edward IV to commemorate the brutal murder of his brother Edmund. Grandest of all though is **Wakefield Cathedral** which was begun in Norman times, rebuilt in 1329 and refashioned in 1470 when its magnificent 247-foot high spire - the highest in Yorkshire - was added. The eastern extension is a 20th-century addition, considered necessary after the church became a Cathedral in 1888. Other interesting buildings in the town include the stately Town Hall, the huge County Hall, the recently restored Edwardian Theatre Royal and many fine Georgian and Regency terraces and squares.

Wakefield's cultural attractions include **Wakefield Art Gallery**, housed in an attractive former Victorian vicarage just a short stroll from the town centre. Collections include many early works by locally born sculptors Henry Moore and Barbara Hepworth along with important work by many other major British modern artists. **Wakefield Museum**, located in an 1820s building next to the Town Hall, was originally a music saloon and then a Mechanics' Institute. It now houses collections illustrating the history and archaeology of Wakefield and its people from prehistoric times to the present day. There is also a permanent display of exotic birds and animals garnered by the noted 19th-century traveller, naturalist and eccentric Charles Waterton who lived at nearby Walton Hall where he created the world's first nature reserve. Also of interest are the **Stephen G Beaumont Museum** which houses an unusual exhibition of medical memorabilia and the **National Coal Mining Museum** at Caphouse Colliery in Overton, a few miles southwest of Wakefield. A visit here includes a guided tour 450 feet underground, indoor exhibitions and videos, out-

Nostell Priory, nr Wakefield

150

door machine displays and some friendly pit ponies.

Over to the southeast from Wakefield, **Nostell Priory** is one of the most popular tourist venues in this area. The word "priory" is misleading, since it evokes the picture of an ecclesiastical structure. But Nostell is in fact a large Palladian building erected on the site of an old Augustinian priory. It was in 1733 that the owner, Sir Rowland Winn, commissioned James Paine to build a grand mansion here. Paine was only 19 at the time and this was his first major project. Thirty years later, only half the state rooms were constructed and Sir Rowland's son, also named Rowland, engaged an up and com-

ing young designer to complete the decoration. The young man's name was Robert Adam and between 1766 and 1776 his dazzling designs produced an incomparable sequence of interiors.

There was a third man of genius involved in the story of Nostell Priory - the cabinet maker Thomas Chippendale. What is believed to be his "apprentice piece", made around 1735, is on display here - an extraordinary Doll's House 6 feet high and replete with the most elaborate detail, every minuscule door, window or desk drawer functioning perfectly. Today, Nostell Priory can boast the most comprehensive collection in the world of Chippendale's work.

The Albion

Chapel Lane,
Clifford,
Nr. Wetherby,
North Yorkshire
LS23 6HU
Tel: 01937 842093

Directions:

From Tadcaster
A659 for about 3
miles west, turn left
on to minor road
signposted Clifford.
From Wetherby A1
south, left on to
A659, 2nd right to
Clifford.

Gerald Bastow and his bride-to-be Amanda put heart and soul into running **The Albion**, situated on an elevated site in the village. Totally refurbished inside and out, the whole place is neat, homely and inviting, and a keen eye for design and good taste is evident in the roomy lounge. Good wholesome fare, with traditional Yorkshire dishes, is served from 12 till 2 Monday to Saturday and from 12 till 4 on Sunday. The popular Sunday lunch menu proposes a choice of half a dozen main courses, typified by roast beef and Yorkshire pudding, farmhouse gammon, vegetarian options and a special such as salmon steak served with a white wine and coriander sauce. Pool, darts, dominoes and chess all have their aficionados in the tap room, and all-comers are welcome for the Sunday night quiz.

Clifford is a village of stone cottages, with a Roman Catholic church built in Romanesque style in 1845 and dedicated to St Edward the Confessor. The Ebor Way passes close by, providing excellent walking in attractive countryside. There are pleasant walks, too, in and around Boston Spa, which still has some handsome Georgian houses from its heyday as a spa resort. The most notable of the grand houses in the region is Bramham Park, one of Yorkshire's most exquisite country houses. The nearest towns, each only minutes away from the Albion, are Wetherby and Tadcaster. The former, once an important stop on the London-Edinburgh coaching run, has retained much of its old-world charm and also offers excellent sport at its National Hunt racecourse. Tadcaster started life as a centre for the mining of limestone but as early as the 14th century brewing became the major industry. John Smith, Samuel Smith and Bass Charrington's Tower Brewery are all based in Tadcaster, and all can be visited with prior booking.

Opening Hours: 12.00-23.00.

Food: Traditional home made fayre

Credit Cards: None

Accommodation: None.

Facilities: Car Park.

Entertainment: Quiz Sunday.

Local Places of Interest/Activities: Tadcaster 5 miles, Wetherby 6 miles.

152 The Buffers

Rakehill Road, Scholes,
Leeds, Yorkshire LS15 4AL
Tel: 0113 273 2455

Directions:
A64 from Leeds, turn right on to minor
road signed Scholes.

One look at the building is enough to tell visitors that this was a railway station. The railway got the chop many years ago, but the memories are still there, and one part of the open-plan bar is adorned with railway memorabilia. Robert and Rachel Varley have been the leaseholders at **The Buffers** for the last two years, and their pub has a very good atmosphere and a welcome for all ages. Their chef Neil Winter prepares an across-the-board selection of dishes served lunchtime and evening Tuesday to Thursday, from noon till 8 o'clock on Friday and Saturday and from noon till 6 o'clock on Sunday. There are seats for about 40, and it's best to book before making tracks for Sunday lunch. Two real ales are always available, and the Mansfield brews are particularly popular. Sky Sports, pool, table football and gaming machines keep the sporty locals busy, and on Friday they get their voices in trim for the weekly karaoke session. On Saturday nights there's live entertainment and a disco. Picnic tables are set out on a patio lawn and the children's play area is where the railway line used to run. The pub has a large car park.

On the map, Scholes seems to be in the shadow Leeds. It very nearly is (less than three miles away) but the setting is pleasantly rural. A little way to the northeast, reached along the A64, Bramham Park is an exquisite country house with gardens modelled on Louis XIV's Versailles. Inside the house are elegant furnishings and fine paintings by masters such as Kneller and Reynolds. On the A63, on the southern edge of Leeds, Temple Newsam House is a Tudor-Jacobean gem set in 1,200 acres of parkland and home to one of the largest collections of Chippendale furniture in the country.

Opening Hours: 12.00-15.00, 17.00-23.00; open all day Friday, Saturday and Sunday.

Food: Bar meals.

Credit Cards: Access, Mastercard, Visa.

Accommodation: None.

Facilities: Car Park.

Entertainment: Karaoke Friday, disco and live music Saturday.

Local Places of Interest/Activities: Leeds 3 miles, Bramham Park 7 miles, Tadcaster 10 miles, Wetherby 12 miles.

The Chequers Inn

Bilton-in-Ainsty,
Nr. Wetherby,
North Yorkshire
YO26 7NN
Tel: 01423 359066

Directions:

From Wetherby take the B1224; after about 5 miles turn right on to minor road that ends at Bilton.

The Chequers Inn, a pub of real character in a pretty little village a few miles out of Wetherby on the road to York, is run by Jane Richardson and her staff. Spotlessly kept, and with every effort made to keep the charm of its 19th century coaching days, the Chequers Inn attracts locals from the surrounding villages as well as townies from Wetherby and York with its warm, relaxed ambience and excellent home cooking. Everything is made on the premises, from light bar snacks to full meals. All the meat is produced locally, but the menu tours the world for inspiration: Monday night is curry night. It's very pleasant to spend an hour or two with the regulars or to pass the evening over a leisurely meal, but with the delights of the countryside all around and the major centres of Wetherby and York an easy drive away, the Chequers is also a good place for a stay overnight. There are three lettings bedrooms - two doubles and a twin - with showers and basins, tv and tea/coffee-making kit. So you can drink here, eat here and sleep here - but you can also shop here! The bar and restaurant are filled with enough interesting objects and bric-a-brac to fill a small shop, and it's all for sale.

The next village along the York road is Long Marston, where in 1644 the Battle of Marston Moor was fought. The night before the battle, the soon-to-be-victorious Oliver Cromwell and his battle chiefs stayed at Long Marston Hall, and the room they occupied is still called the Cromwell Room. South of Bilton (two miles as the crow flies but rather further if he follows the country lanes) is the village of Healaugh, known principally for its 12th century Church of St Helen and St John. It bears a bullet scar reputedly made by a Cromwellian trooper on his way to Marston Moor.

Opening Hours: 12.00-14.30, 18.00-23.00; Sunday 12.00-15.00, 19.00-22.30: closed lunchtime Monday (except Bank Holidays)

Food: Bar meals and à la carte.

Credit Cards: Access, Mastercard, Visa.

Accommodation: 3 rooms.

Facilities: Beer Garden

Entertainment: Quiz nights

Local Places of Interest/Activities: York 10 miles, Wetherby 5 miles, Marston Moor, Tadcaster 10 miles.

154 The Country House Inn

Halifax Road, Hipperholme,
West Yorkshire HX3 8HQ
Tel: 01422 202232

Directions:

Hipperholme lies between Halifax (5 miles) and Bradford (6 miles) on the A58/A644

A fine old stone building standing prominently on the Halifax side of Hipperholme. **The Country House**, which dates from the last part of the 19th century, has a friendly, hardworking owner in Julian Saidy, who gives the impression that he could almost run the place single-handed! The interior of the inn is a pleasing blend of old and new, with priority clearly given to making visitors comfortable and relaxed the moment they walk through the door. In the beautiful 30-cover conservatory restaurant the day starts with breakfast at 8 o'clock. The main menu, served from noon to 8pm Monday to Saturday, covers a selection of classic pub favourites such as chilli, battered scampi, steaks and giant Yorkshire puddings filled with Cumberland sausage or roast beef and gravy. Vegetarians are not forgotten, and their main course choice could include cheese and broccoli bake or chargrilled vegetables with penne pasta. Sunday lunch, served from 1 till 6, offers a choice of starter and dessert framing roast beef or roast chicken with generous vegetables and Yorkshire pudding with gravy. Wines from California are an excellent accompaniment. Pool is played in the bar, summer is enjoyed in the beer garden and three nights a week (at least) are pencilled in for entertainment at this most sociable of pubs - quiz on Tuesday, karaoke on Friday, disco on Saturday and live music from time to time.

Halifax, a short distance to the west, has much for the visitor to see, including the marvellous 18th century Piece Hall, a notable town hall designed by Sir Charles Barry, architect of the Houses of Parliament, museums of industry and textiles, and the splendid Shibden Hall, a distinctive 15th century timber-framed house whose grounds include a collection of horse-drawn vehicles and a recreation of 19th century village life.

Opening Hours: Mon-Sat, 12.00-23.00; Sun 12.00-22.30

Food: Breakfast bookings taken, bar meals; Tue-Thu, 16.00-20.00; Fri-Sat, 12.00-20.00; Sun, 12.00-18.00

Credit Cards: All the major cards.

Accommodation: None.

Facilities: Car Park.

Entertainment: Quiz Tuesday, karaoke Friday, disco Saturday.

Local Places of Interest/Activities: Halifax 5 miles, Bradford 6 miles.

The Drop Inn | 155

29 Town Street,
Guiseley,
Yorkshire
LS20 9DT
Tel: 01943 874967

Directions:

Guiseley is 5 miles
north of Bradford
on the A658/A65

Drop in any lunchtime or any evening to enjoy the hospitality and cheerful ambience of this town-centre pub run for the last three years by John and Gaynor Blair. Behind the distinctive 1960s facade with its stone walls and steeply raked tiled roof, **The Drop Inn** has a warm, inviting atmosphere, and the decor and furnishings in the lounge and public bar are of high quality. John is a chef by trade, and a great choice of dishes is served here every lunchtime and early evening (5-7) Monday to Friday. A specials board supplements the printed menu, and the fine food is complemented by an excellent selection of brews, including the full Tetley range and Red 'C' Taunton cider. Fish dishes are something of a speciality, and on Tuesday and Thursday there's a bargain menu for pensioners. Booking is advisable at the weekend. Darts and pinball machine in the bar; small patio garden; plenty of off-road parking space.

The village of Guiseley is equally well placed for town and country, with the Moors and Dales beckoning all around and the metropolitan areas of Shipley, Bradford and Leeds a short distance to the south. Ilkley Moor is one of the leading local attractions, and close to it is a distinguished 17th century manor house that is well worth a visit: East Riddlesden Hall, in a lovely Aire Valley setting, contains a fine collection of textiles, furniture and pewter and has a magnificent garden. From Guiseley it is on the way to Keighley, a town where modern development rubs shoulders with grand Victorian buildings from the days of industrial prosperity.

Opening Hours: Mon-Sat 11.30-23.00; Sun 12.00-22.30

Food: Bar meals.

Credit Cards: None

Accommodation: None.

Facilities: Car Park.

Entertainment: None.

Local Places of Interest/Activities: Bradford 5 miles, Otley, Ilkley, Keighley.

156   The Featherstone Hotel

Station Lane,
Featherstone,
Nr. Pontefract,
West Yorkshire
WF7 6EW
Tel: 01977 791851

Directions:

From Pontefract
A645 2 miles; from
Wakefield A638
than A645; from
M62 junction 31,
take B6134 then
B6428.

A large and handsome late- Victorian building, impressive both externally and within, easily accessible from Pontefract, Wakefield or the M62 (j31 or 32). The lounge has an inviting period look, its panelled bar front emblazoned with coats of arms. In the main bar the feeling is more contemporary, and there's entertainment aplenty in the shape of a pool table, bar football and a juke box with records to stir middle-aged memories.

The present leaseholders - only the twelfth since the hotel opened its doors in 1894 - are Peter and Sue Green, who have been here since 1985. Their hostelry is popular with both local customers and visitors to the area, the former for the excellent beer and food, the latter for these and for the comfortable overnight accommodation on offer. Food is served lunchtime and evening, and the regular printed menu is supplemented by a long list of home-cooked daily specials that run from chicken to gammon, egg & chips, chilli, rump steak and roast beef with Yorkshire pudding. Sunday lunch is particularly popular, and children are welcome for all meals - they even have their own menu, and there's a special budget menu for OAPs.

The locals have to get their brains into gear three times a week, for the quizzes that the pub hosts every Thursday, Friday and Sunday. The accommodation comprises nine rooms of various sizes, some under the eaves, all with en suite facilities.

Opening Hours: Mon-Sat 11.30-23.00; Sun 11.30-22.30

Food: Bar meals.

Credit Cards: None.

Accommodation: 9 en suite rooms.

Facilities: Car Park. Beer Garden

Entertainment: Quiz nights Thursday and Sunday.

Local Places of Interest/Activities: Pontefract 2 miles, Wakefield 7 miles.

The Flappit
157

Flappit Springs,
Haworth,
West Yorkshire
BD21 5PU
Tel/Fax:
01535 643117

Directions:

12 miles north of
Halifax
signposted off
the A639.

Wayne Lerigo is the hands-on owner of **The Flappit**, a grand old roadside in with a history going back to the 17th century. Behind the sturdy stone facade the interior is smart and inviting, with cosy areas for enjoying a pint and a chat and a spacious section for settling down to a meal. Food is very important here, and the menus offer a quite amazing variety of dishes, with special steak days, fish days and a splendid carvery on Sunday. To accompany the food, or just to quench a thirst, there's an equally generous choice of cask ales and lagers. At the back of the pub is a delightful beer garden that's a great asset when the sun shines. The pub has no accommodation, but an adjacent caravan site has pitches for tourers and motor caravans. The Flappit is the only pub in the county with this unusual name, which goes back to the days when there was a flay pit where animal hides would be prepared for the tannery.

Haworth is known throughout the world for the Brontë connection. Once a bleak, moorland town in a romantic setting that inspired the sisters, it is now a lively, attractive place as well and, of course, the destination of Brontë pilgrims from the four corners of the earth. Their home, the Parsonage, built in 1777, is now a museum, with exhibitions and displays of period material, personal belongings, letters and manuscripts. The Brontë Way, a 40-mile footpath with a series of guided walks, links many of the places which provided inspiration for the sisters; one of the marked paths leads to the deserted ruins of Top Withins Farm, said to have been the inspiration for the setting of *Wuthering Heights*. A vigorous walk through scenery that includes pastoral countryside and wild moorland will build up a thirst and an appetite, and there's no better place to deal with both than Wayne Lerigo's Flappit.

Opening Hours: 12.00-15.30, 18.00-23.00; Friday & Saturday 11.00-23.00, Sunday 11.00-22.30.

Food: Bar meals and à la carte.

Credit Cards: Access, Mastercard, Visa.

Accommodation: Caravan site.

Facilities: Car Park.

Entertainment: Quiz night Monday.

Local Places of Interest/Activities: Haworth (the Brontë experience; HQ of the Keighley & Worth Valley steam railway), Keighley 4 miles.

158 The Fleece Inn

Westgate,
Otley,
West Yorkshire
LS21 3DT
Tel: 01943 462636

Directions:
Otley lies 8 miles
north of Shipley
A6038/A65/A659;
10 miles southwest
of Harrogate on
the A659.

Five minutes walk from the centre of Otley, the **Fleece Inn** dates back to the coaching days of the 18th century. Behind a sturdy stone facade brightened by hanging baskets and window boxes, the inn has a cosy, inviting feel and a good deal of individual character. A central fire with an ornate tiled surround warms the main lounge, and the other ground-floor public rooms comprise a quarry-tiled tap room filled with interesting objects and memorabilia, and a games room with a pool table. Darts, dominoes and board games are also available, and the weekly quiz starts at 10pm on Monday.

David and Sandra have been the leaseholders for 15 years, dispensing hospitality to their regulars and to Otley's many visitors. Sandra does the cooking, providing a good choice at lunchtime and pizzas in the evening (also supper for residents). The overnight accommodation, open all year except the Christmas/New Year period, consists of four upstairs rooms - a double, two twins and a family room - that share bathroom facilities. Families are catered for at lunchtime at the Fleece, and there's a beer garden at the rear, which has a small resident population of goats and pot-bellied pigs. The garden leads down to the River Wharfe, with a fence making it secure for children - and animals.

Otley is part of Leeds Metropolitan District bat has managed to retain much of its individual appeal of earlier days, with a busy cobbled market place and alleyways and courtyards to discover. Its most famous son is Thomas Chippendale, the great furniture maker, who was born here in 1718.

Opening Hours: Mon-Thur 11.30-15.00 and 17.30-23.00; Fri-Sat 11.30-23.00; Sun 12.00-22.30

Food: Bar lunches, pizza suppers.

Credit Cards: None.

Accommodation: 4 rooms with shared facilities.

Entertainment: Quiz night Monday.

Local Places of Interest/Activities: Ilkley 6 miles, Skipton 14 miles, Bradford 8 miles, Harewood House, Leeds 14 miles , Harrogate

Half Moon Inn

Main Street,
Pool-in-Wharfedale,
Yorkshire LS21 1LH
Tel: 0113 284 2878
Fax: 0113 203 7895

Directions:

From Otley 2 miles east on the A659; from Bradford 8 miles north on the A658; from Harrogate 10 miles south on the A61/A658.

This grand old inn dating back to the late 17th century is the first venture into the licensed trade for congenial hosts Jim and Vicki Irvine. Known locally as Minnie's, the **Half Moon Inn** was changed into a temperance hotel by a local vicar at one stage, but reverted to its original role in the 1950s. Inside, the scene is pleasantly traditional, with solid stone walls, a roaring fire, copper-topped tables and an assortment of prints and pictures, framed cigarette cards and gleaming brass ornaments on the walls. It's a convivial, atmospheric setting for enjoying a glass or two of real ale and something to eat - Vicki is the cook, and her printed menu, along with the specials board, offers a good choice of dishes that combine generous servings with excellent value for money. Food is served, either in the bar or in the little non-smoking dining room, every session except Wednesday lunchtime and Sunday evening. With equally access to the countryside and several major towns and cities, the Half Moon is an excellent place to stay for both tourists and business people. The five upstairs rooms all have en suite facilities, and a hearty breakfast gets the day off to a good start. Sunday and Monday nights are written in many local diaries as the days when the pub holds its live music nights (bring along your voice) and quiz night (bring along your brain). The pub has a small car park at the back. The nearest town is Otley, which though part of the Leeds Metropolis has retained a distinctive period character, with a maypole standing in the busy cobbled market place and lots of alleyways and courtyards to explore. Harewood House, one of Yorkshire's top attractions, is only a few minutes drive along the A659. This is one of the grandest country homes in Britain, combining the talents of Robert Adam, Thomas Chippendale (a native of Otley) and the ubiquitous landscaper Capability Brown. The house is a treasury of paintings by such masters as Bellini, Titian, Veronese, Reynolds, Gainsborough and Turner.

Opening Hours: 11.00-15.30 and 17.30-23.00.Closed Wednesday lunchtime. Open all day Sunday

Food: A la carte and bar meals.

Credit Cards: Access, Diners, Mastercard, Visa.

Accommodation: 5 en suite rooms.

Facilities: Car Park.

Entertainment: Live music Sunday night, quiz Monday night.

Local Places of Interest/Activities: Otley 2 miles, Leeds 5 miles, Bradford 5 miles, Ilkley Moor.

160 Hunters Inn

Harrogate Road,
Pool-in-Wharfedale,
Yorkshire
LS21 2PS
Tel: 0113 284 1090

Directions:

From Harrogate 7
miles south A61
then A658, from
Otley 3 miles east on
the A659, from
Bradford 8 miles
north on the A658.

Set back from the Harrogate road just outside Pool, **Hunters Inn** is a long, low building with excellent well maintained patio and hanging baskets and a row of coloured lights along the veranda. Cheerful and inviting from the outside, it is equally agreeable inside, where tasteful stone and timber are used predominately throughout, including the bar and fire surround. David Hamby, manager here for five years, has established the inn as one of *the* places in the area for real ales. Nine cask-conditioned brews are always available from breweries all over the country, as well as a good traditional 'real cider'. The choice is excellent!

Ruth is the leading force in the kitchen, producing wholesome, hearty dishes, often with a local flavour, on a varied lunchtime menu. Tuesday's pie and peas is a surefire winner, and other choices at the head of the favourites list include Cumberland sausages, steaks and giant Yorkshire puddings with a variety of fillings. The pub has ample off-road parking space. Pool-in-Wharfedale is well sited for access to the lovely Yorkshire countryside and also to the big cities and smaller towns.

Otley, only three miles away, is a pleasant place to explore, and there are grand houses at Harewood, east of Pool, and Riddlesden. 17th century East Riddlesden Hall, now a National Trust property, stands in the Aire Valley a little way south of one of the county's most celebrated attractions. Ilkley Moor, immortalised in the song, is a place of scenic beauty and archaeological importance, with many Bronze Age relics. It can be very wild and breezy in winter, so don't go baht 'at!

Opening Hours: Mon-Sat 11.00-23.00; Sun 12.00-22.30

Food: Bar meals 12.00-14.30 (except Tues)

Credit Cards: None.

Accommodation: None.

Facilities: Car Park, wheelchair access

Entertainment: Juke box, pool table

Local Places of Interest: Otley 3 miles, Leeds 8 miles, Bradford 8 miles, Harewood House, Ilkley Moor. Excellent bus service: Otley to Harrogate

The Huntsman Inn **161**

Chidswell Lane, Dewsbury,
West Yorkshire
WF12 7SE
Tel: 01924 275700

Directions:
From the M1(J40) proceed towards
Dewsbury. At the first roundabout turn
right to Batley. After Dewsbury Rugby
League Club, turn right up Windsor Rd
and turn right at the top.

Just five minutes drive from the centre of Dewsbury, **The Huntsman** is a real gem of a place owned and personally run for the last 18 years by Jean and Ian Mann. It started life as a row of farm cottages more than 200 years ago, and there are lovely views of open countryside. The owners have a warm, friendly welcome for all their customers, whether familiar faces or first-timers, and it's a pleasure to step inside a place of great atmosphere and character. A painting of the inn occupies pride of place above the stone fireplace in the main bar, and an old cast-iron Yorkshire Range with a glowing log fire in the Snug, which is always lit during winter. The beams and the walls are filled to the brim with hunting memorabilia, brasses and remnants of the way life used to be. It's the perfect setting for relaxing with a pint of real ale or the local Chidswell bitter, or for settling down to enjoying something from the excellent menu. The pub is closed Monday lunchtime except when it's a Bank Holiday. Monday evening is quiz night, which is informal with proceeds going to local charities. Food is only served Tuesday to Saturday lunchtimes. At Sunday lunchtimes, pork pies and mucky fat and bread are on the bar - free for all customers. The new room - Snug two, is available for small business meetings, celebration parties etc.

Dewsbury is an extremely old-established town with an imposing town hall and a famous open market. According to legend, Dewsbury Minster is situated on the very spot where, in 627AD, St Paulinus baptised converts to Christianity in the River Calder. The church dates from the 12th century but the tower was erected in 1767 to a design of the eminent York architect John Carr. The church is perhaps best known for its custom of tolling the 'Devil's Knell' on Christmas Eve to ward off evil spirits with a bell known as 'Black Tom'.

Opening Hours: 12.00-15.00 and 19.00-23.00
Closed Mon lunchtime; Opens 17.00 Fri

Food: Bar meals 12.00-14.00 Tues-Sat

Credit Cards: None

Accommodation: None.

Facilities: Small function room

Entertainment: Quiz Monday.

Local Places of Interest/Activities: Wakefield 6 miles, Leeds 8 miles.

162   The New Inn

Main Street,
Barwick-in-Elmet,
Leeds
Yorkshire
LS15 4JF
Tel: 0113 281 2289

Directions:

A64 out of Leeds, turn right for Barwick at roundabout before Thorner.

Built as a cottage tavern in the latter half of the 18th century, **The New Inn** has been extended down the years without losing its original character. Peter and Kath Weatherill have held the lease here for 15 years and could not be more friendly or welcoming. The interior of their pub is warm, cosy and absolutely delightful, with beams, wood panelling and settles presenting an old-world scene; the Tap Room and Snug are just as they were, and a unique feature is the tiny low-ceilinged bar at a lower level than the rest of the public area. The main place for diners is the lounge, where Peter and Kath offer an attractive menu of home-cooked dishes for every lunchtime session (Sunday lunch bookings only) and Tuesday to Thursday evenings. Everything on the menu is worth trying, but the steak pie and the chicken, ham and cream pie are extra special. Bar snacks are also served daily, and themed food evenings take place every five or six weeks. Darts and dominoes are the favoured pub games, and Monday night's quiz is open to all-comers, with 10p off the price of a pint and free sandwiches to nourish the brain.

Barwick-in-Elmet was once an important settlement in the Celtic kingdom of Elmet, and the land around the village has yielded considerable evidence of early occupation, including the earthworks at Hall Tower Hill and Wendel Hill. At the top of the village, next to the village cross, stands the historic maypole, which at 90 feet is one of the tallest in Britain. Every third year the maypole is taken down for a spring clean and re-erected with time-honoured ceremony. The nearby All Saints Church dates from the 12th century. The village is a conservation area, and there are many picturesque walks in the vicinity. A network of minor roads leads from Barwick to the A64, A1 and M62, so the pub is in easy reach of many towns, villages and places of interest.

Opening Hours: All day, every day except Sunday

Food: Bar meals.

Credit Cards: None.

Accommodation: None.

Entertainment: Quiz night Monday.

Local Places of Interest/Activities: Leeds 4 miles, Tadcaster 10 miles, Bramham Park.

The New Queen | 163

Lower Mickleton, Methley,
West Yorkshire LS26 9AN
Tel/Fax: 01977 515382

Directions:
A639 from Castleford. After 1 mile take right turn on road signposted Mickleton.

Paula Wright liked this 100-year-old pub so much that she bought it three years, changing its name from The Queen to **The New Queen**. Situated in a little village very close to Methley and the sizeable town of Castleford, the smart white-painted pub has a prominent conservatory to one side and a beer garden with picnic tables to the rear. Paula and her husband Kevin are lucky to have the services of a top-class chef in David Jackson, who has 25 years experience in the business.

Good traditional cooking of tip-top produce is his forte, and his menus always offer plenty of choice, with daily specials and roasts in addition to the standard list. His sauces are a highlight, always well constructed and full of flavour. Booking is essential for Sunday lunch. Food is served lunchtimes and evenings except for Saturday lunch and Sunday evening, and also Monday lunch, when the pub is closed except on Bank Holidays. Diners can choose between the classy conservatory, with its thick carpets and ruched curtains, and the equally appealing lounge. Thirst-quenchers include John Smiths Real Ale and Smooth and three draught lagers. This is very much a place for all the family, and children are always very welcome.

The location, close to the River Aire, offers quick access to the delights of the countryside and to the amenities of the town: Castleford is only minutes away, and Pontefract, Leeds and Bradford are all in easy striking distance.

Opening Hours: Mon 19.00-23.00; Tues-Fri 11.30-15.00 and 17.00-23.00; Sat 12.00-23.00; Sun 12.00-22.30

Food: A la carte.

Credit Cards: None.

Accommodation: None.

Facilities: Car Park.

Local Places of Interest/Activities:
Castleford, Leeds 6 miles.

164   The Red Lion

The Green,
Guiseley,
West Yorkshire
LS20 9BB
Tel: 01943 872052

Directions:

5 miles north of
Bradford A658/A65.

Behind a solid cream-painted frontage on the green at Guiseley, the **Red Lion** (spot him on the Tetley pub sign) is a cheerful, congenial place with excellent hosts in George and Susan Spiby. Several Tetley's brews - Real Ale, Smoothflow, Dark Mild - are served in the well-stocked bar, an attractive room with wood panelling, bright lights and rows of gleaming bottles and glasses. A fire burns in a hearth with massive stone surrounds, and rustic chairs are set neatly at little tables for drinkers and diners.

The pub is open all day, every day, and food is served from opening time until 6pm. Traditional pub grub runs from sandwiches and light snacks to pie and peas, warming soups and satisfying stews. This is one of the most sociable of hostelries for miles around, with pool, darts and dominoes as well as fruit machines, and the four days of the weekend are particularly jolly: on Friday a disco starts at 8 o'clock, varied entertainment on Saturday, a disco at 7 o'clock with a music quiz on Sunday, and occasional darts or dominoes knock-out competitions on Monday.

The Red Lion does not serve food in the evening, but there's another place in Guiseley that does. This is the famous Harry Ramsden's, the original of the ever-growing chain of fish & chip shops. Much of the area round Guiseley is built up, with Shipley, Bradford and Leeds almost falling over each other. Main roads run in all directions, and the Leeds Bradford International Airport is very close to the pub. But there's also plenty of open countryside (Ilkley Moor is a short drive away) and pleasant walks along the Wharfe and Aire rivers and the Leeds & Liverpool Canal.

Opening Hours: All day, every day

Food: Bar meals until 6pm.

Credit Cards: None.

Accommodation: None.

Facilities: Car Park.

Entertainment: Disco Friday & Sunday.

Local Places of Interest/Activities: Otley 2 miles, Shipley 3 miles, Bradford 5 miles, Leeds 6 miles, Ilkley Moor.

The Rose & Crown

165

11 Church Street,
Ilkley,
West Yorkshire
LS29 9DR
Tel: 01943 885911

Directions:

From Leeds A660
then A65 (15 miles
in all); from Skipton
6 miles on A65.

Set back from one of the main streets in town, the **Rose & Crown** is a popular inn with the most hospitable of managers in Michael and Mandy Phillips. After spells in Lancashire, the Midlands and Buckinghamshire, they took over here in the autumn of 2000, and are already making their mark. The panelled bar areas are pleasant spots to meet for a drink and a chat or to settle down to a snack or a leisurely meal. Food is served every day from 12 to 2.30 and from 5 to 7.30 and the menu covers a largely familiar range of the popular pub classics, from sandwiches, jacket potatoes and a healthy bowl of salad leaves with avocado and crispy bacon to a breakfast-style brunch, battered haddock, chicken kiev and giant Yorkshire puddings filled with onion gravy, chilli or sausage and vegetables. Daily specials are dispensed from the servery hatch, and at the weekend the lunchtime carvery always attracts a good crowd - booking is definitely recommended to guarantee a slice of the action. Ilkley is very handily placed for both the tourist and the business visitor, and Michael and Mandy have available five comfortable guest rooms - two doubles, two twins and a family room - all with en suite facilities.

There's plenty to interest the visitor right on the doorstep: originally an Iron Age settlement, Ilkley was later occupied by the Romans, who built a camp to protect their crossing point of the River Wharfe. The spring at White Walls brought visitors to the town in the 18th century, and with the coming of the railways in the 1860s, during a growth period in the woollen industry, Ilkley became a popular commuter town. Many opulent Victorian buildings still grace the town, including a perfectly preserved arcade complete with balconies and potted palms. Most people associate the name of Ilkley with Ilkley Moor, immortalised in the song. This beautiful heathery moor, inviting on a summer's day but bleak and forbidding in winter, is of considerable importance archaeologically, and the determined walker who reaches the middle will discover an ancient stone circle.

Opening Hours: All day, every day

Food: Bar meals.

Credit Cards: Access, Mastercard, Visa.

Accommodation: 5 en suite rooms.

Facilities: Car Park.

Entertainment: Tuesday - Quiz night, Thursday - Live entertainment

Local Places of Interest/Activities: Skipton 6 miles, Leeds 15 miles, Ilkley Moor, Bolton Abbey, Otley 8 miles.

166   The Royal Oak

15 High Street,
Crofton,
Wakefield,
West Yorkshire
WF4 1NF
Tel: 01924 863433

Directions:

Crofton is 3 miles southeast of Wakefield on the A638.

Surveying the village scene from its hilltop position, the **Royal Oak** - originally the Masons Arms - was built in Tudor style in 1842. Behind a very distinctive facade the Tudor look continues in the bar and restaurant, with beams and handsome panelling contributing to the inviting old-world atmosphere, along with leaded windows, an open fireplace with canopy and brick surround and some interesting pictures and prints.

Business partners Clive Sharples and Tony Wray have built up a strong local following during their five years at the helm, and the congenial atmosphere finds new friends all the time - and since it lies on a main road, it attracts many casual visitors. There's an excellent choice for quenching thirsts, including three real ales, many other beers and lagers on draught and a sweet and dry cider on draught. Food is served every lunchtime except Monday, and in the evening (5pm to 8pm) on Thursday, Friday and Saturday. The printed menu provides plenty of variety, and the prices are extremely reasonable. Picnic benches out at the front come into their own in the summer, and a room upstairs can accommodate 70 people for a party or function. The pub is open all day Monday-Saturday and from 12 to 4 and 7 to 10.30 on Sunday. All-comers are welcome to pit their wits against the locals on quiz nights, Sunday and Thursday, and the popular pub version of Play Your Cards Right.

Opening Hours: Mon-Sat 12.00-22.30, Sun 12.00-16.00 & 19.00-22.30.

Food: Bar meals.

Credit Cards: None.

Accommodation: None.

Entertainment: Quiz Sunday & Thursday.

Local Places of Interest/Activities:
Wakefield 3 miles.

The Rustic Arms

Long Lane, Low Ackworth,
Nr. Pontefract,
West Yorkshire WF7 7EZ
Tel: 01977 794136

Directions:

From Pontefract, head southon A639. Turn
right on Station Road at East Hardwick or
left on A628 at High Ackworth.

Some of the buildings date back to the 17th century, but the look is mainly modern at Pat
and Geoff Thompson's splendid combination of pub and restaurant in a quiet setting south
of Pontefract. **The Rustic Arms & Brown Trout Restaurant** stands in an acre of gardens
bordered by a 2½-acre lake where fishing is available for a small fee.

The food is a great attraction in the recently opened restaurant, where the Thompsons
have had the good fortune to acquire the services of Richard Hammond, a top-class chef
with 20 years experience in the business. His high-quality food is served every lunchtime,
evenings Tuesday to Saturday and booking is recommended at the weekend. Local produce
plays a very important part in the cooking, and Richard's menu runs from bar snacks and
light dishes (garlic mushrooms, mussels with garlic and cider) to steak pie, black Cajun
chicken, pan-fried salmon and crispy roast duck breast in a loganberry and brandy sauce.
Fish specials are always worth looking out for, and there's a good choice for vegetarians, as
well as a children's menu. Early diners can get a special deal in mid-week. Lighter lunchtime
fare includes soup, sandwiches and Yorkshire pudding filled with roast beef, beef stew or
home-made sausage. Tables and chairs are set out in the garden, and there's an area where
children can play in safety.

The area has some excellent waymarked walks, some of which start at the Rustic Arms.

Opening Hours: Winter 12.00-15.00 and
17.00-23.00; Summer 12.00-23.00

Food: A la carte, bar meals.

Credit Cards: Mastercard, Visa.

Accommodation: None.

Facilities: Car Park.

Entertainment: None.

Local Places of Interest/Activities:
Pontefract 2 miles, Leeds 10 miles.

168 The Steam Packet Inn

The Bendels,
2 Racca Green,
Knottingley,
West Yorkshire
WF11 8AT
Tel: 01977 677266

Directions:

By the junction of
the A1 and M62
(J33).

The Aire & Calder Canal runs at the bottom of the garden at this sympathetically modernised pub in Knottingley. Should visitors want to arrive by water, there are moorings for six boats at the front, and a feature above the bar is the wooden hull of an old boat.

Old and new (original 18th century timbers, modern brick features) blend harmoniously in the bar, where two real ales and a weekly-changing guest ale are served all day. Home cooking with a strong Yorkshire flavour is available from noon to 5 o'clock. Pool and darts are played in the games area, there's a big-screen TV for sports events, and weekly entertainment includes an artist on Thursday and disco/karaoke (in a a separate room) on Friday, Saturday and Sunday. Colin (Jack) and Margaret Horner took over as tenants in December 2000 and have already put the Steam Packet back on the map. Their plans for the future include longer hours for serving food and the opening of six letting bedrooms for guests wanting to stay overnight.

Knottingley is located near the junction (33) of the M62 and the A1 a mile or so east of Pontefract, where the attractions include the ruined castle, the annual liquorice fair and the racecourse, which stages several flat race meetings in the summer. The town has long associations with liquorice (notably through Pomfret Cakes), and the annual Liquorice Fayre in mid-August includes two days of jousting, archery and battle re-enactments at the Castle.

Opening Hours: 12.00-23.00 every day

Food: Lunchtime bar meals.

Credit Cards: None.

Accommodation: Planned.

Facilities: Car Park.

Entertainment: Artist Thursday, Disco/karaoke Friday, Saturday & Sunday.

Local Places of Interest/Activities: Pontefract 1 mile.

The Stump Cross Inn — 169

Britannia Road,
Morley,
Leeds,
Yorkshire
LS27 0DD
Tel: 0113 253 4655

Directions:

A653 2 miles south of Leeds city centre; Morley is on the A650 Bradford-Wakefield road.

The Stump Cross is a very distinctive building presenting a triangular face to the world on a corner site in Morley. The first pub on the site was a coaching and posting inn, and the pub in its present form dates from 1900. The tenants are David Ward, born and bred in Morley, and his wife Susan - this is their first venture into the licensed trade. This is Rugby League territory, and the Tap Room of the inn has a collection of pictures and prints relating to the sport. Another feature is the Grumpy Old Mens Club Corner. There's very little reason why anyone here should be grumpy, as the whole place is very cosy and inviting, and full of character.

Lunchtime visitors have an extra reason not to grump, as this is when Sue prepares her good wholesome pub food. Tetley's Real Ale and a guest ale, other Tetley's brews, four draught lagers and two draught ciders offer plenty of choice for the thirsty. General knowledge is a useful asset here, as no fewer than three evenings a week are devoted to quizzes: an experienced quizmaster runs the show on Tuesday and Sunday, while on Thursday David hosts a quiz with the additional feature of 'Play Your Cards Right'. The pub has a beer garden and car park.

Morley is no distance at all from the southern edge of Leeds and it's only a short drive to Batley, Dewsbury and Wakefield. Dewsbury has a number of notable public buildings, a famous open market and a well-preserved minster. Wakefield also has much to interest the visitor, including the Cathedral with its magnificent 247ft spire, museums and a fine art gallery with works by locally born sculptors Henry Moore and Barbara Hepworth.

Opening Hours: All day, every day

Food: Bar lunches.

Credit Cards: None.

Accommodation: None.

Facilities: Car Park.

Entertainment: Quiz nights Tuesday, Thursday and Sunday.

Local Places of Interest/Activities: Leeds, Wakefield, Dewsbury, Batley.

170 Tino's Beehive

Main Street,
Thorner,
Leeds
Yorkshire
LS14 3DE
Tel: 0113 289 2711

Directions:

Off theA64, follow signs for Thorner. 5 miles east of Leeds in the direction of York.

More than just a 'pub' pub. That's the claim of **The Beehive**, a former private house in a pretty village on the A64 east of Leeds. Tino is Tino Gonzalez, an ebullient Spanish gentleman who has been in England for 37 years. The last three of those years have been at this splendid pub, which he has made a favourite destination for lovers of good food and good company throughout the region.

The bar and the 38-cover restaurant (also available for private functions) are both warm and inviting, with beamed ceilings and half-panelled walls. Food is served in all parts, and the choice is very wide. The printed menu covers starters/light bites, salad platters, lunchtime sandwiches, 'hot delights' including roast beef, steaks and scampi, and a good selection of vegetarian main courses. But what most people swarm round at the Beehive is the specials board, which always includes some dishes from Tino's native Spain. as well as closer-to-home choices such as goujons of plaice or shoulder of lamb. A typical list might offer boquerones (Spanish-style anchovies), patatas bravas (potatoes in a spicy sauce), lamb chasseur and griddled swordfish steak. Food is served lunchtime Tuesday to Sunday and evenings Tuesday to Saturday. Four real ales and two guest ales are usually available, as well as two draught lagers and Guinness Extra Cold. The pub has a large car park at the back.

Of the many towns and villages within an easy drive, Boston Spa (8 miles) is a pleasant little town on the River Wharfe, and Tadcaster, also on the Wharfe, is a renowned centre of the brewing industry, with John Smith, Samuel Smith and Bass Charrington's Tower Brewery the leading trio.

Opening Hours: Mon-Fri 11.30-15.00 and 18.30-23.00; Sat 11.30-23.00; Sun 12.00-22.30

Food: Bar meals.

Credit Cards: Access, Mastercard, Visa.

Accommodation: None.

Facilities: Car Park and terrace

Entertainment: Quiz night on Tuesdays; karaoke on Fridays; Disco on Saturdays (60's, 70's and 80's)

Local Places of Interest/Activities: Leeds 5 miles, Tadcaster 8 miles, Boston Spa, Wetherby 10 miles.

The Whitakers

49 Kirkgate, Otley,
West Yorkshire LS21 3HN
Tel: 01943 462580

Directions:

From Ilkley on A65 then A660 (7 miles in all); from Harrogate A61/A658/A659 (10 miles).

A former dram house with a history going back to 1744. David and Linda Bradley, leaseholders for the past three years, have made it a very popular place with both local residents and tourists. It stands in the town centre on one of Otley's main streets and is open all day, every day. The bar has an old-world appeal, with beams, half-panelling and an open brick feature wall. But the hidden treasure here is tucked away at the back, where picnic benches are set out on the grass in a lovely secluded garden - created by the Bradleys - with old stone and brick walls and pretty flower beds.

Inside or out, visitors can enjoy an excellent pint (Whitakers Best Bitter is brewed locally for the pub) and a tasty bar meal. David and Linda both cook, and their menu and specials board provide plenty of choice; many of the locals look no further than the splendid hot beef sandwiches. Food is served at lunchtime during the week and from 12 till 6 o'clock on Saturday and Sunday. Brains and memories are tested here not once but twice a week: the 60s, 70s and 80s disco quiz gets under way at 8 o'clock on Wednesdays, while the general knowledge quiz begins at 9pm every Sunday. Daily sport includes darts, dominoes and fruit machines.

Otley is well placed for both business and leisure visitors, with beautiful Dales countryside more or less on the doorstep and the virtual conurbation of Leeds and Bradford a short drive away. Otley itself is a pleasant place to stroll round, with a busy market place and many little alleys and courtyards to discover. Each May the Wharfedale Agricultural Show, founded in 1709, is held in a field close to the centre.

Opening Hours: All day, every day

Food: Bar lunches.

Credit Cards: None.

Accommodation: None.

Entertainment: Quiz night Wednesday and Sunday.

Local Places of Interest/Activities: Harewood House, Skipton 14 miles, Leeds 15 miles, Bradford 12 miles.

172 The White Hart

Wakefield Road,
Denby Dale,
West Yorkshire
HD8 8RT
Tel: 01484 862357
Fax: 01484 866683

Directions:

From Huddersfield
(8 miles) A629 then
A635. From Barnsley
8 miles west on
A635.

Nineteenth century stone-built inn on an elevated site near the junction of the A635 and A636. Donna Brayshaw and her husband Carl run this most sociable of inns, and the mood is always cheerful and relaxed in the carpeted bar, where oak beams, an open log fire and a collection of brass ornaments contribute to an agreeably traditional scene. One corner is a snug little library and there is a separate games room with a pool table. Entertainment is laid on generously, with quiz night on Tuesday, live music on Thursday and karaoke on Sunday. Lovers of good home cooking make a beeline for the **White Hart**, where Donna produces tasty, satisfying dishes at very kind prices. It seems only natural that her steak and ale pie is among the all-time favourites, as Denby Dale is famous high and low for its gigantic meat pies.

The first of these Desperate Dan-sized dishes was produced in 1788 to celebrate the return of George lll to sanity and later ones marked the victory of Waterloo and Queen Victoria's Jubilee. The 1928 monster was baked in order to raise funds for the Huddersfield Royal Infirmary but the festivities were in danger of being scuppered when it was discovered that a large part of the pie had gone bad. The offending section was removed (by the barrowload!) and the event went ahead, but it was not until 1964 that the baking resumed, this time to celebrate four royal births. Another monster bake-in took place in 1988 and the dish used for that pie is now on display just outside the village. The pie to end all pies was baked for the Millennium, weighing in at a prodigious 12.16 tonnes. A few miles up the A636 towards Wakefield is the village of Clayton West, where a popular attraction is the Kirklees Light Railway, a 15" gauge steam railway which runs along the old Lancashire & Yorkshire Clayton West branch line. A little further away, close to junction 38 of the M1, is the Yorkshire Sculpture Park, which draws in some 200,00 visitors each year with its changing exhibitions of sculpture set in beautiful parkland.

Opening Hours: 12.00-23.00.

Food: Bar meals.

Credit Cards: None.

Accommodation: None.

Facilities: Car Park.

Entertainment: Quiz Tuesday, live music Thursday, karaoke Sunday, disco Friday

Local Places of Interest/Activities: Barnsley 8 miles, Huddersfield 8 miles, Clayton West 3 miles.

Wills o' Nats

Blackmoorfoot Road,
Meltham,
Holmfirth,
West Yorkshire
HD9 5PS
Tel: 01484 850078

Directions:

From Huddersfield
B6108 3 miles to
Meltham then turn
right on to B6107.
The pub is ¾ mile
west of Meltham on
the road to Marsden.

The husband and wife team of Chris and Melanie Laws have recently taken over the reins at this most delightful 100-year-old pub, which enjoys a picture-postcard setting just west of the village. Old and new elements combine to great effect in the bar, which features lots of pine, an open log fire and an antique stove. The pub is very much food driven, with good wholesome dishes served lunchtime and evening drawing on local, British and modern European recipes. The value for money is outstanding, and the food is complemented by excellent wines and a regularly changing choice of cask ales. Regular entertainment is provided by a pianist with the locals joining in a singalong. Outdoor fun is to be had in the beer garden, where the attractions include an adventure playground and a mini-farm with ponies, goats and birds. The name **Wills o' Nats** hails from the original owners of the pub, a father and son called William and Nathaniel.

Meltham is a typical Pennine wool town, mostly Victorian but with a handsome Georgian parish church. Only two mills have survived but the Meltham Mills Band, founded in 1845, is still thriving and has won many competitions throughout the country. Some customs from the past have also managed to survive: on Collap Monday (the day before Shrove Tuesday) the shopkeepers give away sweets to the children, there is carol singing on Christmas Eve in the centre of the village; and on Whit Monday members of all the churches and chapels join in a walk accompanied by the brass band. A few miles away is the village of Holmfirth, the setting for *The Last of the Summer Wine*. Another attraction here is the Postcard Museum.

Opening Hours: 12.00-23.00

Food: Bar meals.

Credit Cards: Access, Mastercard, Visa, Solo.

Accommodation: None.

Facilities: Children's play area, beer garden

Entertainment: Piano singalong.

Local Places of Interest/Activities: Huddersfield 3 miles, Holmfirth 5 miles.

174 The Yorkshire Penny

Cobblers Lane, Pontefract,
West Yorkshire WF8 2LL
Tel: 01977 602894

Directions:

From junction 32 of the M62 take the A639 south to Pontefract. The Yorkshire Penny is a short walk from the centre of town.

A short walk from the centre of Pontefract, the **Yorkshire Penny** is a modern pub offering a traditional atmosphere, with new tenants John and Vicky Young here since the end of 2000. The main eyecatching feature of the building is a spacious conservatory restaurant that overlooks an outside seating area with picnic benches. The pub is open Monday to Thursday from 6 o'clock (all day in the summer months) and all day at the weekend. Food is served in the non-smoking dining area until 9 o'clock in the evening. John and Vicky are maintaining and strengthening the pub's reputation as a lively, cheerful place, with quiz nights on Wednesday and Sunday evenings and occasional live entertainment and karaoke evenings. The pub has a private room for functions and parties, and also available is a mobile pub-style bar that opens out from the back of an articulated truck.

The town of Pontefract - Pomfret to William Shakespeare - has long been a place of influence and power, often visited in earlier times by monarchs and their retinues. The Castle, built in the 11th century, was one of the most formidable fortresses in the north of England; today it stands a gaunt ruin with only sections of the inner bailey and the lower part of the keep surviving intact. The town is best known for its Pontefract cakes, and the town celebrates this heritage with a five-day liquorice fayre in mid-August that includes medieval sporting at the Castle. Many of the streets of Pontefract evoke memories if its medieval past with names such as Micklegate, Beast Fair, Shoe Market, Salter Row and Ropergate.

Opening Hours: 18.00-23.00 Monday-Thursday (all day in summer); 11.00-23.00 Friday-Sunday.

Food: Bar meals.

Credit Cards: Mastercard, Visa.

Accommodation: None.

Facilities: Car Park.

Entertainment: Quiz Wednesday and Sunday.

Local Places of Interest/Activities: Pontefract Castle, Pontefract Races (Flat), Leeds 9 miles.

6 South Yorkshire

PLACES OF INTEREST:

PUBS AND INNS:

The Hidden Inns of Yorkshire

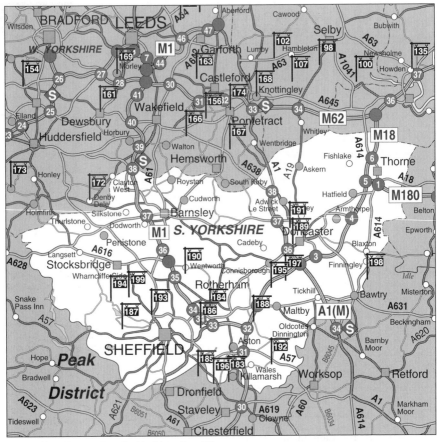

© MAPS IN MINUTES ™ 2001   © Crown Copyright, Ordnance Survey 2001

183 The Angel Hotel, Spinkhill	**192** The Loyal Trooper, South Anston
184 The Atlas, Brinsworth	**193** New Barrack Tavern, Sheffield
185 The Bridge Inn, Ford	**194** The Plough, Low Bradfield
186 The Crown, Blackburn	**195** The Plough Inn, Micklebring
187 The Crown & Glove, Stannington	**196** The Prince of Wales, Eckington
188 The Double Barrel, Thurcroft	**197** The Red Lion, Braithwell
189 Hexthorpe House, Hexthorpe	**198** The Ship Inn, Newington
190 The Horse & Tiger, Thorpe Hesley	**199** The Shoulder of Mutton, Worrall
191 John Bull Inn, Thorne	

Please note all references refer to page numbers

Lacking the spectacular scenery of the Yorkshire dales, moors or coastline, South Yorkshire tends to be overlooked as a tourist venue. But there's a great deal here to occupy and entertain the visitor. Its main centre, Sheffield, quite rightly claims to be England's greenest city, and the wild open spaces of the Pennine moors roll right up to its western boundaries. The city boasts many open spaces and gardens, some excellent museums and galleries and, for shoppers, a choice that ranges from the small independent shops in Orchard Square to the shopaholic's paradise of Meadowhall, one of the largest shopping malls in the UK. Heritage sites in South Yorkshire include Roche Abbey, Conisbrough Castle and the appealingly faded Victorian grandeur of Brodsworth Hall.

PLACES OF INTEREST

BARNSLEY

The county town of South Yorkshire, Barnsley stands on the River Dearne and derived its Victorian prosperity from the rich seams of coal hereabouts. It has an appropriately imposing Town Hall, although the building is comparatively recent, completed in 1933. Nearby, the **Cooper Gallery** is a lively centre for the arts which hosts a varied programme of exhibitions throughout the year as well as housing a fine permanent collection.

The town's most impressive museum is actually located a few miles to the west, in the village of Cawthorne. **Cannon Hall** is a magnificent 18th-century country house set in formal gardens and historic parkland. It offers unique collections of pottery, furniture, glass-

Cannon Hall, Barnsley

ware and paintings, along with the "Charge Gallery", which documents the story of the 13th/18th Royal Hussars.

About a mile to the south of Barnsley is the **Worsbrough Mill and Country Park**. The Grade II listed mill dates from around 1625. A steam mill was added in the 19th century, and both have been restored to full working order to form the centrepiece of an industrial museum. The mill is set within a beautiful 200-acre country park which also includes the Wigfield Farm rare breeds centre.

Another three miles to the southeast, situated in attractive South Yorkshire countryside just off the M1 (J36), the **Elsecar Heritage Centre** is an imaginative science and history centre which is fun and educational for all the family. Visitors can discover hands-on science in the Power House; nostalgic travel on the Elsecar Steam Railway; the history of South Yorkshire in the "Elsecar People" exhibition; and interactive multi-media in the "Newcomen Beam Engine Centre". The centre is also the base for several working craftspeople who make and sell their products here. Special events include "Friends of Thomas the Tank Engine" days.

CADEBY

Listed in the Domesday Book as *Catebi*, this pleasant little village is surrounded on all sides by prime agricultural land. For centuries Cadeby had no church of its own - its residents had to travel the two miles to the parish church in Sprotbrough. Then in 1856 the owners of the huge Sprotbrough estate, the Copley family, paid for a church to be built in Cadeby. It was designed by Sir George Gilbert Scott, the architect of St Pancras Station in London, and resembles a medieval estate barn with its steeply pitched roofs and lofty south porch. A century and a half later, Cadeby is again without a church, since Sir George's attractive church has recently been declared redundant.

CONISBROUGH

The town is best known for the 11th-century **Conisbrough Castle** (English Heritage) which features prominently in one of the most dramatic scenes in Sir Walter Scott's novel *Ivanhoe*. The most impressive medieval building in South Yorkshire, Conisbrough Castle boasts the oldest circular Keep in England. Rising some 90 feet and more than 50 feet wide, the Keep stands on a man-made hill raised in Saxon times. Six huge buttresses some 6 foot thick support walls that in places are 15 feet deep. Visitors can walk through the remains of several rooms, including the first floor chamber where the huge open fireplaces give one a fascinating insight into the lifestyle of Norman times. The castle also offers a visual presentation, a visitor centre and a tea room.

One of Conisbrough's latest places of interest is the Earth Centre, adjacent to the railway station. The Earth Centre has as its aim "to inspire understanding of sustainable development and to help people become involved in achieving it in their own lives and for the world". This is achieved with fascinating exhibits, interactive tours and exciting activities.

Conisbrough Castle

DONCASTER

The Romans named their riverside settlement beside the River Don, *Danum*, and a well-preserved stretch of the road they built here can be seen just west of Adwick le Street. The modern town boasts some impressive buildings, notably the **Mansion House** built in 1748 and designed by James Paine. The parish church was rebuilt in 1858 by Sir Giles Gilbert Scott and it's an outstanding example of Gothic revival architecture with its lofty tower, 170 feet high and crowned with pinnacles. The lively shopping centre is enhanced by a stately **Corn Exchange** building and a market which takes place every Tuesday, Friday and Saturday. Doncaster was also one of the most important centres for the production of steam engines. Thousands were built here, including both the *Flying Scotsman* and the *Mallard*. The *Mallard* still holds the record for the fastest steam train in the world, achieving a top speed of 125mph in July 1938.

There is no one connected with the racing fraternity who has not heard of the St Leger, one of the oldest classic races, which has been held at Doncaster since 1776. Doncaster, in the Yorkshire tradition, provides a magnet for all horse-racing enthusiasts and there are a total of 26 meetings each year.

On the northwestern outskirts of the town Cusworth Hall is home to the **Museum of South Yorkshire Life** (free). The Hall is a splendid Georgian mansion built in the 1740s and set in a landscaped park. The interior features varied displays on the social history, industry, agriculture and transport of the area.

Another 3 miles or so to the northwest of Doncaster, **Brodsworth Hall** (English Heritage) is a remarkable example of a Victorian mansion that has survived with much of its original furnishings and decorations intact. When Charles and Georgiana Thellusson, their 6 children and 15 servants moved into the new hall in 1863 the house must have seemed the last word in both grandeur and utility. A gasworks in the grounds supplied the lighting and no fewer than 8 water-closets were distributed around the house, although rather surprisingly only two bathrooms were installed.

More immediately impressive to visitors were the opulent furnishings, paintings, statuary and decoration. The sumptuous reception rooms have now a rather faded grandeur and English

Brodsworth Hall, nr Doncaster

tually an island since it is surrounded by rivers and canals and can only be entered by crossing a bridge.

It's a charming village with a striking medieval church famous for its elaborately carved Norman doorway, an ancient windmill and a welcoming traditional inn.

PENISTONE

Perched 700 feet above sea level, Penistone forms a gateway to the Peak District National Park which extends for some 30 miles to the south of the town. Penistone's oldest building is the 15th-century tower of its parish church which overlooks a graveyard in which ancestors of the poet William Wordsworth are buried. Later centuries added an elegant Dissenters' Chapel (in the 1600s) and a graceful Cloth Hall in the 1700s.

ROTHERHAM

The town's most striking building is undoubtedly the **Church of All Saints**. With its soaring tower, pinnacled buttresses and battlements, and imposing porch, it is one of the finest examples of Perpendicular architecture in Yorkshire. It dates mainly from the 15th century although there is evidence of an earlier Saxon church on the site. A church here was listed in the Domesday Book and in 1161 the monks of Rufford Abbey were granted the right to prospect for and to smelt iron, and to plant an orchard, and from that day industry has existed side by side with agriculture.

Seventy-five per cent of the Borough of Rotherham is actually rural but it was heavy industry that put the town on the map. From the mid-18th century, the Walker Company of Rotherham was famous for cannons, their products featuring to lethal effect in the American War of Independence and at the Battle of Trafalgar. They also built bridges, amongst them Southwark Bridge in London and the bridge at Sunderland. Another famous bridge builder was born here in 1901. Sir Donald Coleman Bailey invented the Bailey Bridge which proved to be of great military value, especially during the Second World War.

The town also had lighter manufactures. Rockingham Pottery, produced here in the late 18th and early 19th century, is now highly prized by collectors. There's a fine collection at

Heritage has deliberately left it so, preserving the patina of time throughout the house to produce an interior that is both fascinating and evocative. A vanished way of life is also brought to life in the huge kitchen and the cluttered servants wing. The Hall stands in 15 acres of beautifully restored Victorian gardens complete with a summer house in the form of a classical temple, a Target Range where the family practised its archery, and a Pets Cemetery where the family dogs - and a prized parrot bearing the unimaginative name of "Polly" - were buried between 1894 and 1988.

FINNINGLEY

A unique feature of this pleasant village close to the Nottinghamshire border is its five village greens, the main one having a duck pond complete with weeping willows. Finningley is a living village with a well-used Village Hall, originally a barn but which later served as the village school. Finningley has a beautiful Norman church with a rectors' list dating back to 1293 and a post office which has been in the same family for five generations. Just before World War II, Finningley RAF airfield was built to the west of the village and although the airfield is no longer in regular use it provides the venue for an annual **Air Show** which includes some spectacular flying displays.

FISHLAKE

Set along the banks of the River Don, which is known here as the Dutch River, Fishlake is vir-

180

the **Clifton Park Museum**, a stately building whose interior has changed little since it was built in 1783 for the Rotherham ironmaster, Joshua Walker. The most breathtaking piece is the spectacular Rhinoceros Vase which stands almost 4 feet high. In addition, the museum houses a collection of other Yorkshire pottery, English glass, silver and British oil paintings and water-colours. The grounds around Clifton House form the largest urban park in the Borough which has 10 urban parks altogether, along with 3 country parks, 7 golf courses, 10 swimming pools and a leisure centre.

Another museum of interest is the **York and Lancaster Regimental Museum** in the Central Library. The regiment had strong ties with South Yorkshire, its recruits drawn mainly from Barnsley, Sheffield and Rotherham. The displays include historic uniforms, campaign relics and over 1,000 medals, among them nine Victoria Cross groups. There are also sections on local militia, rifle volunteers and territorials.

The palatial 18th-century mansion **Wentworth Woodhouse** boasts the longest frontage in England, some 600 feet long. The house is not open to the public, but is clearly visible from its Park. Also visible are a number of follies and monuments dating from the 1700s. The most curious of these is the Needle's Eye which consists of a tower with a stone urn on top and is pierced by a carriageway. Legend says it was built in response to a wager by the Marquis of Rockingham, owner of Wentworth Woodhouse, that he could drive through the eye of a needle. One structure which *is* open (on Sunday afternoons during the season) is the Wentworth Mausoleum, which was built in 1788 in memory of the 2nd Marquis.

Roche Abbey

A little further afield, near the village of Maltby, are the dramatic ruins of **Roche Abbey** (English Heritage). The abbey dates from the 12th century and takes its name from the rocky limestone of the riverside site. The majestic remains of this great abbey stand in a landscape fashioned by "Capability" Brown in the 1770s as part of the grounds of Sandbeck Park, home of the Earls of Scarborough.

SHEFFIELD

In recent years Sheffield has re-invented itself. England's fourth largest city, it is still busy with its steel, cutlery, engineering and toolmaking industries, but is also a vibrant, international, multi-cultural city whose image was given a fillip by the worldwide success of *The Full Monty* which was filmed in and around the city. Sheffield is also a world-class centre for sport, a base

Sheffield Town Hall

for the Government backed UK Sports Institute and boasting an impressive array of international venues. There are excellent facilities for swimming, athletics, ice skating, dry skiing as well as two indoor climbing centres.

The city's premier museum is the **Kelham Island Museum**, which tells the story of Sheffield in a living museum. Visitors can see the mighty River Don Engine in steam - the most powerful working steam engine in Europe; reconstructed workshops; the "Little Mesters" working cutler; and craftspeople demonstrating traditional "Made in Sheffield" skills. For children up to 9 years old, "The Melting Shop" provides an interactive experience where they can "clock on" to become a piece of steel - including being rolled and hammered!

Sheffield's industrial heritage is also celebrated at **Abbeydale Industrial Hamlet**, which includes a typical workman's cottage and (considerably grander) manager's home as they would have been in the late 19th century, and a counting house where the prices and quantities of the steel scythes produced on the site where measured and recorded. The **City Museum and Mappin Art Gallery** (free) in Weston Park houses the city's collection of cutlery, metalwork, ceramics, coins, archaeology and natural history. The Mappin Art Gallery has a permanent display of Victorian paintings and organises an imaginative programme of temporary exhibitions.

One of Sheffield's newest attractions is the **Magna Science Adventure Centre**, where children of all ages can enjoy a hands-on experience of water cannons, G-Force, JCB diggers and more in this multi-storey, multi-media museum.

Sheffield's most picturesque museum is undoubtedly the **Bishop's House Museum**, which dates from around 1500 and is the earliest timber-framed house still standing in the city. Many original features survive, and the Bedchamber and Great Parlour are furnished in the style of the home of a prosperous 17th-century yeoman. There are also displays on Sheffield in Tudor and Stuart times, and changing exhibitions on local history themes. A museum of a very different nature is the **Sheffield Bus Museum**, housed in the Tinsley Tram sheds on Sheffield Road. The collection includes many

types of bus and other transport-related exhibits such as destination blinds, old timetables and models. The museum also houses the Tinsley Model Railway layout.

Of related interest is the **South Yorkshire Railway** in Meadowbank. As well as displaying more than 60 locomotives, there are vintage carriages and wagons, and a signal box. Plans are under way to run a steam-hauled passenger service on the 3½ miles line from Meadowhall to Chapeltown.

Sheffield has three outstanding galleries devoted to the visual arts. The **Millenium Galleries** on Arundel Gate opened in 2001 and house the fascinating collection formed for the people of Sheffield in 1875 by the Victorian artist, critic and sage John Ruskin, previously held in the city's Ruskin Gallery. It includes paintings, water-colours and drawings, minerals, plaster casts and architectural details, illuminated manuscripts and books. Other galleries here display changing exhibits from London's Victoria & Albert Museum and other famous collections, exhibits detailing the history of Sheffield's proud steel and silver heritage, and changing displays of modern jewellery and crafts. Nearby, the **Graves Art Gallery** (free) holds a wide-ranging collection of British art from the 16th century to the present, along with European paintings and a fine collection of water-colours, drawings and prints. One of its major treasures is the Grice Collection of Chinese ivories, which forms the centrepiece of a display of non-European artefacts. Another gallery of interest, the **Site Gallery** (free), is devoted to photographic and new media exhibitions and events. One of the largest contemporary visual art and media centres in the country, the gallery also offers darkroom and digital imaging facilities, as well as photographic and digital courses in the recently created education suite.

SILKSTONE

The travel writer Arthur Mee dubbed Silkstone's parish church "The Minster of the Moors" - and it is indeed a striking building. Parts of the church date back to Norman times but most of it was built during the golden age of English ecclesiastical architecture, the 15th century. Outside, there are graceful flying buttresses and wonderfully weird gargoyles. Inside, the ancient

Bishop's House Museum

oak roofs sprout floral bosses on moulded beams, and old box-pews and lovely medieval screens all add to the charm.

The old stocks just outside **The Ring o' Bells** are another sign of the antiquity of this former mining village. The Ring o'Bells itself dates back to the 1700s and it was here, in 1842, that the first Mines Union meeting took place.

THURLSTONE

Thurlstone developed when the first settlers realised that the nearby moors provided extensive grazing for sheep and the lime-free waters of the River Don were ideal for the washing of wool. Today the village still has some fine examples of the weavers' cottages which sprang up during the early 19th century, the best of which can be seen on Tenter Hill. Here the finished cloth would have been dried and stretched on "tenters" - large wooden frames placed outside on the street which gave the road its name.

The village's most famous son was Nicholas Saunderson, born in 1682, who was blinded by smallpox at the age of two. He taught himself to read by passing his fingers over the tombstones in Penistone churchyard - 150 years before the introduction of Braille. Nicholas went on to attend grammar school and rose to become Professor of Mathematics at Cambridge University.

WALES

A mile or so to the west of Wales, the **Rother Valley Country Park** provides excellent facilities for water sports including sailing, windsurfing, canoeing and jet skiing, as well as a cable water ski tow. Visitors can hire equipment or use their own, and training courses from beginner to instructor level are available in various water sports. Other attractions include a lakeside golf course, a Craft Centre with craftspeople at work, cycle hire, gift shop and cafeteria.

About 3 miles northeast of Wales is the **Tropical Butterfly House, Falconry and Wildlife Centre**. Here you can, if you wish, hold a tarantula or fondle a snake. Children can cuddle a bunny or bottle feed a calf. The Centre includes a well-stocked tropical butterfly house, a Bird of Prey centre which has regular flying demonstrations, an Animal Nursery, Farmyard Corner, Nature Trail, children's play area and gift shop.

WHARNCLIFFE SIDE

Nestling in the valley below **Wharncliffe Crags**, Wharncliffe Side is a community of some 2,000 souls and a popular location for commuters to Sheffield and Stocksbridge. An old tradition in the village tells of the "Dragon of Wantly" which lurked in the recesses of the crags and terrorized the local people until a knight by the name of More did battle with the monster and killed it. A cave up on the crags is still called the "Dragon's Den" and local children experience an enjoyable frisson of terror by shouting into its depths. Another ancient tradition in the village is the Whitsuntide walk when Sunday school children process around Wharncliffe Side stopping at various points to sing hymns.

The Angel Hotel

26 College Road,
Spinkhill,
Sheffield,
South Yorkshire
S21 9YB
Tel: 01246 432315
Fax: 01246 431095

Directions:
Spinkhill lies 8 miles
south-east of
Sheffield off the
A616.

A white-painted brick building at the heart of a village at a junction of minor roads between Killamarsh and Renishaw, close to the Yorkshire-Derbyshire border. In the convivial bar there's a good variety of beers to quench thirsts - two real ales and the occasional guest, plus John Smiths Smooth, Guinness, lagers and dry Blackthorn cider.

Judy and St John are the tenants, and Judy does the cooking: home-made soups, lasagne and meat & potato pie are among the favourites on the menu, which is supplemented by daily blackboard specials. Food is served from 12 to 2 and from 6 to 8.45 either in the bars or in the 50-cover restaurant. Judy and St John also offer comfortable overnight accommodation in four high-grade letting bedrooms - a single, two doubles and a family room. A quiz is held every Thursday starting at 9.30.

The Angel has a pleasant beer garden. Sheffield is an easy drive away, and even nearer, almost on the Derbyshire border, is the large, sprawling village of Eckington. Between Eckington and Renishaw is Renishaw Hall, seat of the Sitwell family, who made a fortune in the iron industry. The house was built in 1625 and later transformed, and in its grounds are what is said to be the world's most northerly vineyard.

Opening Hours: 12.00-15.00 Tues-Sun; 18.00-23.00 Mon-Sat

Food: Bar meals.

Credit Cards: Mastercard, Visa.

Accommodation: 4 rooms.

Facilities: Beer garden

Entertainment: Quiz night Thursday.

Local Places of Interest/Activities: Sheffield 8 miles, Renishaw Hall 5 miles.

Internet/Website: sj@angel.force9.co.uk

184

The Atlas

Bawtry Road,
Brinsworth,
Rotherham,
South Yorkshire
S60 5DN
Tel: 01709 377458

Directions:

1 mile south of
Rotherham on the
A631.

The Atlas is a handsome and substantial white-painted building standing on the main road through the village. Built as a mine captain's residence towards the end of the 19th century, it later became a hotel and finally a public house. A former inn on the site was the place where prisoners were kept for the night before appearing in front of the beak in nearby Sheffield. Today's captive audience is the responsibility of Mick Deakin, who took over the tenancy towards the end of 2000. When he moved in, the pub was open all day for drinks, but as we went to press Mick had many plans, including the introduction of food. Pool, snooker and darts are played in the bar, and there's a function room for private parties, with seats for up to 100. A disco operates from 8.30pm on Saturdays, and on Sunday nights the regulars clear their throats for the weekly karaoke session.

The large town of Rotherham, literally just along the road, has an industrial heritage that runs from the manufacture of cannons and bridges (Southwark Bridge in London among them) to the prized Rockingham pottery. There's an impressive collection of pottery, glass, silver and paintings in the Clifton Park Museum, and another museum of interest is the York and Lancaster Regimental Museum. A well-known landmark at Catcliffe, just south of Brinsworth, is a 70ft brick cone built in 1740 for glass-making.

Opening Hours: 12.00-23.00 Mon-Sat; 12.00-22.30 Sun

Food: Planned for the future

Credit Cards: None.

Accommodation: None.

Facilities: Function room

Entertainment: Disco Saturday, karaoke Sunday.

Local Places of Interest/Activities: Rotherham 1 mile, Sheffield 2 miles.

The Bridge Inn

Ford, Ridgeway,
Sheffield,
South Yorkshire
S12 3YD
Tel: 01246 433217

Directions:

From Sheffield
A616 on to B6056;
minor road to Ford.

Licensed in 1845, but an alehouse before that, the Bridge Inn has also seen service as a sickle and scythe factory and a button workshop. For the past ten years it has been in the excellent hands of tenants Jim and Sally Robinson, who welcome visitors of all ages to their delightful pub in the picturesque village of Ford, which lies just east of Mosborough and north of the B6056. Behind the handsome stone facade the Bridge Inn's public rooms are splendidly traditional, with many eyecatching features including a collection of hats, a display of more than 100 golf balls and a snug little area - half stonewalled, half panelled - called RAF corner, with cups, medals and prints of famous fighting aircraft.

It's a very popular place to come for a meal, so it's always worth booking ahead. Jim is a skilled and enthusiastic chef, and his printed menu supplemented by the specials board is available all sessions except Sunday and Monday evenings. Jim's specialities are fish dishes, salads and dishes with an Italian slant, but there really is something for everyone. The pub stands next to a little river, and an old mill race runs through the gardens. Families are very welcome, and children have their own safe play area. Tuesday's general knowledge quiz offers pints for prizes, and proceeds from Thursday evening's 60s and 70s music quiz go towards the village bonfire night.

The village of Ford has seen various activities down the years, including iron production as long ago as the 14th century, charcoal burning and the manufacture of sickles, scythes and reaping hooks. Local places of interest include the Rother Valley Country Park and the village of Renishaw on the Yorkshire-Derbyshire border. Renishaw Hall contains an art gallery, the Sitwell family museum, and a display of sculpture in the Georgian stables; all these can be visited, along with the beautiful Italian gardens and the 300-acre park.

Opening Hours: 12.00-23.00 Mon-Sat; 12.00-22.30 Sun

Food: Bar meals

Credit Cards: None

Accommodation: None

Facilities: Beer garden, play area

Entertainment: Qizzes

Local Places of Interest/Activities:

186 The Crown

88 Blackburn Road,
Blackburn,
Rotherham,
South Yorkshire
S61 2DR
Tel: 01709 560498

Directions:

From Junction 34,
Meadowhall turning,
take the Sheffield
road and follow signs
to Blackburn.

The Crown is a sturdy stone building in a village setting between Rotherham and Sheffield. Just a stone's throw from the M1 (Junction 34, the Meadowhall exit), this hidden gem is run by Jason and Louise, who took over the reins in the summer of 2000. Jason has been in the trade for 10 years, running premises in Sheffield, Leeds and Bradford. Open all day every day, the pub is an excellent place to pull in for a pleasant break. Three real ales are among the wide range of beers and lagers on offer in the bar, and a good choice of food is served lunchtime and evening Monday to Friday and lunchtime on Sunday. The printed menu and specials board provide something for everyone, and in the evening great-value special deals offer two main courses for £5. Sunday lunch of one, two or three courses is very popular, so it's advisable to book.

This is a place where brainpower is put to the test several times a week, with a general knowledge quiz starting at 9.30pm on Thursday and Sunday and a music quiz on Wednesday. Friday brings Fun Fortune and a disco, and Saturdays alternate between karaoke and other live entertainment. This hidden gem has its own hidden gem in the form of a super rear garden with a brick-built barbecue. Rotherham, which is just along the road, has several notable museums and historic buildings, including a 15th century four-arched stone bridge; the York and Lancaster Regimental Museum; Clifton House, with an important collection of local Rockingham pottery; and the 15th century All Saints Church with its soaring tower, pinnacled buttresses and battlements and fine fan vaulting.

Opening Hours: 12.00-23.00;

Food: Bar meals.

Credit Cards: None.

Accommodation: None.

Facilities: Car Park.

Entertainment: Quiz Wednesday, Thursday, Sunday; disco Friday, karaoke Saturday.

Local Places of Interest/Activities:
Rotherham 3 miles, Sheffield 4 miles.

Internet/website:
crown.blackburn@btinternet.com
uk.geocities.com/theonlycrown

The Crown & Glove | 187

96 Uppergate Road,
Stannington,
Sheffield,
South Yorkshire
S6 6BY
Tel: 0114 234 5522

Directions:

2 miles west of
Sheffield off the
A57.

Eighteenth century cottages were converted almost 200 years ago into a roomy public house of great character, with imposing bay windows on either side of the white-painted entrance. There's a terraced area to the front and a lawn to one side, and the elevated position commands lovely views.

The Crown & Glove is the first venture into the licensed trade for enthusiastic leaseholders Kath and Mick Ashmore, who plan improvements as they settle in to their new surroundings. The interior of the pub has a well-kept period look, and an open fire, carpets and plenty of comfortable chairs make an inviting setting for enjoying one of a selection of traditional cask bitters, or perhaps one of the 30+ malt whiskies kept at the bar. Excellent food is available lunchtime and evening every day, with dishes on the printed menu and specials board cooked by Kath and Mick. Sunday lunch, with traditional roasts, should be booked in advance. Children are welcome. Quiz nights Monday and Wednesday.

This outstanding pub is popular with walkers as it is on the edge of the Moors and the High Peaks. A mile and a half beyond Stannington, the Rivelin Nature Trail starts, running through valleys and by the gloriously scenic Ladybower Reservoir. A little further along, the A57 runs through Hope Forest and the rugged Snake Pass. Stannington is more or less part of Sheffield, where tourists will find plenty of interest including several art galleries and museums dealing with the steel industry, local history and transport.

Opening Hours: Mon-Sat 12.00-23.00; Sun 12.00-22.30

Food: Bar meals.

Credit Cards: None.

Accommodation: None.

Entertainment: Quiz nights Monday & Wednesday.

Local Places of Interest/Activities: Sheffield 2 miles, nature trails, walks.

188   The Double Barrel

Woodhouse Green,
Thurcroft,
Rotherham,
South Yorkshire
S66 9AN
Tel: 01709 703571

Directions:

From J32 of the M1
take minor road to
B6060 to Thurcroft.

Kevin and Gail Mozley have completed four years as tenants of **The Double Barrel**, which stands very close to Junction 32 of the M1 a short distance from Rotherham. The premises date from 1971, and beyond the long, low frontage there are plenty of tables and chairs in the roomy carpeted bar and dining area. The pub is open all day for drinks, and food is served from 12 till 8 Monday to Wednesday, 12 till 9 Thursday to Saturday and 12 till 4 on Sunday. Hot baps with fillings such as liver and onions or bacon and mushrooms make super quick snacks, while main courses run from an all-day breakfast to fried cod, chilli, chicken tikka masala, lasagne, omelettes and steak pie. A full meal could end with an all-time favourite such as fruit trifle, treacle sponge or classic jam roly poly - all served with cream, ice cream or custard. The food is a major part of the business here, providing not only plenty of variety but also exceptional value for money, and when the eating is done the entertainment starts; Wednesday is 60s/70s music night, with money off a pint after 8 o'clock; Thursday is quiz night; Friday and Saturday are disco nights; and a duo performs live on Saturday.

The urban attractions of Rotherham and Sheffield are short drives away, but there are several places of interest in the countryside around Thurcroft. Three miles to the east, near the village of Maltby, are the dramatic ruins of Roche Abbey; the Abbey dates from the 12th century and takes its name from the rocky limestone of the riverside site. The ruins stand in a landscape fashioned by Capability Brown as part of the grounds of Sandbeck Park, home of the Earls of Scarborough. At Tickhill the splendid Church of St Mary contains a remarkable early Renaissance monument in the shape of the alabaster tomb of Sir Thomas Fitzwilliam.

Opening Hours: 12.00-23.00 Mon-Sat; 12.00-22.30 Sun

Food: Bar meals, à la carte.

Credit Cards: Mastercard, Visa.

Accommodation: None.

Facilities: Car Park.

Entertainment: Disco Friday & Sunday, quiz Thursday, live music Saturday.

Local Places of Interest/Activities: Rotherham 5 miles, Sheffield 10 miles, Roche Abbey 3 miles, Tickhill 10 miles.

Hexthorpe House

189

*68 Urban Road,
Hexthorpe, Doncaster,
South Yorkshire
DN4 0EE
Tel: 01302 321926*

Directions:

From Doncaster town
centre head west towards
Balby and the A1(M);
turn right at T-junction
before Balby and follow
road to Hexthorpe.

Bright and cheerful on the outside, invitingly traditional within, **Hexthorpe House** stands on its own a short drive out of Doncaster town centre. Patricia and Roy Richards, helped by their daughter Charlene, took over the management in March 2000 and have ambitious plans to widen the appeal of an already very pleasant hostelry. Real ales, keg ales and smooth ales are all available, along with a good selection of lagers and cider, and home-cooked food is served lunchtime and evening seven days a week; the pub, open lunchtime and evening as the new management took over, might soon be open throughout the day. The interior of Hexthorpe House is delightful, with wood panelling for the bar counter, wood features in the lounge and sporting prints on the walls. Doncaster, founded by the Romans by the River Don, is a largely modern town but has some impressive old buildings, notably the Mansion House built to a James Paine design in 1748 and the parish church rebuilt in Gothic Revival style by Sir Giles Gilbert Scott in 1858.

Doncaster was once a great railway centre, and in its works some of the finest steam locomotives were built, including both the A3 Flying Scotsman and the A4 *Mallard*, holder of the world speed record for steam engines at 125mph. Doncaster still is a leading centre for horseracing, with fixtures throughout the year that include important National Hunt races, the first flat race meeting in March (the Lincoln), and the St Leger meeting in September, when the oldest classic, the St Leger, has been run since 1776. On the outskirts of town, the Museum of Yorkshire Life is well worth a visit, and a little further out is the sumptuous Victorian mansion Brodsworth Hall, set in beautifully restored grounds that include a classical temple, an archery target range and a pets cemetery. Pat had worked locally in the licensed trade for three years, but Hexthorpe House is her first time as manager; she and her family deserve great success at this very appealing pub.

Opening Hours: Mon - Sat, 12.00-23.00; Sun, 12.00-22.30

Food: Bar meals.

Credit Cards: None

Accommodation: None.

Facilities: Car Park.

Entertainment: None.

Local Places of Interest/Activities:
Doncaster (horseracing) 2 miles, Brodsworth Hall.

190 The Horse & Tiger

Brook Hill,
Thorpe Hesley,
Rotherham,
South Yorkshire
S61 2QA
Tel: 0114 2468 072
Fax: 0114 2258 886

Directions:

From Rotherham 2 miles northwest along the A629; Thorpe Hesley is signposted on the B6086. The village is seconds from the M1 (J35).

Roger and Sue Stevenson, local people with a background in office equipment, took over the lease at the end of 1999 and immediately started to bring back the good old days at this splendid village pub. **The Horse & Tiger** takes its name - unique among pubs - from an incident which occurred in the late 19th century when a circus was visiting the area. A tiger got loose and attacked a horse; the event was well documented and the pub got its name! Open all day every day, the Horse & Tiger serves Tetley's and a guest real ale as well as a wide range of other beers, lagers and ciders. Sue's home cooking has won a large circle of friends and her menus, available from 12 till 7 every day except Sunday, take their inspiration from all over the world with English classics and dishes from Italy, Mexico, China and India. Fish and chicken specials are particularly good, and Sue's corned beef pie is always in demand. Children are very welcome and can romp in safety in their own play area.

Roger and Sue are great supporters of local charities and hold special theme nights every month. There's something going on almost every night of the week, with pool on Monday; darts, cribbage and dominoes on Tuesday; a noughts and crosses quiz on Wednesday; a music quiz and karaoke on Thursday and a combination of quiz and bingo (quizingo!) on Sunday. A big TV screen shows the important sporting events, with free chip butties provided for viewers at half-time. The pub fields teams for darts, cribbage, dominoes, pool and football - and they're always on the lookout for new local talent.

Thorpe Hesley lies very close to the M1 (J35), with easy access to Sheffield and Barnsley. Attractions in the immediate vicinity include the palatial 18th century mansion Wentworth Woodhouse, which boasts the longest frontage (some 600 feet) in England. Also at Wentworth is a folly known as the Needle's Eye, a tall pyramid-shaped stone tower with a carriageway running through it.

Opening Hours: 12.00-23.00

Food: Bar meals.

Credit Cards: Most major cards

Accommodation: None.

Facilities: Car Park.

Entertainment: Games and quizzes most nights.

Local Places of Interest/Activities: Barnsley 8 miles, Rotherham 4 miles, Sheffield 6 miles, Wentworth 2 miles.

John Bull Inn

Waterside, Thorne,
Nr. Doncaster,
South Yorkshire
DN8 4JQ
Tel: 01405 814677

Directions:

From Doncaster A630 north then M18 to Thorne; or leave the M18 at J6 and follow signs.

The John Bull Inn is a free house with a history going back to 1630. Waterside was, in its heyday, a centre for shipbuilding on the River Don, and this grand old pub once stood right by the river. It takes its name not from the personification of the British bulldog but from the steamer *John Bull*, which was built in the early years of the 19th century to ply the route from Thorne Quay to Hull. Locals and travellers made good use of the quayside inn, and still do, though the diversion of the river in the early 1940s took it away from Waterside.

Behind a distinctive beige-painted frontage on the corner of Quay Road, the John Bull, managed for the past year by Julie and Steven Davison, has enormous old-world charm, with whitewashed walls contrasting with black beams, a fire with brick and beaten copper surround, and a feature open-brick pillar in the charming function room. Open all day every day for the dispensing of hospitality and John Smith's and other excellent ales (Monday to Friday between 5 and 7 is happy hour), the pub serves food lunchtime and evening, with Julie and two full-time chefs sharing the cooking duties. An extensive menu with over 70 main dishes as well as Sunday roasts is available, and booking is necessary for Friday and Saturday evenings and the roast Sunday lunch.

The river and the adjacent Stainforth & Keadby canal still hold plenty of interest. Thorne itself has been a port since at least 1500, with ships sailing to Hull, York, London and Europe. In the builders' yards vessels of up to 400 tons were constructed. As late as 1987 some boat-building yards were still at work here, but in that year they were finally closed and the area is being carefully developed to preserve the heritage. A little way along the river, Fishlake is a charming village with an imposing church and an ancient windmill, while Stainforth stands on the Don and also on the banks of the canal, which has a well-preserved dry dock and a 19th century smithy.

Opening Hours: 12.00-23.00 Mon-Sat; 12.00-22.30 Sun

Food: Bar meals.

Credit Cards: All major cards

Accommodation: None.

Entertainment: Occasional

Local Places of Interest/Activities: Fishlake 2 miles, Stainforth 3 miles, Doncaster 8 miles.

192 The Loyal Trooper

34 Old Sheffield Road,
South Anston,
Sheffield,
South Yorkshire
S25 5DT
Tel: 01909 562203

Directions:

8 miles east of
Sheffield on
the A57.

In February 2000 Ken and Beryl Weston exchanged their role from managers to leaseholders at this handsome white-painted inn on the Old Sheffield Road. **The Loyal Trooper** dates back to the late 17th century and takes its name from a yeomanry barracks that once stood nearby. There's a military theme in the front bar, where four real ales head the list of beers.

Beryl is the cook, and her printed menu and daily specials are available Monday to Saturday lunchtime and Monday to Thursday evenings. One of the most popular orders is the Trooper Smokie Sandwich with smoked bacon and mature cheddar cheese. Children are welcome when eating. The pub is open every lunchtime and evening Sunday to Friday and all day Saturday. Pool, darts, tv and a piano provide in-house entertainment, and there are two quiz nights - general knowledge on Monday and noughts & crosses on Wednesday.

The Loyal Trooper lies a short drive from Sheffield close to the borders with Derbyshire and Nottinghamshire. Sheffield, still busy with its steel, cutlery, engineering and toolmaking industries, is now also a vibrant, international city with an impressive array of sports and cultural amenities. The story of Sheffield is told in a number of city museums, notably the Kelham Island Museum with its mighty River Don steam engine and the Bishop's House Museum in an ancient timber-framed house. Specialist museums include the Sheffield Bus Museum and the South Yorkshire Railway at Meadowbank.

Opening Hours: 12.00-15.00; 18.00-23.00

Food: Bar meals.

Credit Cards: None.

Accommodation: None.

Facilities: Function room with bar (80 max).
Large car park. Beer garden

Entertainment: Quiz Monday and Wednesday.

Local Places of Interest/Activities: Sheffield 8 miles, Worksop 6 miles.

New Barrack Tavern

193

601 Penistone Road,
Sheffield,
South Yorkshire
S6 2GA
Tel: 0114 234 9148

Directions:

In the northwest of
the city on the A61.

Distinguished by a sturdy red brick and yellow stone facade, the 100-year-old **New Barrack Tavern** stands on the A61 Penistone Road a short drive or brisk walk from the centre of Sheffield. The interior is full of character, with carpets and plush banquettes in one part, and bare slatted wooden floor and kitchen furniture in another.

James Birkett and his chef Nicola Harris have made this an outstanding pub in a number of respects. The selection of real ales is without doubt the best in the area, with nine brews that include guest ales from all over the country, draught lagers and 3 draught Belgian beers, hand-pulled scrumpy cider, a fine variety of more than 30 Continental bottled beers and anything up to 80 malt whiskies to please the connoisseur. The food certainly shares the honours with the drinks, and Nicola's across-the-board offers dishes that are all freshly prepared and full of flavour. Wednesday is theme night, with tapas one week, curry the next and Continental specialities the other weeks. There's always a vegan option on the main menu. Food is not served on Saturday or Sunday evenings. The inn has a beer garden at the rear. Children are always welcome.

The places of interest in Sheffield, England's fourth largest city, are many and varied, including several important art galleries and museums covering the topics of steel, local history and road and rail transport. Out to the west the glorious scenery of the Peak National Park beckons serious walkers, energetic cyclists and motorists.

Opening Hours: 12.00-23.00, Sun to 22.30.

Food: Bar meals.

Credit Cards: None

Accommodation: None.

Facilities: Beer garden

Entertainment: Folk session 1st Monday of the month, Jazz nights 1st Tuesday of the Month, Quiz nights every Thursday, Live bands every Saturday night

Local Places of Interest/Activities: Sheffield 1 mile, Peak National Park, nature trails, waymarked walks.

194 | The Plough

New Road,
Low Bradfield,
Sheffield,
South Yorkshire
S6 6HW
Tel: 0114 285 1280

Directions:

From Sheffield take
the B6079, B6077
then a minor
road to Low
Bradfield.

The Plough enjoys a gloriously scenic location at a crossroads in the pretty village of Low Bradfield, set in thousands of acres of open countryside yet only a few miles from the fourth largest city in England. A large, dignified brick and stone building dating back over 200 years, it started life as a farmhouse but has been licensed for most of that time. The exterior suggests impressive proportions within, and indeed some of the features are on a grand scale, notably a gigantic stone hearth and massive stone walls under roof timbers.

The leaseholders are Matthew and Alison Riley, and Alison's superb cooking is the best of many reasons to visit this atmospheric inn. Traditional fare, including splendid Sunday roasts, is available from 11.30 to 2.30 and 6.30 to 8.30 (later in summer). The pub is open all day Saturday and Sunday, and all day most days in the summer season; it is closed Monday lunchtime in winter. Children are welcome if eating, and the pub has a secure beer garden. Quiz night is Thursday.

This is walking territory par excellence, and the High Peak area of northwest Derbyshire is practically on the doorstep, with some of the finest scenery in the whole country. This is an area of desolate moorland and high peaks, dry-stone walls and deep river valleys. Many reservoirs were created in the early years of the 20th century by flooding the valley of the River Derwent. Several of these surround the Bradfields, but the largest of all is a few miles to the southwest. Ladybower Reservoir, whose creation necessitated the flooding of two villages. The Derwent Dam, built in 1935, was the practice site for the Dambusters' bouncing bomb.

Opening Hours: 12.00-15.00 and 18.30-23.30 Mon-Fri; 11.30-23.30 Sat; 12.00-23.00 Sun

Food: Bar meals.

Credit Cards: Mastercard, Visa.

Accommodation: None.

Facilities: Beer garden, large car park

Entertainment: Quiz Thursday.

Local Places of Interest/Activities: Sheffield 6 miles, Ladybower Reservoir 6 miles.

The Plough Inn

Greaves Sike Lane,
Micklebring,
Nr. Rotherham,
South Yorkshire
S66 7RR
Tel: 01709 812710

Directions:

From M18 (J1) go through Hellaby Industrial Estate and beyond for about a mile.

Highly recommended for both its atmosphere and its food, Jim and Marie's **Plough Inn** enjoys a superb setting in open countryside not far from Rotherham. The handsome 1930s building, white-painted and with a steeply raked tiled roof, commands a fine view from the front that stretches over the M18 and for miles across the plain. Inside, all is agreeably traditional, with wheelback chairs set at neat little tables, plush carpeting and a tiled floor section round the wood-panelled bar. Real fires add to the homely appeal. Jim is a trained chef, but he also uses the services of a full-time professional in producing meals that are served lunchtime and evenings every day of the week. The pub is very popular over a wide local area, and it's best to book to be sure of a table in the non-smoking restaurant. The printed menu and blackboard specials offer plenty of choice, and the specialities include steaks and vegetarian dishes. Tempting special deals such as 2 for 1 off the specials board are available Monday to Friday lunchtime and early evening, and there are regular theme evenings.

A free buffet accompanies the Monday quiz, which starts at 9 o'clock on the dot. Three real ales are served, along with numerous other beers and lagers and a draught stout. Children are welcome, and the pub has a large garden. Rotherham is only a few minutes away by car, and among its many attractions are the striking Church of All Saints and a museum with a marvellous collection of the famous local Rockingham pottery. there are also several imposing ruins nearby, including Roche Abbey and Conisbrough Castle.

Opening Hours: 12.00-15.00 and 18.30-23.00 (closes 22.30 on Sunday)

Food: Bar meals.

Credit Cards: Mastercard, Visa.

Accommodation: None.

Facilities: Car Park.

Entertainment: Quiz Monday.

Local Places of Interest/Activities: Rotherham 4 miles, Roche Abbey.

196   The Prince of Wales

11 Church Street,
Eckington,
Sheffield,
South Yorkshire
S21 4BG
Tel: 01246 435678

Directions:

From Sheffield, A616
about 3 miles then
right on to B6056; 2
miles to Eckington.

Through capital investment, hard work and enthusiasm, Paul and Christine Taylor have put the 100-year-old Prince of Wales firmly back on the map since acquiring the premises at the end of 1999. The red-shuttered stone building has a cheerful, welcoming look, and the promise of the exterior is amply fulfilled within. In the dining area, with wheelback chairs set at neatly arranged tables, or in the bar, food is served from 12 till 2 and from 5 till 7 in the winter, and from 12 straight through to 7 in the summer. Christine is a fine cook, and among her many excellent dishes the savoury pies are something of a speciality. The Sunday carvery is keenly priced and very popular, so booking is advisable.

The pub, which is open all day, every day, is very much geared to families, and in the large, secure beer garden there is a bouncy castle and plenty of toys to keep the children busy and happy. Entertainment for grown-uos includes Friday and Sunday discos for the over-25s, live shows from top performers on Saturday, pool, darts and a big-screen TV for major sporting events. A short drive away, on the A616 just before it meets the M1, is the village of Renishaw, which gives its name to Renishaw Hall, home of Sir Reresby and Lady Sitwell. The beautiful formal Italian gardens and 300 acres of wooded park are open to visitors, along with a nature trail and a Sitwell family museum, an art gallery, and a sculpture display in the Georgian stables. Sheffield, City of Steel, is a short drive to the north, while in the other direction is the ancient town of Chesterfield with its famous crooked spire.

Opening Hours: 12.00-23.00 daily

Food: Bar meals.

Credit Cards: None.

Accommodation: None.

Facilities: Car Park.

Entertainment: Disco Friday & Sunday, live show Saturday.

Local Places of Interest/Activities: Sheffield 4 miles, Chesterfield 6 miles, Renishaw 4 miles.

The Red Lion

Holywell Lane,
Braithwell,
Rotherham,
South Yorkshire
S66 7AF
Tel: 01709 812886

Directions:

From M8 Junction 1, A631 to Maltby, B6427 to Braithwell

Kevin and Margaret Holmes are in their first year as leaseholders at the **Red Lion**, which occupies a corner site in a village equidistant from Rotherham and Doncaster. Behind the neat exterior - half redbrick, half white-painted - there are two bars, the public bar where pool, cards and dominoes are played, and the feature lounge and bar with plenty of banquettes and comfortably upholstered chairs at little tables, and a collection of plates adorning the walls. Margaret is a fine cook, and her printed menu, supplemented by daily specials, is available seven days a week. Pub classics are to the fore, including cod in batter, scampi, gammon and pineapple and giant Yorkshire puddings. Margaret's steak pie is a particular favourite, as is the traditional Sunday lunch of roast beef or pork with all the trimmings. Value for money is impressive, especially on the two meals for £5 offer. Children are welcome if eating, and the pub has a large, secure garden. Wednesday is quiz night, and Sunday spells karaoke.

The historic village of Braithwell is close to the motorway and main road networks, putting Rotherham, Sheffield and Doncaster within easy reach. Even closer are a number of places of historical interest. Near Maltby, the imposing ruins of Roche Abbey stand in a Capability Brown landscape. At Tickhill, where a famous battle was waged in the 14th century, are the ruins of one of the five castles licensed by Richard l for the staging of tournament, and the remains of a 13th century priory. Yet another ruin is that of Conisbrough Castle, which is mentioned in Sir Walter Scott's *Ivanhoe*.

Opening Hours: 12.00-14.00, 18.30-23.00 Mon-Fri; 12.00-23.00 Sat; 12.00-22.30 Sun

Food: Bar meals.

Credit Cards: None.

Accommodation: None.

Facilities: Car Park.

Entertainment: Quiz Wednesday, karaoke Sunday.

Local Places of Interest/Activities:
Rotherham 8 miles, Doncaster 6 miles, Tickhill, Roche Abbey.

198   The Ship Inn

Newington,
Nr. Bawtry,
South Yorkshire
DN10 6DJ
Tel: 01302 710334

Directions:
From the south leave the A1 at the junction with the A614; follow this road through Bawtry to a sharp lefthand turn at the beginning of Austerfield; go straight on along the Misson road following the pub signs. From Doncaster, A638 to Bawtry

For a great night out, good food and a friendly country welcome, the **Ship Inn** has few equals in the area. And that's also true in the daytime, as this 400-year-old inn located in the tiny hamlet of Newington is open all day, every day with a cheerful greeting for all-comers. Tony and Jane Jacques, in the licensed trade since 1989, have been here four years, regaling guests with a range of quality real ales and some excellent food. Behind its smart white-painted facade, the Ship is particularly warm and inviting, and hungry customers can turn up at any time, any day: the traditional home-cooked food is a big draw here, with the main menu and specials served Monday to Saturday from noon till 9, and Sunday (bookings only) 5.30 to 8.30; the carvery every evening; Sunday lunch (no bookings) 11.30 to 3; special lunchtime deals Monday to Friday from the carvery; and a '2 Meals for a Fiver' offer Monday evening and Saturday lunchtime. Early booking of a table is recommended for the Saturday night cabaret. Children are very welcome at the Ship, and the garden has one of the biggest play/adventure areas of any pub, with dozens of things to explore, swing on or climb through. There is also a "Little Munchers" menu for children priced at £2.50 with free ice cream.

The nearby River Idle was once an important waterway for the transportation of goods such as ironware and cloth, and Bawtry, a mile to the west of Newington, became a prosperous river port and market town, thanks to both its proximity to the river and its strategic position on the Great North Road. The opening of the Chesterfield Canal in 1777 and the coming of the railways in the next century marked the end of the great days, but Bawtry remains a delightful little market town well worth taking time to explore. Also nearby is the pleasant village of Finningley, best known for its annual air show.

Opening Hours: 11.00-23.00.

Food: Bar meals, carvery.

Credit Cards: Mastercard, Visa.

Accommodation: None.

Facilities: Car Park. Extensive play area

Entertainment: Cabaret Saturday night.

Local Places of Interest/Activities: Bawtry 1 mile, Doncaster 8 miles, Finningley 4 miles.

Internet/Website:
e-mail: theshipinn@btinternet.com

The Shoulder of Mutton 199

19 Top Road, Worrall,
Sheffield,
South Yorkshire
S35 0AQ
Tel: 0114 286 2101

Directions:
Worrall lies just off the A616 about 3 miles northwest of Sheffield city centre.

In the attractive commuter village of Worrall, northwest of Sheffield, Barry and Julie Kitchen are the leaseholders of a pub of real character and distinction. Known locally as the Top House, **The Shoulder of Mutton** has a long greystone facade, and interior features include an old stove,, exposed stone walls, panelling, stained glass and a wall tapestry.

Julie's home cooking is a major draw here, and her skills can be appreciated every session except Sunday evening. Fish and duck dishes are among the specialities, but everything on the menu is worth trying. The standard menu includes classic starters such as garlic mushrooms or paté served with toasted ciabatta, while main courses run from fish & chips or salmon with a tomato hollandaise to super pies, liver & bacon, steaks and always some vegetarian main courses. Delicious desserts round things off in style. Booking is recommended in the non-smoking restaurant on Friday and Saturday, and also for the very popular Sunday lunch, with three roast meats and a fish and a vegetarian option. Wines are available by the bottle or glass, and there's a good range of real ales, beers and lagers. Wednesday is quiz night. The inn has a beer garden, patio and terrace.

Oughtibridge, the next village, lies on the west bank of the River Don looking across to the tree-covered slopes of Wharncliffe Wood. After Oughtibridge is Wharncliffe Side, another commuter village where a fearsome dragon was killed (in days of yore, naturally!) by a knight called More. A cave up on the hills is called the 'Dragon's Den' and local children give themselves a fright by shouting into its echoy depths. Another ancient tradition in the village is the Whitsuntide Walk when Sunday school children process around the village stopping off here and there to sing hymns. Sheffield, England's fourth largest city, has three outstanding galleries and a number of museums telling the story of steel and local history. Transport fans will make tracks for the Bus Museum and the collection of old locomotives and rolling stock at the South Yorkshire Railway in Meadowbank.

Opening Hours: Mon-Fri 12.00-15.00, 17.30-23.00; Sat 12.00-23.00; Sun 12.00-15.00, 19.00-22.30

Food: A la carte menu.

Credit Cards: Mastercard, Visa.

Accommodation: None.

Facilities: Beer garden

Entertainment: Quiz Wednesday.

Local Places of Interest/Activities: Sheffield 3 miles, Wharncliffe 2 miles.

200   *ALPHABETIC LIST OF INNS*

ALPHABETIC LIST OF INNS

ACCOMMODATION

ALL DAY OPENING

CHILDRENS FACILITIES **207**

208 | *CREDIT CARDS ACCEPTED*

CREDIT CARDS ACCEPTED

210 GARDEN, PATIO OR TERRACE

GARDEN, PATIO OR TERRACE **211**

RESTAURANT/DINING AREA 213

214   *RESTAURANT/DINING AREA*

INDEX OF PLACES OF INTEREST | 215

Hidden Inns Order Form

To order any of our publications just fill in the payment details below and complete the order form *overleaf*. For orders of less than 4 copies please add £1 per book for postage and packing. Orders over 4 copies are P & P free.

Please Complete Either:

I enclose a cheque for £ ☐ made payable to Travel Publishing Ltd

Or:

Card No: ☐

Expiry Date: ☐

Signature: ☐

NAME: ☐

ADDRESS: ☐

POSTCODE: ☐

TEL NO: ☐

Please either send or telephone your order to:

Travel Publishing Ltd   Tel : 0118 981 7777
7a Apollo House   Fax: 0118 982 0077
Calleva Park
Aldermaston
Berks, RG7 8TN

The Hidden Inns of Yorkshire

	PRICE	QUANTITY	VALUE
Hidden Places Regional Titles			
Cambs & Lincolnshire	£7.99	....	....
Chilterns	£8.99	....	....
Cornwall	£8.99	....	....
Derbyshire	£7.99	....	....
Devon	£8.99	....	....
Dorset, Hants & Isle of Wight	£8.99	....	....
East Anglia	£8.99	....	....
Gloucestershire & Wiltshire	£7.99	....	....
Heart of England	£7.99	....	....
Hereford, Worcs & Shropshire	£7.99	....	....
Highlands & Islands	£7.99	....	....
Kent	£8.99	....	....
Lake District & Cumbria	£7.99	....	....
Lancashire & Cheshire	£8.99	....	....
Lincolnshire	£8.99	....	....
Northumberland & Durham	£8.99	....	....
Somerset	£7.99	....	....
Sussex	£7.99	....	....
Thames Valley	£7.99	....	....
Yorkshire	£7.99	....	....
Hidden Places National Titles			
England	£9.99	....	....
Ireland	£9.99	....	....
Scotland	£9.99	....	....
Wales	£11.99	....	....
Hidden Inns Titles			
Central and Southern Scotland	£5.99	....	....
South East England	£5.99	....	....
South of England	£5.99	....	....
Wales	£5.99	....	....
West Country	£5.99	....	....
WelshBorders	£5.99	....	....
Yorkshire	£5.99	....	....
TOTAL			

For orders of less than 4 copies please add £1 per book for postage & packing. Orders over 4 copies P & P free.